Since 1962 *Ottone M. Riccio* has published more than 600 poems, short stories, articles, and editorials, as well as two books of poetry. He is the editor and publisher of six different poetry periodicals and series, conducts Hellric House writing workshops, and teaches at the Boston Center for Adult Education. In addition, he has sponsored numerous poetry lectures, seminars, and workshops for universities and high schools in the New England area.

The Intimate Art of Writing Poetry

Ottone M. Riccio
Foreword by Stephen Minot

Prentice-Hall, Inc., Englewood Cliffs, New Jersey 07632

Library of Congress Cataloging in Publication Data

Riccio, Ottone (date).
   The intimate art of writing poetry.

   (A Spectrum Book)
   Bibliography: p.
   Includes index.
   1. Poetics.   2. Poetry—Authorship.   I. Title.
PN1042.R5   808.1   80-12708
ISBN 0-13-476846-9
ISBN 0-13-476838-8 (pbk.)

©1980 by Prentice-Hall, Inc., Englewood Cliffs, New Jersey 07632.
All rights reserved. No part of this book may be reproduced in any
form or by any means without permission in writing from the publisher.
A Spectrum Book. Printed in the United States of America.

10 9 8 7 6 5 4 3

Editorial/production supervision
and interior design by Eric Newman
Cover design by Ira Shapiro
Manufacturing buyer: Cathie Lenard

Prentice-Hall International, Inc., *London*
Prentice-Hall of Australia Pty. Limited, *Sydney*
Prentice-Hall of Canada, Ltd., *Toronto*
Prentice-Hall of India Private Limited, *New Delhi*
Prentice-Hall of Japan, Inc., *Tokyo*
Prentice-Hall of Southeast Asia Pte. Ltd., *Singapore*
Whitehall Books Limited, *Wellington, New Zealand*

For Dolores —
with
me
on
every
word.

A poet must love the Tradition; otherwise
he will not love poetry. He must love
language and be tender and reverent with
it, as well as bold; or he will never
have mastery of its secrets.

                                        GILBERT MURRAY
                        The Classical Tradition in Poetry

Contents

FOREWORD by Stephen Minot, xi
PREFACE, xv
ACKNOWLEDGMENTS, xvii

BEING
1. The Engagement, 3
Your commitment to poetry; your uniqueness; understanding your motives, desires, and need to write. Gaining perspective and critical objectivity toward your own work. The mystery and mystiques of poetry. Reading other poets, past and present.

BODY AND SOUL
2. Brain and Heart, 15
Conscious and subconscious, memory, dreams, experiences, emotions, and feelings. Thematic sources outside the self.

3. Physiognomy, 27
Descriptions of lyric, epic, narrative, dramatic, classical, romantic, objective, subjective, humorous, and surreal poetry.

4. Bone and Muscle, 62
Organization of structural elements, traditional forms, free verse, contemporary forms (including concrete and found).

5. The Nervous System and the Middle Ear, 133
Rhythm and meter (including classical meter).

6. The Voice, 155
Language; diction; tone.

7. Life Signs, 175
Rhyme; metaphor; simile; other poetic devices; symbols.

EXPRESSION
8. The Consummation, 209
Writing your poems. Writing techniques.

9. The Nurturing, 226
Self-discipline; ways to work; value of assignments; idea provokers. Appropriateness between theme and expression—content and form; experimentation.

10. The Weaning, 240
Releasing your poems; reading before an audience; preparation of manuscripts; marketing techniques; seeing your work through an editor's eyes; putting together a book

manuscript; whether or not to have an agent; the value of contacts; alternative modes of publishing; how to reach the reviewers; selling your book at your poetry readings.

Appendix i, 265
Recommended reading list of 100 books, well-known journals, university quarterlies, "little magazines"; recorded and taped poetry.

Appendix ii, 274
Market listing sources; information sources for poets and writers.

Appendix iii: The Workshop Connection, 278
A look at a workshop in action.

INDEX, 283

Foreword

"Being a poet," Ottone Riccio writes, "means one cares about language and finds joy working with it." Here is the balance of concern that differentiates this volume from others: On the one hand is *care*, which means mastering craft, learning techniques, studying the anatomy of the genre; on the other is *joy*, which wells up from within, the emotion that makes all that effort worthwhile.

Writing poetry takes work. It is not like humming or doodling with a pencil. There are marvelously intricate things that have been done with language, and none of us can really understand them until we analyze the techniques employed and attempt to use them in our own voice.

Mr. Riccio reminds us that we cannot be fresh and inventive until we have familiarized ourselves with the best of what has been done in the past. As he puts it, "In art nothing dies." That is, the contemporary poet may draw on techniques of rhythm, rhyme, stanza, or metaphor from the work of centuries before. What we think of as a "new" approach—free verse, for example—often has its roots in poetry that was written more than two thousand years ago. A good poet sees this heritage not as a burden but as a continually unfolding source.

While mastering the craft involves effort, it should also, he reminds us, be joyous work. It must never be too far removed from the spontaneous. Every accomplished poet draws on his or her unconscious, and this volume helps the reader to listen for those signals and allow them to influence not only images selected but the auditory effects of rhythm and rhyme and the nuances of tone. What we may think of as chance phrasing may reflect our deepest feelings. The joy of creation comes when we tap these sources and are then able to apply our knowledge of technique to the shaping of a line that is unmistakably "right."

The extended metaphors with which this book is organized are unique. They deserve special attention because they are a key to the author's view of the creative process. First, the "engagement," the commitment. Here at the very outset we are told that "writing poetry is a worthwhile experience for its own sake." What a welter of misconceptions this sweeps aside! Yes, it is unfortunate that poets are not paid a living wage for their art; but those who are committed rely on other rewards. For them the act itself is a pleasure—first the writing and then the performing, the public reading. Publication is a concern, but it is not a poet's primary motive.

The author next presents the anatomy of the creative process: the conscious and unconscious sources are like "brain" and "heart" respectively; specific forms such as lyric and narrative poems are like "the physiognomy," the outer appearance. Structural elements are presented to us as the "bone and muscle" without which expression would be subjective ramblings. Rhythm and meter are seen as "the middle ear"—that intricate source of balance. Then "the voice," which includes diction and tone. Under "life signs" he includes all those figures of speech and symbolic suggestions that give a poem the sense of being alive.

After that anatomy comes "the consummation," the actual process of composition, and "the nurturing," which includes sound and practical advice on how to achieve self-discipline and how to conquer the dreaded writer's block. His final section is appropriately "the weaning," the entire process of sending your work forth into the world.

The balance between hard work and the joy of creation that characterizes this volume is as important for the novice as it is for the accomplished poet. I once visited a college that serves as a "second chance" for students who have failed in one or more other institutions. Morale, of course, was a major problem. And nowhere was it more needed than in the lowest of courses, remedial English. Since all traditional methods had failed, the teachers turned the problem over to a group of more gifted seniors. Their solution: spend the first two weeks writing a villanelle! True, it took reading, analysis, and discussion; it took work. But what these students learned was that a complex literary form can be mastered with no more effort than it takes to learn an intricate disco step. Few of them returned to that particular verse form, but they drew from their effort a new confidence, a sense of accomplishment, and the personal proof of what a delight language can be.

This volume should serve as an ideal text for poetry classes. It is the kind of book most students will want to keep, to review long after graduation. It should also be of real value to those who are writing on their own. Although there is no substitute for working with a group, this book can serve as a buffer against isolation. The tone is warm, supportive, and enthusiastic.

There is no mistaking the fact that Ottone Riccio is a man who "cares about language and finds joy working with it." With his help, the reader will also.

Stephen Minot
Author,
*Three Genres: The Writing of Poetry, Fiction, and Drama,
Second Edition*

Preface

This book is the one for which I searched, at the time of the beginning, and could not find. All you poets just beginning or writing in solitude, looking for the rituals of poetry, the word made music, the mystery of technique, the quickness of knowing, doing, living the poem; all you poets gathered in classes, workshops, discussion groups, seminars, wherever; all you poets recording the history of the universe; all you poets reaching out of the darkness of desire toward the spurt of creation; you poets and teachers of poets who come to review and renew—this is your book now.

This book of yours has swum back to beginnings; there lies renewal. Some forget, lose sight of poetry's essence, its multitudinous features. Some admire only the mystique of poetry, not the demanding craft. Some would rather be published than strive to write poems. Some are unwilling to place their hands on poetry's essence. This is not their book. But those of you who are unafraid, who dare touch the pulse of poetry, this book is yours now.

Poetry is insistent paradox. It articulates that which cannot be articulated.

Words refute their boundaries. Syllables fire energies,

omnidirectional; their dynamic waves swell, repel, merge, overcome, outride individual profiles, creating an overcompassing sea.

There is a poetry magic, magic rising from the poem. The poet is Merlin; poetry is illusion, sleight of mind. The magicians know their craft, and we believe.

Acknowledgments

I wish to express my gratitude to Mary E. Kennan, editor of Spectrum Books, for her interest, patience, and expert guidance throughout this entire project, and for suggesting the idea initially; to my wife, Dolores, for her careful reading of the manuscript and for her many helpful criticisms and suggestions; to Alice C. Harvey, who deserves my sincere appreciation and thanks for her valuable and insightful contributions to this book; to Eric Newman, who watched over the production of this book with a refined eye; and to the members of the workshops I've moderated—poets who have been generous with their material and from whom I've learned a great deal.

Acknowledgment is made to the following for granting permission to reprint material:

The poem "Query" by Joyce Carol Oates is included here with the permission of the poet.

The poem "Penance" by Laura Marlin, published in *Ab Intra* #1, 1972, ©1972 by Hellric Publications, is reprinted here by permission of the publisher.

The poem "Players" by Josephine Miles, from *Poems 1930-1960* by Josephine Miles, published by Indiana University Press, 1960, ©1960 by Josephine Miles, is reprinted here by permission of the poet.

xviii *Acknowledgments*

"Lament in Spring" by John Logan, from his book *Spring of the Thief, Poems 1960–1962*, published by Alfred A. Knopf, Inc., ©1960, 1961, 1962, 1963 by John Logan, is reprinted here by permission of the poet.

"Love Poem" from *The Iron Pastoral* by John Frederick Nims. Copyright 1947 by John Frederick Nims. By permission of William Morrow & Company.

"Twinned Heart," published in *Poems 1968–1970* by Doubleday and Company. Reprinted by permission of Curtis Brown, Ltd. Copyright ©1971 by Robert Graves.

"Morning and Evening Song" by Dolores Stewart was first published in *South and West*, vol. 1, #2, Winter 1962, and is reprinted by permission of the publishers.

"Praise for an Urn" is reprinted from *The Complete Poems and Selected Letters and Prose of Hart Crane* by permission of Liveright Publishing Corporation. Copyright 1933, ©1958, 1966 by Liveright Publishing Corporation.

The poem "Sergeant Brandon Just, U.S.M.C." by Bryan Alec Floyd was first published by *The Beloit Poetry Journal* and is reprinted by permission of the publishers; ©1974 by *The Beloit Poetry Journal*.

Excerpt from *Alcestis* reprinted by permission of the publishers from *The Complete Greek Tragedies*, ed. by David Grene & Richmond Lattimore, Vol. III "Euripides," Chicago, Illinois, University of Chicago Press ©1959 (*Alcestis* ©1955) by the University of Chicago; translation of *Alcestis* by Richmond Lattimore.

"Unfortunate Coincidence" from *The Portable Dorothy Parker*. Copyright 1926 by Dorothy Parker, renewed 1954 by Dorothy Parker. Reprinted by permission of Viking Penguin, Inc.

The poem "Quartet in One Movement" is reprinted from *On Pain of Discovery* by Ottone M. Riccio by permission of Hellric Publications, ©1968 by Hellric Publications.

The lines from *Pale Fire* by Vladimir Nabokov, published by G. P. Putnam's Sons, ©1962, are reprinted here by permission of the publisher.

The excerpt from *The Divine Comedy* of Dante Alighieri, taken from *The Comedy of Dante Alighieri the Florentine*, 3 vols., translated by Dorothy Sayers, published by Basic Books, Inc., ©1962 by Anthony Fleming, is reprinted here by permission of the publishers.

"Let Me Enjoy" from *Collected Poems* of Thomas Hardy (New York: Macmillan, 1953).

Acknowledgments xix

The lines from "Heart's Needle" by W. D. Snodgrass, published 1959 (reprinted 1969) by Alfred A. Knopf, Inc., are used here with the permission of the publishers.

The excerpts from *The White Goddess* by Robert Graves, published by Faber and Faber, London, 1948, are reprinted here by permission of the publishers.

"Salutation" and "Sestina: Altaforte" (based on a poem by Bertrand de Born) both from *Personae*, by Ezra Pound. Copyright 1926 by Ezra Pound. Reprinted by permission of New Directions. Reprinted by permission of Faber and Faber Ltd. from *Collected Shorter Poems* by Ezra Pound.

The Poems of Emily Dickinson, "#712," is reprinted by permission of the publishers and the Trustees of Amherst College from *The Poems of Emily Dickinson*, edited by Thomas H. Johnson, Cambridge, Mass.: The Belknap Press of Harvard University Press, copyright ©1951, 1955 by the President and Fellows of Harvard College.

The first triad from "Pythian 2," translated by Frank J. Nisetich, is taken from *Pindar's Victory Songs*, translated by Frank J. Nisetich, published by John Hopkins University Press, ©1980 by John Hopkins University Press, and is reprinted here by permission of the publishers.

"Parting at Dawn" copyright 1924 by Alfred A. Knopf, Inc. Copyright 1952 by John Crowe Ransom. Reprinted from *Selected Poems*, Third Edition, Revised and Enlarged, by John Crowe Ransom, by permission of Alfred A. Knopf, Inc.

"Sonnet of Fishes" by George Barker. Reprinted by permission of Faber and Faber Ltd. from *Collected Poems: 1930–1955* by George Barker.

The poem "Wrinkles/gray hair, dry bones" by Mary Terrell, published by *Pyramid* #8, 1970, ©1970 by Hellric Publications, is reprinted here by permission of the publisher.

The translation of the tanka by Fujiwara Teika is reprinted from *Japanese Court Poetry*, by Robert H. Brower and Earl Miner, with the permission of the publishers, Stanford University Press. ©1961 by the Board of Trustees of the Leland Stanford Junior University.

The three Haiku by Buson, Taigi, and Bashō are taken from *The Four Seasons. Japanese Haiku, Second Series* Peter Pauper Press, 1962, ©1962 by Peter Pauper Press; the Haiku by Boncho is taken from *Japanese Haiku* Peter Pauper Press, 1955–1956, ©1955–1956 by Peter Pauper Press; all four Haiku reprinted by permission of the publisher.

Acknowledgments

"Do not go gentle into that good night" is taken from *The Poems* of Dylan Thomas. Copyright 1952 by Dylan Thomas. Reprinted by permission of New Directions.

"227-2272" copyright ©1974 by Barbara L. Greenberg. Reprinted from *The Spoils of August* by permission of Wesleyan University Press.

"In Memory of W. B. Yeats," copyright 1940 and renewed 1968 by W. H. Auden, and "Paysage Moralise" ("Hearing of harvest rotting"), copyright 1937 and renewed 1965 by W. H. Auden, are reprinted from *W. H. Auden: Collected Poems*, by W. H. Auden, edited by Edward Mendelson, by permission of Random House, Inc. "In Memory of W. B. Yeats" and "Paysage Moralise" reprinted by permission of Faber and Faber Ltd. from *Collected Poems* by W. H. Auden.

The poem "After a Game of Squash" by Samuel L. Albert, from *New Poems by American Poets* #2, edited by Rolfe Humphries, copyright 1957 by Ballantine Books, Inc., is reprinted here by permission of the poet.

"Hearing Margaret, Aged Four" from *The Fortune Teller* by John Holmes. Copyright ©1960 by John Holmes. Reprinted by permission of Harper & Row, Publishers, Inc.

The poem "Ghosts" from *All My Pretty Ones* by Anne Sexton, copyright ©1961, 1962 by Anne Sexton. Reprinted by permission of Houghton Mifflin Company and the Sterling Lord Agency.

The poem "The Invention of Comics" by LeRoi Jones is taken from *The Dead Lecturer* by LeRoi Jones, published 1964 by Grove Press, ©1964 by LeRoi Jones, and is reprinted here by permission of the publishers and the Sterling Lord Agency.

The concrete poem "Love" by Ottone M. Riccio, published in *Pyramid* #4, ©1969 by Hellric Publications, and the poem "The Memory Bottle" by Ottone M. Riccio, published in *Pyramid* #5, ©1969 by Hellric Publications, are reprinted here by permission of the publisher.

The concrete poem by Valerie Jayne, published in *Pyramid* #4, 1969, ©1969 by Hellric Publications, is reprinted by permission of the publisher.

The poem "Personals" by Dolores Stewart, published in *Pyramid* #8, ©1970 by Hellric Publications, is reprinted here by permission of the publisher.

The poem "Thin Ice" by Ottone M. Riccio was first published in *Choice* #6, 1970, ©1970 by *Choice* Magazine, Inc., and is reprinted here by permission of the publishers of *Choice* Magazine.

The excerpt from the poem "Hands" by Siv Cedering Fox, taken from *Cup of Cold Water*, New Rivers Press, 1973, ©1973 by Siv Cedering Fox, is reprinted here by permission of the poet.

"The Fish" reprinted by permission of Macmillan Publishing Co., Inc., from *Collected Poems of Marianne Moore* by Marianne Moore. Copyright 1935 by Marianne Moore, renewed 1963 by Marianne Moore and T. S. Eliot. Reprinted by permission of Faber and Faber Ltd. from *The Complete Poems of Marianne Moore*.

The poem "The Place of the Carp" by Stanwood K. Bolton, published in *Pyramid* #1, 1968, ©1968 by Hellric Publications, is reprinted here by permission of the publisher on behalf of the poet.

"Aiming" by Richard Gillman appears in *Lunch at Carcassonne*, X Press, 1976, by Richard Gillman, and is included here by permission of the poet.

"Poem on His Birthday" from *The Poems* of Dylan Thomas. Copyright 1952 by Dylan Thomas. Reprinted by permission of New Directions.

The poem "The Zamosc Rebbetzin's Birthday" by John Reed, published in *Pyramid* #10, ©1970 by Hellric Publications, is reprinted here by permission of the publisher.

The excerpt by W. H. Auden, taken from his essay "Making and Judging Poetry," published in *The Atlantic Monthly*, January 1957, copyright ©1956, by the Atlantic Monthly Company, Boston, Mass. Reprinted with the permission of the Atlantic Monthly Company and Curtis Brown Ltd.

I, Being

1. The Engagement

By deciding to write poetry, you've made a commitment to express your contemporary life and environment. Language is your medium. Content is achieved through the words you employ, the constructs of language you use, your application of the techniques of craft based upon a knowledge of the elements of prosody. In the true poem, medium and content become one; keep this foremost in your mind. This is your goal. Writing poetry is a worthwhile experience for its own sake. Worthwhile experience, however, does not come easily. There are risks. This fact will not deter you. You have responded to the attraction, the lure of poetry. Poetry welcomes your commitment; it will not abandon you unless you default on your pledge.

Who will become the great poets of our age? No one can predict exactly who among the present practitioners of the art will represent our era to generations of the future. To become a fine poet takes a combination of talent, sensitivity, pride and humility, knowledge and insight, and a fascination with the process of language as a living phenomenon. To become a great one requires also genius and the gift of prophecy.

Whether or not you become a great poet, you will—given

the least spark of insight into the meaning and beauty of the art—experience moments of joy and deep satisfaction when a particular poem flashes through your mind or grows step by painstaking step on the page, nurtured by your effort and increasing skills. Many of us are happy to settle for such moments.

Some beginners fear that writing may rupture their privacy, their personal lives. They worry about the effect their writing may have on their intimates.

To avoid revelations of the self entirely is impossible for any writer. But there is no reason why such revelations need to be embarrassingly blatant. Young writers (and young readers) often assume that the protagonist must be the author. This is not always the case. Autobiography has its place in poetry, but it is expressed by the author's design. All poetry is not autobiographical, although some poets are—eternally. You need not be when you'd rather not be. Inventiveness, the exercise of imagination, and outright fictionalizing will serve you in the expression of your emotions and experiences. The trick is to be able to recall your reactions to certain stimuli and to express sensitively those reactions in fictionalized parallel experiences. Don't lose sight of the fact that you live in a world abounding in material from which you are free to choose subject matter for your poems.

If your work is to have integrity not only in technique but in content as well, you must be emotionally honest in your writing, however much it may be necessary for you to alter factual data. The sensing aura about your writing should be in tune with your vision of the world. Anything less becomes apparent to even a moderately perceptive reader. The risks go with the territory; such is the nature of commitment.

Doubt is another condition that continually afflicts the good writer. Only the naive writer sees excellence in every line. Real poets are frequently forced by doubt to question and to reassess the value of their efforts. For writers made of stern poet-stuff, this kind of doubt can be beneficial. They will be strict with themselves and will refuse to settle for anything less than the very best they can produce. If you are this type of individual, welcome to the real world of poetry. Be cautioned, however, that if dissatisfaction with your work goes too far, nothing will ever be finished. Learn to recognize when revision after revision is actually helping your poem achieve its greatest potential. But learn as well when the time to stop revising comes. Keep in mind that your goal is to complete the poem.

The other kind of doubt writers contend with concerns the potential relationship between their work and the audience they envision for it—actually the contribution they see themselves making to the art in general. At times, you will not be able to refrain from asking yourself: Is what I'm attempting worth doing at all? Isn't it merely ego serving to try to express in poetry what others already have expressed better than I shall ever be able to do? Why should anyone be interested in what I have to say?

These recurring doubts are natural. Don't let them frighten you. Your personal devil stands at your left shoulder, but your personal angel stands at your right.

UNIQUENESS

One of the splendid attributes of human nature is that each of us is endowed with an individual set of perceptions; the mode and character of your perceptions are different from those of anyone else. In the creative arts, this proves to be one of the artist's most valuable strengths. You are you, and there is only one you in the entire universe. Your ways of hearing, seeing, feeling, thinking, absorbing, experiencing, and expressing yourself are not like the ways of any other individual. Depending on how well you do your work, your contribution will be valuable because of these differences, this uniqueness that only you can offer as your personal vision.

MOTIVES

Examining your motives for wanting to write poetry may enable you to write with more confidence and clarity. Why the urge to express yourself in this fashion? Is poetry the goal? Or is it the means to a goal? Do you feel the need to be noticed, to perform, to obtain publicity? Is it important for you to live the life of a poet? Do you look upon poetry as therapy? Have you something important to say that you believe you alone can communicate? Are you unable to resist imagining, daydreaming, inventing, turning the blank page into meaningful art? Do you need to create something where nothing existed before? Are you challenged to exploit and experiment with language, to exhort it to expanded perimeters?

Poems result from a combination of these motives plus many others. The process is so complex that time does not permit us to examine it here in any real depth. But for the best poets, the desire to make the poem is the chief motive for writing, with other considerations (fame, therapy, *la vie bohème*) taking second place. The great poet loves the medium—the language. For him or her, words are personal entities; the language matters more than the message. It's not what the poet has to say so much as how he or she will say it that will make the reader wake to the subject or experience. Many a poem has urged a loved one to return love, but only one has said

> Had we but world enough, and time,
> This coyness, Lady, were no crime.

which brings in the argument and the whole transitory nature of humanity in just two lines—and they rhyme!

If you are honest in assessing your own motives, you may be able to channel them into such fertile waters.

PERSPECTIVE AND OBJECTIVITY

Your unique way of thinking enables you to achieve an individual perspective. This results in a personal vision of life unlike that of anyone else. Your poems should exhibit, along with a sense of spontaneity, the shape and direction of such personal vision. Try to understand the sources of your "intuitions," your private symbols and their meanings, the developmental logic of your expressions.

The element of spontaneity bears further comment. Now and then, a poem comes from a truly spontaneous conception, and when that happens it's wonderful. More often, a great deal of thought and work goes into *making* the poem, and in a good poem, "spontaneity" is the *result of such effort*. In other words, however much sweat and work go into the making of a poem, the labor must not show in the final version; the poem must create the illusion of spontaneity.

Having achieved an understanding of your aims and impulses, you should be able to take a more objective view of your work. If you find it difficult to encourage this view initially, you will have to *practice* being objective for the first few times. Imagine yourself as a magazine editor and the poems as the work of someone who is unknown to you. Your task is to review the work critically, taking into account all the things an editor might. After you've tried this awhile, you'll be able to detect weaknesses and faults in your poems and thereby will be in a position to correct them. It may help you further to make a list of things an editor would look for: interest factor, universality, theme, emotional content, diction, tone, form, visual presentation, sound, logic, order, and so on. As a result of doing this exercise several times, you will learn the process well enough to be able to make critical judgments more easily—of the work of others as well as your own.

To do anything well takes training and practice. Gaining objectivity about your writing is no exception.

MYSTERY

However much we may analyze or dissect a poem, there remains, at times, a quality that defies investigation. This is one of the mysteries of poetry and one of the mysteries in making poems. Analysis can never be truly complete in a real poem. Prose summations, paraphrases, explanations, and the like cannot take the place of the poem. They approximate only, providing us points of entry in our attempt to comprehend the poem as a compositional unit. Although analysis cannot deliver the poem, neither can it harm it unless the poem is a bad one, in which case it is better given its proper burial. The true poem rises, intact once more, after we've divided it into as many parts as possible. In a way, this can be considered one of the tests of a successful poem; we may call it the "mystery of result."

Another mystery is involved in the poem's conception: Where does the idea come from? What made the poet select this particular form? Where have his or her illustrating images originated? Although scholars are eternally teased into trying to explicate such matters, the answers to these and similar questions remain elusive. We can look at the completed poem and arrive at the author's intent and meaning, and we are able to appreciate the poem's shape and sound, the success of its style, diction, and mood; but the remaining mystery is in the very act of creation itself. Of course, we are considering the writer's real poems, those that start inside the self, and not those executed merely as assignments to improve personal skills or to fit a particular occasion.

These mysteries are part of the natural evolution of the poem; unfortunately, they sometimes become associated with certain pitfalls of which the beginner should be aware. Moody vagueness, superficial philosophic musings, profundity without depth (a paradox too often encountered), and deliberate obscurity do not add mystery—they only detract from it. The true mystery of a poem is rarely evident to the poet until he or she has completed the work.

If you do your work well, there will evolve from a wide range of your efforts a series of related symbols and the development of certain themes that are especially important to you—your personal mythology. This further outlines your uniqueness: you are reshaping the world in accord with your private terms. If, because of your methods of expression and your ability to convince, your readers or listeners are compelled to accept such a world, you have succeeded in an important aspect of the relationship between poetry and audience. Gaining the readers' acceptance, in spite of the fact that they find elements of logic or reality eluding them, reveals that you have captured the 3-M facet of poetry: mystery, myth, and magic.

Mystery should not be confused with *mystique,* however, the latter a term we find applied to cults that form around some popular or precious poet, some experimental style, or some artistic cause. In its literal sense, mystique is concerned with mystical beliefs and attitudes centered around some person or idea. In poetry, this frequently shapes itself into a school in which lesser poets attach themselves to a major poet or style and practice the art of imitation. Imitators seldom surpass those they imitate. And when you have imitators imitating each other, you have a sorry state of affairs. Keep in mind that *your* greatest assets are your personal vision and your uniqueness. Almost everything else about art can be learned, but you must bring these qualities with you.

Imitation is a legitimate part of the learning process. But the writer must differentiate between being involved in a learning process and chasing a popular bandwagon. Popular taste in poetry (as in anything else) shifts rapidly. Striving to satisfy that taste may leave the writer trailing far behind. Be aware of what's going on, and be aware of your potential audience; but don't chase after it.

READING OTHER POETS

This is an important part of your life as a poet. Read as much poetry as you can, both past and contemporary. It cannot harm you (as some beginners fear it will), and it may help you considerably. Do not read to "copy" except as an exercise. Read to see how other poets express themselves, how they achieve their effects, how they put the elements of their work together—in other words, how poets *make* poems.

You may ask yourself why you really don't like some poems that have been revered throughout time and are included in anthology after anthology. Can I really be a poet, you wonder, if I don't understand or appreciate as others do? It is natural to dislike certain poems and to feel misgivings about such dislike. Liking is a subjective affair. We don't all like the same things; there's no reason why all of us should like the same poems. It is more honest to admit not liking a poem than to pretend to like it because everyone else seems to like it. It would be naive to accept all famous works indiscriminately. As your own writing and critical skills develop, you will detect faults in many favorite poems.

On the other hand, there is nothing to be ashamed of if tomorrow you discover what a fine piece of work a poem is, whereas yesterday it appeared to be dull and obscure. It could be that in the meantime your taste and appreciation have gained in sophistication. Even bad poems are of value if you learn to ferret out the reasons for their badness. Such understanding serves you well when you're working on your own material. If you strive to avoid the pitfalls other poets stumbled into, you will be the better poet for it.

In considering the ivory-tower syndrome today, one is both intrigued and repelled—with just reason. Although it is appealing to contemplate the unbounded privacy such isolation affords, it can also be disastrous for any kind of a writer to separate himself or herself entirely from surrounding life. Most writing must be done in isolation, at least the early drafts; but one should guard against being tempted to make isolation a way of life. Poets who are out of touch with the world are likely to turn out to be bland or uninteresting. Worse, they may find themselves to be anachronisms.

In most areas there exists a poetry community of some sort. Become a part of it. You can benefit from such association; the interchanges among writers are both stimulating and challenging. Often, they lead writers to do some of their best work. Discuss with your poet-friends the poets you are reading. Analyze the methods of these poets in meetings with your peers. Examine the experimental poetry appearing in the avant-garde journals. You may discover that you have ideas for enlarging upon or developing further the suggestive enticements of some of these experiments. Above all, be daring rather than timid, in your work as well as in discussion.

You have considered the import of the things we've discussed so far and have not been dissuaded from following your intent. You have given your pledge, and poetry has accepted your commitment. This is the jumping-off place. Now you can only go on to write your poems.

II. Body and Soul

2. Brain and Heart

In writing your poems, you will call into play all levels of yourself—those readily available and some for which you will have to reach into yourself. You will rely on your thinking *and* your feelings; one without the other is addressing only half the process of creating a poem.

CONSCIOUS AND SUBCONSCIOUS

In each of us there is an underworld of the mind. Occasionally, for one reason or another, our conscious level is moved to probe this place, to try to pull some of its stored matter to the surface. At other times, bits and pieces float upward of their own accord, assuming vague shapes in beginning light. Most often, this subterranean material remains in its own darkness, protecting itself from the probing light of the conscious mind; attempts to reveal such material require effort and patience.

Much has been written about this deep place, but it has yet to be explained satisfactorily. The general assumption seems to be that the function of the subconscious is to shield us from too strenuous an emotional threat. Now and then we are driven to slice away at the protective coating with our conscious scapels, laying bare old hurts and fears. This other part of ourselves, this lurking underworld, can be frightening at times. It also happens to be one of the most productive resources available to the creative intellect. Time and again, it has been mined for use in artistic creation and expression. No doubt, in some cases, it has been overmined.

The poet who makes use of material from the subconscious part of the mind learns that the impulse to create originates from the same area. The conflicting desires to express and to repress, the revelations that filter through our censor and make themselves known to us accompany this creative effort. The result of the artistic process, the work itself, is rarely shaped and organized by the subconscious. From the exuberant outpouring of its origin, the poem is shaped into a manifest form through the sobering influences of the conscious mind and the application of poetic skills—skills learned and practiced during the poet's appreticeship. In a way, this critical process illuminates the ideas emerging from that darker side of the mind.

It is not unusual to experience difficulty in facing some of these things about ourselves that have been coaxed from our deeper recesses. If we can keep fears in check, we will learn to deal with these alarming facets of nature and to direct them toward contributing to creative output.

Consider your subconscious a dimly lit storehouse whose contents are being continually sorted, rearranged, catalogued, and suggested for your consideration. Make yourself receptive to these offerings, and you will be able to draw on this rich, extensive inventory. And the data become yours to shape and transform into a work of art. Protect yourself, however, from mere spillage. Invariably, the material furnished from this deep place is *raw;* it needs *to be made into art* by the application of your poetic skills.

MEMORY AND DREAMS

An individual's memory store occupies both parts of the mind. Parts of this store sink into the subconscious and are more resistant to recall. They lie hidden until some trigger—a sound, view, word, or feeling—reactivates them and makes them accessible once more to the conscious level of the mind. Other parts of the memory lie fairly close to the surface and are easier to recall. The poet makes use of both states of memory, as well as what is called "racial memory." This individualization in a poet's work lends the poems a continuity, the authority of reality. Racial memory, the phenomenon that furnishes the species' continuum, is stored so deeply in the individual's subconscious that it requires diligent effort to reach and examine it consciously. Paradoxically, it surfaces quite readily and naturally by disguising itself as intuition and instinct. Instinct and intuition reside somewhere between the realms of the conscious and the subconscious. Although they appear to be innate, they originate from external influences and inputs that have been well absorbed, individually and racially.

From the time of our conception until our death, everything we experience or learn becomes an item in memory. Each item is continually processed and stored. Its retrieval, when and if retrieval becomes necessary, is conditioned by our emotional state and attitude at the time of retrieval, which is influenced, in turn, by the degree of urgency that inspires the desire to retrieve. Poets frequently force or encourage such retrieval to take place so they can make use of the information in their writing.

A great amount of material unearthed in this fashion masquerades as art while seldom achieving art. Only a small portion becomes transformed, in its final form, into poetry.

If poems stemming from such individual material rely entirely on the personal aspects of experience to the exclusion of the needs of the reader to identify with the poem's elements, they are likely to prove failures because they will lack universality. They will probably end up being "in" poems of the era;

they may sound "arty," and unless the reader is one of the people mentioned in the poems or knows the private references and jargon, the poems will mean little. Intensely personal or exclusive poetry tends to be incestuously inbred, obscure, and rather snobbish. Some of the beat poets of the fifties were often guilty of this kind of poem; the members of some groups seemed to be talking only to each other, and the general audience was hard put to understand why publication was necessary at all, since the reader was kept out of the material. The real poet handles personal material in such a way that it achieves a universal quality that includes the reader in the work's experience. By all means, avail yourself of the treasures your experience storehouse can offer you, but keep in mind your responsibility for refining, distilling, and transforming that raw material into art, and the fact that your reader needs to empathize and participate in your poem.

Hidden elements of memory also reveal themselves at times through dreams. Dreams appear to be an enactment or a "working out" process in problem solution. Because of their dramatic presentations, dreams are sometimes transcribable into poems. It is not unusual for poets to keep notebooks by their bedsides in which to record dreams as soon as possible upon waking.

Some poems prompted by dreams turn out to be fine works. In a few cases, a dream may produce a masterpiece, as demonstrated by the following example.

Samuel Taylor Coleridge (eighteenth–nineteenth centuries)
Kubla Khan

In Xanadu did Kubla Khan
   A stately pleasure-dome decree:
Where Alph, the sacred river, ran
Through caverns measureless to man
   Down to a sunless sea.
So twice five miles of fertile ground
With walls and towers were girdled round:
And here were gardens bright with sinuous rills,
Where blossomed many an incense-bearing tree

And here were forests ancient as the hills,
Enfolding sunny spots of greenery.

But oh! that deep romantic chasm which slanted
Down the green hill athwart a cedarn cover!
A savage place! as holy and enchanted
As e'er beneath a waning moon was haunted
By woman wailing for her demon-lover!
And from this chasm, with ceaseless turmoil seething,
As if this earth in fast thick pants were breathing,
A mighty fountain momently was forced;
Amid whose swift half-intermitted burst
Huge fragments vaulted like rebounding hail,
Or chaffy grain beneath the thresher's flail:
And 'mid these dancing rocks at once and ever
It flung up momently the sacred river.
Five miles meandering with a mazy motion
Through wood and dale the sacred river ran,
Then reached the caverns measureless to man,
And sank in tumult to a lifeless ocean:
And 'mid this tumult Kubla heard from far
Ancestral voices prophesying war!

    The shadow of the dome of pleasure
        Floated midway on the waves;
    Where was heard the mingled measure
        From the fountain and the caves.
It was a miracle of rare device,
A sunny pleasure-dome with caves of ice!

    A damsel with a dulcimer
        In a vision once I saw:
    It was an Abyssinian maid,
        And on her dulcimer she played,
    Singing of Mount Abora.
    Could I revive within me
    Her symphony and song,

> To such a deep delight 'twould win me,
> That with music loud and long,
> I would build that dome in air,
> That sunny dome! those caves of ice!
> And all who heard should see them there,
> And all should cry, Beware! Beware!
> His flashing eyes, his floating hair!
> Weave a circle round him thrice,
>   And close your eyes with holy dread,
>   For he on honey-dew hath fed,
> And drunk the milk of Paradise.

The story goes that Coleridge, who had not been feeling well, was sitting in a chair reading *Purchas His Pilgrimage*. The medicine he'd taken made him drowsy, and after reading the reference to Cublai Can's building a stately palace in Xanadu, Coleridge dozed off. By his own report, he had a dream in which the elements that were to find their way into the poem's beginning appeared to him. He began to write but was called out, and when he returned, he found it difficult to recall more of the dream in specific details.

Unfortunately, not all poems triggered by dreams turn out to be masterpieces, or even good poems. One comes across many poems resulting from dreams that are nothing more than the details of the dreams arranged to look like poems. We learn that dreams, also, provide material in raw form. There is no escaping the requirement that *we* have to turn it into art.

Sometimes dreams are interpreted as "prophetic visions." Whether there's any prophetic aspect to some dreams is, as yet, debatable. But we can be fairly sure that the dream demonstrates potential resolution to some individual problem by recombining elements and projecting toward such results. We do much the same thing while awake if we're trying to solve a puzzle or difficulty. The advantage in having the process occur during sleep lies in the fact that our personal censor is not interfering, permitting more creative solutions to be dramatized. What concerns us as poets is that we recognize the value of dream material and use it to artistic ends. If we, as clever artisans, can imbue the poems' thrusts with a sort of prophetic magic, all the better.

Dreams also reinforce our uniqueness. As an individual viewpoint makes a way of perceiving, thinking, and interpreting entirely different from others, so our dreams are individualized dramatizations of things on our minds. In using dream material for poetry, we are encouraging our uniqueness of expression. We must take care, however, to avoid sounding too wrapped up in self, too ego placating. Transcribing and editing dream data into poetry also calls for a wise application of skills.

EXPERIENCES AND EMOTIONS

We experience in various ways: (1) directly and physically by sense contact through sight, sound, touch, smell, taste; (2) vicariously through a combination of the poem's emotions and feelings and our own; and (3) again vicariously through our intellect and imagination and by empathizing with the poem's content. These methods of experiencing overlap, interweave, and alter each other to achieve various combinations.

The store of experience for each of us is composed of direct impressions resulting from having lived through events, occurrences, situations, relationships, and the like; it is the sum of the history of our individual lives. All your experiences become integrated into your being in some fashion or other. Frequently, you will find yourself using such experience directly—by drawing on events from memory—or indirectly—by using your imagination, your inventiveness, to create fictional events similar to, or even opposite from, real events that have actually occurred in your life. Your point of view, attitudes, prejudices, and so forth are likely to undergo some subtle changes as you assimilate further experiences. This maturation will reveal itself in your poems, both in your images and the logic behind them and in the continuing ways you express yourself through language.

Study yourself. Appreciate what a truly fantastic entity

your mind and body unite to form. Listen to your own heartbeat, your inner rhythms, the silences within you. Separate, analyze, and understand each of your bodily processes, mental as well as physical. Let your body reveal to you how experience is absorbed and assimilated. Consider the manner in which your senses pick up data. Even your skin functions as a continuously receiving antenna, flowing over the extent of your body. Regard the way your intellect assesses events or sensations and assigns them storage levels within your internal computer bank. And consider how your experiencing affects your emotions and feelings.

EMOTIONS AND FEELINGS

Although these terms are often used as synonyms for each other, here they are used with the following distinctions: *emotion*—any one of the states designated as fear, anger, joy, surprise, grief, disgust, hate, and so on; *feeling*—appreciative recognition, a sensing, a partly physical and partly mental response that is painful or pleasurable or both in some degree.

Emotion provides the atmosphere of a poem. Feeling is imparted by you, as the writer, through the poem to your audience, reaching that audience on a physical *and* emotional level. And while you are transmitting the poem's feelings in this way, the meaning, or abstract sense, is being directed by the poem's structural and technical features to the audience's intellect for interpretation. It is never quite so cleanly divided, of course—rather an overlap of the two. As you develop your skills, you will be able to control more and more the ratio of projected sense and feeling to suit your purposes.

The following poem by Joyce Carol Oates, which appeared in *The Missouri Review* in the spring of 1978, is not lacking in emotion, but the direct appeal seems biased more toward the reader's intellect.

Query

For instance, why
does the blood coagulate:
why does the tiny mouth of a wound

turn prim when touched by air:
why don't we drain away
like fluid in cracked vases?

And why is it an axiom
that the posthumous move
among us airy of spirit:
why do they claim more,
claim us:
why are their grins earth-full
and wicked?

Why are there certain weathers
that contract giants to shadows:
that reduce the splendor of our cries
to echoes: the blossom of our souls
to mere seeds?

On the other hand, this poem by Laura Marlin, which appeared in *Ab Intra* #1, 1972 (Hellric Publications), is aimed right to the solar plexus:

Penance

oh heaven
stab once more
this hand held
bleeding against
the spin of
the man in front
I have seen
his glazed look
snip off my
dress my skin
I shudder
as scaled with
sperm wasted
in washrooms
his stiff hand

> he would now
> have me touch
> my own hand
> still bleeding
> from one knife
> left blade up
> in the tray

This amazing assemblage of resources, all contained within your individual storehouse, constitutes the greatest reserve on which you can draw. Dip into this storehouse as often as you like; you will never exhaust material demanding poetic expression, because you have in you the *living* inventory. And above all, don't be hesitant about altering facts for the benefit of composition. *Your role is that of a poet, and your responsibility is to express the truth of perception rather than the truth of experience.*

THEMATIC SOURCES OUTSIDE THE SELF

Rich and enticing as your own store of resources may be, you are by no means limited to only those sources; nor should you be. Let your imagination loose upon the environment and on situations involving others. Better yet, invent situations in which you play no part at all, except, perhaps, as observer. Appreciate subjectively, but appraise objectively. All around you exist thousands of reasons for poems: people with whom you come in contact or read or hear about; events you witness; relationships you observe: the child and parent, playmates, siblings, adults at war, adults in love; the phenomena of the natural environment; the industrial, militaristic, socialistic, or whatever society you view, ponder, interpet, report on; the past, future, or present. As a writer you have the obligation to listen, watch, take notes (mentally, at least), evaluate, and understand in the context of an event's happening.

In this external world, as well as in your private internal

one, everything is still in a raw state, so here, too, you have to transform elements into a poetic composition. In some of these poems, you will invest the details with feelings you recall associated with similar events or situations in your own life. For instance, if you are writing of your protagonist's love for another person, you may find the best way to express that love is to recall feelings you had when you loved that way at that age. In other words, you would apply the same criteria to subjective and objective poems, but in the latter, you maintain a narrator's or observer's distance.

In the following poem, Josephine Miles does not interject her presence in the situation; she maintains the stance of invisible observer. Whether she actually witnessed such a scene or only imagined it really doesn't matter. What does matter is how she executes the poem so that it has meaning for the reader and communicates on all the levels a poem should.

> *Players*
> Into the spacious bay the sun of afternoon
> Shone,
> And there two people, a man with a beard and a woman
>   without, were playing
> At cards alone.
>
> Lake traffic, line traffic, pine, plain traffic all around them
> Presided,
> Roared but soft, rushed but not
> Into the window, many-sided,
>
> Looking for a game to play, a war to win, some sort of
>   magnificent errand
> To be done;
> While the spadebeard took easily a trick
> Already a century won.

The way that second stanza communicates the scene's atmosphere is marvelous. Can't you just feel the loudness of that rough traffic for the rest of the world and how hushed and far away its existence is for the two players? It is accomplished not only because of the curious juxtaposition of some of the words but by their very sounds as well.

While striving to be as objective as possible in some of your poems, remember that pure objectivity is not possible. You can keep your poems free of interpretive phrases, conclusions, editorial comments, and the like, but the very selection and arrangement of details are subjective and will indicate or imply your point of view and your sympathies. Don't worry about this; readers don't expect you to be as impersonal as a tape recorder. Nor would they want you to be. They want to feel in contact with a warm-blooded creature, not some machine. They expect your poem to include feeling and attitude, however much subdued they may be. Otherwise, your work will resemble a technical report.

Extending the range of theme and subject interest outside your personal experience not only affords you much more material from which to draw and a greater variety of modes of expression but also results in an extension of experience itself. In dealing with the external world, you make that experience your own, in effect. As you can see, you are actually increasing the inventory in your storehouse when writing about others.

To write poems, one needs commitment, an analytical appreciation of self, a compulsive urge to express oneself in language, a critical assessment of the results of such expression, a knowledge of the state of poetry and an awareness of what its future directions may be, a respect for one's personal storehouse of experience and feelings, and a greedy reaching to the outside world for more material to assimilate, digest, and use. These needs must be met, but in themselves they are not enough to ensure that one will become a poet, however many poems one may write. To be a true poet, one must have, in addition to all the foregoing, a strong sense of ego, yet a realistic understanding of one's place with respect to the rest of the world, literary and public, as well as a thorough knowledge of the craft of poetic expression.

To deal more concretely with this last requirement, let's make a closer examination of the different kinds and styles of poetry.

3. Physiognomy

There should be *shape* to any poem, whether that shape is determined by a traditional form like that of the sestina, by an organic form resulting from the use of free verse or syllabics, or by the design that evolves in working with open techniques. In addition to shape, a poem also possesses a *nature*, an inner quality that is its essence. The combination of shape and nature gives the poem its *appearance*, using the term to mean "that by which a thing is truly known."

Since a poem is a composition in which all parts contribute to its total aesthetic effect, and since the removal of any one part would destroy the poem, we are responsible for ensuring the concord between shape and nature in any piece we write. Whereas the use of metaphor, meter, or rhyme, for instance, is optional in the making of poetry, shape and nature must be present.

Although we realize that poetry itself still defies definition, we have become aware that the line between fine poetry and fine prose has all but disappeared. A good many prose pieces surpass in poetic quality much contemporary work that passes for poetry. Writers such as James Joyce, Franz Kafka, Herman Melville, Anaïs Nin, Virginia Woolf, John Hawkes, and Alan Paton (to name only a few) are not known primarily as poets. Yet can anyone doubt that these writers possess the poet's sensitivity to a high degree and that the masterful and loving use they make of language, mood, and other poetic devices raises their work well above the structure and effect of ordinary prose?

Let us, for our purposes here, tolerate a temporary definition—a working definition, you might say—of poetry: A poem is an integrated literary composition, tightly expressed, that is not restricted to discursive progression and logic but operates on a radiational level. It has form, shape, pattern, and agreement (as used here) as well as theme and subject.

Since metaphor, rhythm, density and compression, formal structure, and pattern are often found in fine prose, how does one distinguish between poetry and prose at all? In the final analysis, *recognizing* poetry is dependent on "the feel"—a knowing at a deeper than usual level that *one is in the presence of poetry;* that poetry is language in living action as complex as life itself; that it is directional and nondirectional, particular and universal at the same instant. We could add that true poetry has an unknown or X quality nourished by its earliest history rooted in magic, myth, and music. Yet we realize that even comprehension that relies on intellectual and intuitive impulses is merely an approximation of the understanding of any poem worthy of the name. And be warned: even with all these criteria, there's no certainty, because they may all be present, as well, in a superb literary novel.

How does one come to know this chameleon, poetry, at all? One of the aids to knowing is to become familiar with the history, traditions, and development of the art. This is too broad a subject to cover here, but the offerings that follow are designed to whet your appetite, and the hope is that you will be motivated to do further research on your own. You have no doubt asked yourself why it's necessary to explore the past (of poetry) in such great detail, since most of the poems you read today are written in free verse or open style. The past explains (in many cases, through implication) the directions of the present and future.

In addition, traditional forms do appear from time to time

in some journals, and they are a welcome relief. It is especially pleasing when the contemporary writer does something new with an established form. In art, nothing dies; it merely moves through change. The past offers possible approaches. And it is through exploring these approaches that we will come to know something about this chameleon, poetry.

Conventions, traditions, these offer temporary reference points—temporary because conventions and traditions also change with development and experimentation. Stylistic devices, persistent character types, forms, themes, patterns, manner and style in the presentation of various subject matter—these, appearing again and again in poetry, develop into conventions. Adherence to a particular set of conventions for a period of time leads to the establishment of a tradition. In turn, traditions are influenced by further development and experiments. And through such cycles, the art of poetry continues to lead a healthy life.

If you will allow yourself to experience some of the exquisite examples from the long line of our poetic heritage, you will develop a better *feel* for what poetry is and will more easily recognize it when it occurs in our time. The forms and natures of poems reveal to us how they acquire their shapes, their faces, their bodies, their pulses, their appearances. And recognition depends on appearance, the outer *and* the inner.

The qualities of lyricism, narration, and drama—these are the principal divisions of the nature of poetry.

There is always the temptation to label a poem as a lyric, narrative, or dramatic one. In rare instances, a poem may indeed have just one of these qualities, but most often elements of all three are present in various ratios; and if we describe the nature of a poem as dramatic, we really mean that the dramatic aspect is the dominant one. Even poems whose natures are referred to as descriptive or didactic are seldom entirely so. For example, Hamlet's speech to the players, which amounts to a didactic prose-poem, is certainly dramatic as well and by no means lacking in lyricism.

> Speak the speech, I pray you, as I pronounced it to you, trippingly on the tongue: but if you mouth it, as many of your players do,

I had as lief the town-crier spoke my lines. Nor do not saw the air too much with your hand, thus; but use all gently: for in the very torrent, tempest, and, (as I may say) whirlwind of your passion, you must acquire and beget a temperance that may give it smoothness. O, it offends me to the soul to hear a robustious periwigpated fellow tear a passion to tatters, to very rags, to split the ears of the groundlings; who, for the most part, are capable of nothing but inexplicable dumbshows, and noise: I would have such a fellow whipped for o'er-doing Termagant; it out-herods Herod: pray you, avoid it.... Be not too tame neither, but let your own discretion be your tutor: suit the action to the word, the word to the action; with this special observance, that you o'er-step not the modesty of nature: for any thing so overdone is from the purpose of playing; whose end, both at the first, and now, was, and is, to hold, as 'twere, the mirror up to nature; to show virtue her own feature, scorn her own image, and the very age and body of time, his form and pressure. Now, this overdone, or come tardy off, though it make the unskilful laugh, cannot but make the judicious grieve; the censure of which one, must, in your allowance, o'er-weigh a whole theatre of others. O, there be players, that I have seen play,—and heard others praise, and that highly,—not to speak it profanely, that, neither having the accent of Christians, nor the gait of Christian, pagan, nor man, have so strutted and bellowed, that I have thought some of nature's journeymen had made men, and not made them well, they imitated humanity so abominably.

As you can see, didactic poetry intends to "teach" or "instruct." Examples of other didactic poems are Wordsworth's "The Excursion," the works of Cowper in general, and Alexander Pope's *Essay on Man* and *Essay on Criticism*. These lines from the latter poem will give the flavor of Pope's didacticism:

> 'Tis hard to say, if greater want of skill
> Appear in writing or in judging ill;
> But, of the two, less dangerous is the offence
> To tire our patience, than mislead our sense.
> Some few in that, but number err in this;
> Ten censure wrong for one who writes amiss;

> A fool might once himself alone expose,
> Now one in verse makes many more in prose.
>
>   'Tis with our judgments as our watches, none
> Go just alike, yet each believes his own.
> In poets as true genius is but rare,
> True taste as seldom is the critic's share;
> Both must alike from Heaven derive their light,
> These born to judge, as well as those to write.
> Let such teach others who themselves excel,
> And censure freely who have written well.
> Authors are partial to their wit, 'tis true,
> But are not critics to their judgment, too?
>
> . . . .
>
>   Of all the causes which conspire to blind
> Man's erring judgment, and misguide the mind,
> What the weak head with strongest bias rules,
> Is pride, the never-failing vice of fools.

Satire, too, is a species of didactic poetry, and along with Pope, we have Swift, Butler, Dryden, and Burns as major exponents of poking fun at our mores and hoping to teach through ridicule.

The term *didactic* is sometimes used as a negative criticism. Obviously, this is not entirely fair. A great deal of fine poetry is didactic in intent, if not in expression. In such great works as *The Divine Comedy, Paradise Lost,* and even some of the poetry in the Bible, for that matter, the didacticism is sublimated, which makes it less intrusive. But one can't deny that their authors intended us to learn from their poems. One suspects that every poet hopes his or her work will influence readers, and that is teaching of a sort. When we apply the term *didactic* in a negative sense, it generally refers to work that is clumsily executed so that the moral or lesson sticks out in an ungainly fashion. Dante, Milton, and others placed such emphasis on the music and the dramatic and narrative aspects in their work that their lessons are painless for most readers.

Descriptive poetry is another borderline category. Details of character, scene, event, and so forth are hardly absent entirely from any poem. But poems in which description seems to be the dominating feature are often classed as descriptive poetry. *Polyolbion* by Drayton, *Windsor Forest* by Pope, and Goldsmith's *The Deserted Village* belong in this group, as do Milton's "Il Penseroso" and "L'Allegro." Another species of descriptive poetry is the *pastoral,* a poem dealing with the innocence (real or imagined) of rural life and in which the figures are shepherds and maidens. The pastoral has all but gone out of fashion in our time.

Keeping in mind that the three main divisions of the nature of poetry do not maintain their separate distinctions, let's have a closer look at the major categories.

The term *lyric* is too often applied as if it designated a form. It refers more properly to the nature of the language, tonality, mood, and emotional expression in the poem—which is why narrative and dramatic poetry may, at the same time, be lyrical. The forms and styles most often included in this category are songs, hymns and psalms, ballads, elegies, odes, sonnets, pastorals, idylls, epitaphs, dramatic short pieces, reflections, drinking songs, and poems on the subjects of religion, love, friendship, nature, patriotism, war, childhood, and other preoccupations of our daily lives.

Of the three major divisions, lyric poetry constitutes the most extensive category by far. Generally, lyric poems are shorter and more manageable than narrative or dramatic poems, which seem to enjoy longer treatments. Narrative poetry is concerned primarily with telling a story. Dramatic poetry usually presents the story in a dramatic form such as a verse play or in forms structured as dramatic "lyrics," monologues, or dialogues. Dramatic poetry is epitomized by the plays of Shakespeare.

Early epics and heroic poetry combined lyricism, narration, and drama in admirable fashion. Such epics usually dealt with elevated themes, important national undertakings, or the adventures of some famous hero. Classic epics include *Beowulf, The Iliad* and *The Odyssey* of Homer, Virgil's *Aeneid,*

The Divine Comedy by Dante, and Milton's *Paradise Lost* and *Paradise Regained*.

Such poems as Ariosto's *Orlando Furioso*, *The Faerie Queene* by Edmund Spenser, Byron's *Childe Harold's Pilgrimage*, and Tennyson's *Idylls of the King* are known as romantic epics. There is also a humorous version of the epic called a mock epic, which takes some neglibible theme or trifling subject and elevates it to an exaggerated importance and dignity. Byron did this in *Don Juan*, and Pope did it in *The Rape of the Lock*.

Folk ballads are usually narrative in nature and humorous, gruesome, or tragicomic in tone. Most literary ballads (ballads composed by known poets rather than by anonymous tradition) are fictitiously narrative, as are Chaucer's "The Pardoner's Tale," "Tam o' Shanter" by Robert Burns, "The Eve of St. Agnes" by John Keats, and Oscar Wilde's *Ballad of Reading Gaol*.

The verse play has enjoyed varying degrees of popularity during different eras. It has persisted from the dramatic presentations of the ancient Greek playwrights to (among other contemporary poets indulging in the genre) T. S. Eliot, Robert Lowell, William Butler Yeats, and Federico García Lorca. Some of the verse plays by contemporary poets play very well on stage. Others are primarily dramatizations of *ideas* and do not fare so well when acted out. Such plays, known as "closet plays," are better read than witnessed in a theater, but quite often the poetry is of a high order of exellence.

As you develop your personal level of discrimination, you will be able to select what is worth your while to study.

Let's pretend that we are attending a concert of language in the form of poetry. See if you can determine how the following poets developed the narrative, expressed the dramatic, and sang the lyrical quality in their works. Some of these examples will be familiar, at least in part. Others may be unknown to you. Perhaps you will be moved to delve deeper into the work of those poets to whom you respond most readily. Most selection is a strongly subjective process. You will certainly exercise your own subjectivity in your future reading, and that is as it should be. For the present, savor the lyric, narrative, and dramatic traits in these few poems.

LYRIC

The principal quality of lyric poetry is its melodic tonality working in accord with its rhythms.

Sappho (ancient Greece)
Beauty
Translated by D. G. Rossetti.

I.
Like the sweet apple which reddens upon the topmost bough,
Atop on the topmost twig,—which the pluckers forgot, somehow,—
Forgot it not, nay, but got it not, for none could get it till now.

II.
Like the wild hyacinth flower which on the hills is found,
Which the passing feet of the shepherds forever tear and wound,
Until the purple blossom is trodden into the ground.

Robert Herrick (seventeenth century)
Julia
(also known as "Upon Julia's Clothes")

Whenas in silks my Julia goes
Then, then (methinks) how sweetly flows
That liquefaction of her clothes.

Next, when I cast mine eyes and see
That brave vibration each way free;
O how that glittering taketh me!

William Wordsworth (nineteenth century)
A Slumber Did My Spirit Seal

A slumber did my spirit seal;
   I had no human fears:

  She seemed a thing that could not feel
    The touch of earthly years.

No motion has she now, no force;
    She neither hears nor sees,
Rolled round in earth's diurnal course,
    With rocks, and stones, and trees.

John Logan (contemporary)
Lament in Spring

Oh I have felt these same
yearnings in myself—
the tiny dark and yellow
hairs lit with wet
at the center of the May Day
violets Elizabeth held
in her seven-year-old fist
some six or seven years before
the grace she gave the afternoon

(her hand stemmed in mine)
at the topaz time of day
when children doze and she,
Elizabeth, waits breath-
less at the edge of the well.
She was my brother's girl,
and so I let her go.
For who can stand these old stirrings
in himself, and that one too?

John Frederick Nims (contemporary)
Love Poem

My clumsiest dear, whose hands shipwreck vases,
At whose quick touch all glasses chip and ring,
Whose palms are bulls in china, burs in linen,

And have no cunning with any soft thing

Except all ill-at-ease fidgeting people:
The refugee uncertain at the door
You make at home; deftly you steady
The drunk clambering on his undulant floor.

Unpredictable dear, the taxi drivers' terror,
Shrinking from far headlights pale as a dime
Yet leaping before red apoplectic streetcars—
Misfit in any space. And never on time.

A wrench in clocks and solar systems. Only
With words and people and love you move at ease.
In traffic of wit expertly manoeuvre
And keep us, all devotion, at your knees.

Forgetting your coffee spreading on our flannel,
Your lipstick grinning on our coat,
So gayly in love's unbreakable heaven
Our souls on glory of spilt bourbon float.

Be with me, darling, early and late. Smash glasses—
I will study wry music for your sake.
For should your hands drop white and empty
All the toys of the world would break.

Perhaps the most melodic of all lyric poems are those described as *songs*. Poetry abounds with songs; from the very beginning—when poetry was actually (and naturally) sung—its inventory has included songs of love, prayer, grief, patriotism, family love, and so forth, with those of love occupying the lead. In the song, sacred or secular, language is used in its simplest manifestations, with reliance placed on emotional content and implication to enhance the richness of the words even further. There is form, of course, but here there is no time or patience to puzzle over intellectual phrases. Here is time to sound forth, directly and clearly.

The Old Testament of the Bible is filled with fine songs like the Song of Songs, the Psalms of David, the songs of

Miriam and of Deborah. Here are a few other examples from the literature of poetry.

William Shakespeare (Elizabethan period)
from *Twelfth Night*

O mistress mine, where are you roaming?
O, stay and hear; your true love's coming,
   That can sing both high and low:
Trip no farther, pretty sweeting;
Journeys end in lovers' meeting,
   Every wise man's son doth know.

. . . .

What is love? 'tis not hereafter;
Present mirth hath present laughter;
   What's to come is still unsure:
In delay there lies no plenty;
Then come kiss me, sweet and twenty,
   Youth's a stuff will not endure.

William Blake (eighteenth century)
Nurse's Song
(the version from *Songs of Experience*)

When the voices of children are heard on the green
And whisp'rings are in the dale,
The days of my youth rise fresh in my mind,
My face turns green and pale.

Then come home, my children, the sun is gone down,
And the dews of night arise;
Your spring & your day are wasted in play,
And your winter and night in disguise.

William Butler Yeats (nineteenth–twentieth centuries)
The Lake Isle of Innisfree

I will arise and go now, and go to Innisfree,
   And a small cabin build there, of clay and wattles made:

Nine bean-rows will I have there, a hive for the honeybee,
And live alone in the bee-loud glade.

And I shall have some peace there, for peace comes dropping slow,
Dropping from the veils of the morning to where the cricket sings;
There midnight's all a glimmer, and noon a purple glow,
And evening full of the linnet's wings.

I will arise and go now, for always night and day
I hear lake water lapping with low sounds by the shore;
While I stand on the roadway, or on the pavements grey,
I hear it in the deep heart's core.

Robert Graves (contemporary)
Twinned Heart

Challenged once more to reunite,
    Perfect in every limb
But screened against the intrusive light
    By ghosts and cherubim,

I call your beauty to my bed,
    My pride you call to yours
Though clouds run maniac overhead
    And cruel rain down pours,

With both of us prepared to wake
    Each in a bed apart,
True to a spell no power can break:
    The beat of a twinned heart.

Dolores Stewart (contemporary)
Morning and Evening Song

that girl who combs her hair
in that long mirror there
combs in the fern and fennel spells
the silkworm spinning spells

       combs in the wires of the sun
       the green vines on the ground
       and in the mirror combs
       the languorous willow wands
       the cries of winnowing birds
       who combs her daughter's hair
       combs in the lyres and the harps
       the blossoms of nine trees
       sits on the rocks and combs her hair
       in that deep mirror there
       the seaweed coming back from sleep
       the drowned ships sailing down
       combs in the weaving and unraveling
       the white moths putting out the lights
       the whirr of owls in the woods
       who combs her hair alone
       who combs her daughter's hair

    Before going on, it may be worth your while to read these examples again, this time aloud. Actually voicing the poems best brings out the music in them.

    We are fortunate that Rossetti was such a sensitive translator of poems. In the piece by Sappho, note the very real stretching effect of the proximity and repetition of the words such as *topmost, atop,* and *topmost* again. Think of the primary sense of the words themselves, and of the feel of them, quite apart from their context. Granted, they are Rossetti's words. One hopes the originals worked as well. This is what the business of poetry is about.

    In the poem by Herrick, the special timbre and liquidity of the word *liquefaction* is astoundingly precise, a truly inspired word selection.

    In "A Slumber Did My Spirit Seal," appreciate the contrast between the smoothness of the first stanza and the extremely subtle disturbance in the rhythm of the second, reinforcing the heavy, sad tone; the hesitation occasioned by the comma before *no force* and the mournful pacing of that last line, brought about by the combination of commas and conjunctions—a masterful development of mood.

Looking at John Logan's poem, we see that lyric poetry need not have true rhymes to create music. There are some exquisite modulations in *rhyme sounds* in many of the line endings (the long *a* sounds in *same, day;* the short *e* in *myself, yellow, wet, held, well;* the *o*'s in *before, afternoon, go,* and *too,* recalling the second syllable of *yellow* in the third line; the *r* sounds in *girl* stretched in *stirring*) that definitely make this a rhymed poem through the use of vowel and consonant rhymes.

Nims, in "Love Poem," rhymes the second and fourth lines of each stanza. The number of *l*'s, *m*'s, and *n*'s in this gently teasing poem reinforce its musical quality to an extraordinary degree. Notice how deftly the poet establishes the starting mood: in the opening line, the words *clumsiest* and *shipwreck* indicate the tone immediately. But the love is there, along with the teasing; and when the poem nears its end, it takes on—in the last two lines—a somber note. The skill of this poet is further revealed by the way he maintains the integrity of detail throughout the poem; the choice of the word *toys* is apt because it does not violate the poem's diction and prevents the poem from turning overly sentimental.

One of the greatest singers in verse in recent times was William Butler Yeats. In "The Lake Isle of Innisfree," notice how the pauses in the middles of the first three lines of each stanza emphasize by contrast the uninterrupted rhythm of the fourth lines. In this poem, written in 1890, Yeats felt that for the first time, his own music revealed itself. The lightness and playfulness of the detail are overcome by the poem's dignity and reverence, which are developed through the pacing and rhythm and through the contrasts in rhyming (the more fragile rhyme sounds in the middle stanza are bracketed by the heavier rhymes of the other two stanzas). "I will arise and go now, and go to Innisfree" recalls strongly the line from the New Testament of the Bible: "I will arise and go unto my father." It is also interesting to observe that image phrases like "the bee-loud glade" and "in the deep heart's core" foreshadow the deeply resonant singing of Dylan Thomas.

Although these simple lyrics and songs are not confined to any one specific form, the elements of pattern give each poem a structural unity that makes it a true composition. In many cases, the pattern development coincides with the development of other aspects—subject or theme, mood, form, or character delineation. In Logan's poem, for instance, there is a concentration of three-beat lines at the beginning. In the middle, where emotion becomes intensified in the presence of the memory's poignancy, the lines themselves are "intensified" (extended) to four beats. Then there is a release back to three-beat lines as the moods of regret and surrender make themselves felt, and a final tentative and quiet "burst" of energy implicit in the last two lines. Throughout the poem, the rhythmic elasticity elaborates the tension which invests the sense of the lines.

In "Morning and Evening Song," the repetition of elements and detail, the sounds of the words, and the arrangement of lines as dance measure give the Stewart poem an unmistakable music. The motion suggested by the three-beat and four-beat lines (more alternating than in the Logan poem) is not unlike the gentle tug and release of a quiet sea, one of the poem's elements. This hypnotic poem provides the feeling that one could keep going back to the beginning and let the music continue indefinitely.

During classical times, the term *elegy* designated any poem written in elegiac couplets (pairs of lines, each with six metrical feet or six in the first line and five in the second). Greek and Roman poets used the elegy form to express themes of death, war, and love. Since the sixteenth century, the term has come to identify any poem written to express an exalted mourning of either death in general or the death of a particular person. The nature of the elegy is lyrical and dignified. Elegies appear throughout the long repertoire of poetry. More recent ones include Whitman's "When Lilacs Last in the Dooryard Bloom'd," "Anne Rutledge" by Edgar Lee Masters, W. H. Auden's "In Memory of W. B. Yeats," and Rainer Maria Rilke's *Duino Elegies*. Here are two samples—one from the last century, the other from this one.

Sir Walter Scott
Coronach from *The Lady of the Lake*
A *coronach* is a Highland funeral lament. In this one, the poet mourns the death of Duncan. Given are the first and last stanzas.

He is gone on the mountain,
   He is lost to the forest,
Like a summer-dried fountain,
   When our need was sorest.
The font, reappearing,
   From the rain-drops shall borrow,
But to us comes no cheering,
   To Duncan no morrow!

. . . .

Fleet foot on the correi,[1]
   Sage counsel in cumber[2]
Red hand in the foray,
   How sound is thy slumber!
Like the dew on the mountain,
   Like the foam on the river,
Like the bubble on the fountain,
   Thou art gone, and forever!

The shift to direct address in the last stanza is in accord with the emotional intensification. Note, too, that many lines begin with a strong beat—a convention of elegiac verse from its earliest times.

Hart Crane (1899–1932)
Praise for an Urn
In Memoriam: Ernest Nelson.

It was a kind and northern face
That mingled in such exile guise
The everlasting eyes of Pierrot

---

[1]*Correi:* hollow side of a hill where game usually lay.
[2]*Cumber:* trouble or difficulty.

And, of Gargantua, the laughter.

His thoughts, delivered to me
From the white coverlet and pillow,
I see now, were inheritances—
Delicate riders of the storm.

The slant moon on the slanting hill
Once moved us toward presentiments
Of what the dead keep, living still,
And such assessments of the soul

As, perched in the crematory lobby,
The insistent clock commented on,
Touching as well upon our praise
Of glories proper to the time.

Still, having in mind gold hair,
I cannot see that broken brow
And miss the dry sound of bees
Stretching across a lucid space.

Scatter these well-meant idioms
Into the smoky spring that fills
The suburbs, where they will be lost.
They are no trophies of the sun.

In this section on the lyrical nature of poetry, you have heard many tonalities; and you have witnessed and felt some shapes of poems, for there always is shape, however free the form. The progress of lyric poetry is a record of the changing music of poetry.

NARRATIVE

Keeping in mind that the primary characteristic of narrative poetry is to tell a story in verse form, consider the following samplings.

Anonymous (later Middle Ages)
The Twa Corbies[a]

As I was walking all alane,
I heard twa corbies making a mane;[b]
The t'ane unto the t'other say,
"Where sall we gang and dine to-day?"

"In behint yon auld fail dyke,[c]
I wot there lies a new slain knight;
And naebody kens that he lies there,
But his hawk, his hound, and lady fair.

"His hound is to the hunting gane,
His hawk to fetch the wild-fowl hame,
His lady's ta'en another mate,
So we may mak our dinner sweet.

"Ye'll sit on his white hause-bane,[d]
And I'll pike out his bonny blue een;
Wi ae lock o his gowden hair
We'll theek our nest when it grows bare.[e]

"Mony a one for him makes mane,
But nane sall ken where he is gane;
Oer his white banes when they are bare,
The wind sall blaw for evermair."

William Morris (nineteenth century)
The Haystack in the Floods (opening lines)

Had she come all the way for this,
To part at last without a kiss?
Yea, had she borne the dirt and rain

---

[a]*Corbies:* ravens.
[b]*Mane:* moan.
[c]*Fail:* turf.
[d]*Hause-bane:* neck bone.
[e]*Theek:* thatch.

44

That her own eyes might see him slain
Beside the haystack in the floods?

Along the dripping leafless woods,
The stirrup touching either shoe,
She rode astride as troopers do;
With kirtle kilted to her knee,[1]
To which the mud splashed wretchedly;
And the wet dripped from every tree
Upon her head and heavy hair,
And on her eyelids broad and fair;
The tears and rain ran down her face.

Bryan Alec Floyd (contemporary)
Sergeant Brandon Just, U.S.M.C.

He was alive with death:
Her name was Sung
and she was six years old.
By slightest mistake of degrees
on an artillery azimuth
he had called for rockets and napalm.
Their wild wizardry of firepower
expired her mistake of a village,
killing everyone except her,
and napalm made her look
like she was dead among the dead,
she alone alive among their upturned corpses
burning towards the sky.
He and the platoon
got to them too late,
removing only her
to a hospital inside of his base, Da Nang.
In the months that followed him,
when he could make it back from the boonies,

---

[1]*Kirtle:* dress or skirt.

he always went to visit Sung.
Finally he was ordered to a desk job at the base.
He visited her every day,
though he accused himself of being alive
and would stand in a slump,
breathing his despair,
before entering the children's ward.
But he would enter.
Sung, knowing it was him,
would turn towards the sound of his feet,
her own, seared beyond being feet,
crisply trying to stand on shadows,
cool but unseen.
And as he could come in,
Sung would hobble up to him
in her therapeutic cart,
smiling even when she did not smile, lipless,
her chin melted to her chest
that would never become breasts.
He would stand
and wait for her touch upon his hand
with her burn-splayed fingers
that came to lay a fire upon his flesh.
Sung was alive
and would live on despite life,
but even now her skull
seemed to be working its way through
the thin, fragile solids of wasted, waxen skin.
Her head was as bald as a bomb
whose paint had peeled.
She had no nose
and her ears were gone.
Her eyes had been removed,
and because they were not there,
they were there
invisibly looking him through.

> Sung was child-happy
> that he came and cared,
> and when he would start to leave,
> she would agonize her words
> out of the hollow that was her mouth.
> Her tongue, bitten in two while she had burned,
> strafing his ears,
> saying, without mercy,
> I love you.

The way Floyd has revealed the story in this poem portrays the horrors of war much more vividly than any editorial or peace propaganda ever could. For another treatment of war experience in our time, you might have a look at *Obscenities*, a volume of poems about Vietnam by Michael Casey, which won the 1972 Yale Younger Poets Award.

DRAMATIC

The dramatic monologue (Browning, who brought the form to perhaps its greatest development, coined for it the term *dramatic lyric*) is a poem consisting of the words of a single speaker who reveals the dramatic situation and his or her own character. The elements of time, place, and events described are made known by the poem itself.

We are fortunate that dramatic poetry's long history has given it a repertoire so extensive and varied. The most familiar verse plays, however, are still those of ancient Greece and of the Elizabethan period. The following examples illustrate different styles of treatment. (In the example by Browning, although the poet included the word *soliloquy* in his title, the poem has all the features of the dramatic monolgue.)

> Robert Browning (nineteenth century)
> Stanzas 1, 2, and 9 of *Soliloquy of the Spanish Cloister*
>
> > Gr-r-r—there go, my heart's abhorrence
> > Water your damned flower-pots, do!

If hate killed men, Brother Lawrence,
  God's blood, would not mine kill you!
What? your myrtle-bush wants trimming?
  Oh, that rose has prior claims—
Needs its leaden vase filled brimming?
  Hell dry you up with its flames!

At the meal we sit together:
  Salve tibi! I must hear
Wise talk of the kind of weather,
  Sort of season, time of year:
Not *a plenteous cork-crop: scarcely*
  Dare we hope oak-galls, I doubt:
What's the Latin name for "parsley"?
  What's the Greek name for Swine's Snout?

. . . .

Or, there's Satan!—one might venture
  Pledge one's soul to him, yet leave
Such a flaw in the indenture
  As he'd miss till, past retrieve,
Blasted lay that rose-acacia
  We're so proud of! Hy, Zy, Hine . . .
'St, there's Vespers! *Plena Gratia,*
  Ave Virgo! Gr-r-r—you swine!

Euripides (480–406 B.C.)
from *Alcestis*
Translated by Richmond Lattimore.
[Alcestis is speaking.]

ALCESTIS
Let me go now, let me down,
flat. I have no strength to stand.
Death is close to me.
The darkness creeps over my eyes. O children,
my children, you have no mother now,

not any longer. Daylight is yours,
my children. Look on it and be happy.

ADMETUS
Ah, a bitter word for me to hear,
heavier than any death of my own.
Before the gods, do not be so harsh
as to leave me, leave your children forlorn.
No, up, and fight it.
There would be nothing left of me if you died.
All rests in you, our life, our not
having life. Your love is our worship.

ALCESTIS
Admetus, you can see how it is with me. Therefore,
I wish to have some words with you before I die.
I put you first, and at the price of my own life
made certain you would live and see the daylight. So
I die, who did not have to die, because of you.
I could have taken any man in Thessaly
I wished and lived in queenly state here in this house.
But since I did not wish to live bereft of you
and with our children fatherless, I did not spare
my youth, although I had so much to live for. Yet
your father, and the mother who bore you, gave you up,
though they had reached an age when it was good to die
and good to save their son and end it honorably.
You were their only one, and they had no more hope
of having other children if you died. That way
I would be living and you would live the rest of our time,
and you would not be alone and mourning for your wife
and tending motherless children. No, but it must be
that some god has so wrought that things shall be this way.
So be it. But swear now to do, in recompense,
what I shall ask you—not enough, oh, never enough,
since nothing is enough to make up for a life,
but fair, and you yourself will say so, since you love

these children as much as I do; or at least you should.
Keep them as masters in my house, and do not marry
again and give our children to a stepmother
who will not be so kind as I, who will be jealous
and raise her hand to your children and mine. Oh no,
do not do that, do not. That is my charge to you.
For the new-come stepmother hates the children born
to a first wife, no viper could be deadlier.
The little boy has his father for a tower of strength.
(He can talk with him and be spoken to in turn.)
But you, my darling, what will your girlhood be like,
how will your father's new wife like you? She must not
make shameful stories up about you, and contrive
to spoil your chance of marriage in the blush of youth,
because your mother will not be there to help you
when you are married, not be there to give you strength
when your babies are born, when only a mother's help will do.
For I must die. It will not be tomorrow, not
the next day, or this month, the horrible thing will come,
but now, at once, I shall be counted among the dead.
Goodbye, be happy, both of you. And you, my husband,
can boast the bride you took made you the bravest wife,
and you, children, can say, too, that your mother was brave.

John Milton (seventeenth century)
Lines from *Samson Agonistes*

SAMSON
A little onward lend thy guiding hand
To these dark steps, a little further on;
For yonder bank hath choice of sun or shade.
There I am wont to sit, when any chance
Relieves me from my task of servile toil,
Daily in the common prison else enjoined me,
Where I, a prisoner chained, scarce freely draw
The air, imprisoned also, close and damp,
Unwholesome draught. But here I feel amends—

The breath of heaven fresh blowing, pure and sweet,
With day-spring born; here leave me to respire.

. . . .

O loss of sight, of thee I most complain!
Blind among enemies! O worse than chains,
Dungeon, or beggary, or decrepit age!
Light, the prime work of God, to me is extinct,
And all her various objects of delight
Annulled, which might in part my grief have eased.
Inferior to the vilest now become
Of man or worm, the vilest here excel me:
They creep, yet see; I, dark in light, exposed
To daily fraud, contempt, abuse, and wrong,
Within doors, or without, still as a fool,
In power of others, never in my own—
Scarce half I seem to live, dead more than half.
O dark, dark, dark, amid the blaze of noon,
Irrecoverably dark, total eclipse
Without all hope of day!

. . . .

But who are these? for with joint pace I hear
The tread of many feet steering this way;
Perhaps my enemies, who come to stare
At my affliction, and perhaps to insult—
Their daily practice to afflict me more.
CHORUS
This, this is he; softly a while;
Let us not break in upon him.
O change beyond report, thought, or belief!
See how he lies at random, carelessly diffused,
With languished head unpropt,
As one past hope, abandoned,
And by himself given over,
In slavish habit, ill-fitted weeds

O'er-worn and soiled.
Or do my eyes misrepresent? Can this be he,
That heroic, that renowned,
Irresistible Samson?...

Samson Agonistes was labeled "A Dramatic Poem" by Milton; it could be classed as a closet drama. This is a good example of the way in which poets may transfer feelings about conditions of their own to the main figure in the poem. The blind Milton presents a blind Samson in a very convincing manner.

There is no question that the following excerpt from Shakespeare's *Romeo and Juliet* plays as well as it reads:

ROMEO
If I profane with my unworthiest hand
    This holy shrine, the gentle fine is this,
My lips, two blushing pilgrims, ready stand
    To smooth that rough touch with a tender kiss.

JULIET
Good pilgrim, you do wrong your hand too much
    Which mannerly devotion shows in this;
For saints have hands that pilgrims' hands do touch,
    And palm to palm is holy palmer's kiss.

ROMEO
Have not saints lips, and holy palmers, too?

JULIET
    Ay, pilgrim, lips that they must use in prayer.

ROMEO
O, then, dear saint, let lips do what hands do;
    They pray, grant thou, lest faith turn to despair.

JULIET
Saints do not move, though grant for prayers' sake.

ROMEO
Then move not, while my prayer's effect I take.
Thus from my lips by thine my sin is purged.   [*kissing her.*]

JULIET
   Then have my lips the sin that they have took.
ROMEO
   Sin from my lips? O trespass sweetly urged!
   Give me my sin again.
JULIET
                 You kiss by the book.

The first fourteen lines of this dialogue form a modified sonnet. The scene is a superb blend of drama, narrative, and lyric poetry.

For a more cerebral treatment of the verse drama, you might consider Goethe's *Faust;* and for a whimsical approach reminiscent of Byron, read *Venus Observed* by Christopher Fry.

CLASSICAL / ROMANTIC

The term *classical poetry* is rather ambiguous. Originally referring to poetry intended for the upper classes, it became the name for those poems deemed worthy of presentation to the elite and of being studied by scholars, who were also charged with the poems' preservation. The term is also applied to the poetry of the early Greeks and Romans and to any poems written in imitation of such poetry. Today we most readily recognize the use of the term *classical* to describe works of high achievement that display balance and restraint, unity, proportion, and purity of form. *Classical* is distinguished from *romantic* in that it depends on its own organizational elements to stimulate emotional response, whereas the romantic poems rely for their effect on ideas that coalesce and expand in the reader's mind. In classical poetry, one usually notes a dignified approach to universal themes.

    The term *romanticism* suggests a faith in the goodness of humanity, believing that people individually are well intentioned but that civilization corrupts them. The difference between the two terms may be summarized as follows: Romantic poetry is largely subjective and personal; classical poetry is objective and universal.

The era of romantic poetry is described as occurring during the nineteenth century, when poets pitted the imagined world of truth, goodness, and beauty against the actual world of "ugly reality." The three major English poets of this period were Wordsworth, Keats, and Shelley, but such poets as Byron, Coleridge, and Scott were no less important to the romantic period.

If one makes the distinction that classical poets are in absolute control of their material whereas romantic poets are the tools of their emotions, then all poets must be considered, to some degree or other, romantic. (Again, it's important to remember that labels only serve convenience in understanding; boundaries, where they do exist, are most often blurred.) True objectivity is an impossibility; as we noted earlier, the facts of selection and arrangements reveal a subjective bias, however much the writer may strive for objectivity.

Romantic poets see themselves at the center of a personal conflict or struggle; they suffer because of an imperfect world. Classical poets assume more distance between themselves and their subject matter: they will assign the personal role to a protagonist, if such assignment is required, who may be a real-life hero or a mythic one. The hero is often a victim of destiny, tragic because the evil forces leading to destruction are not under his or her control and do not originate with that hero (as demonstrated in the early Greek dramas). Or classical subject matter may be unconnected (on an overt level) with any personal stake in the development of the play's situation or the poem's theme other than a philosophic interest in it by the writer.

Romantic poetry frequently exhibits a lushness that is a further contrast to the spare beauty associated with the best of classical poems. The romantic poet is more concerned with self in relation to life, whereas the classical poet is attracted by the larger, universal themes.

Can you, without reference to any specific time period, determine which poems used as samples in this chapter would fit into the classical category and which into the romantic?

HUMOR

Ranging from subtle ironies to burlesques and caricatures, humor is a welcome component in many poems. For our own time, you might consider Robert Frost and Ogden Nash as practitioners of the two extremes of humor.

Humor is often an important feature of dramatic poetry. Shakespeare made use of the entire gamut, from some pretty bawdy stuff to the gentle teasing in the excerpt from *Romeo and Juliet* included earlier in this chapter. Humor is also useful as a revealer of character, as in the Browning example. T. S. Eliot's "The Love Song of J. Alfred Prufrock" is a fine example of another sort of humor—perhaps a wry sort of Leopold Bloom.

Here are some short poems displaying various facets of humor:

Anonymous
A Toast

Here's to ye absent Lords, may they
Long in a foreign country stay
Drinking at other ladies' boards
The health of other absent Lords.

Robert Herrick
Clothes Do But Cheat and Cozen Us

Away with silks, away with lawn,
I'll have no scenes or curtains drawn;
Give me my mistress as she is,
Dress'd in her nak'd simplicities.
For as my heart e'en so mine eye
Is won with flesh, not drapery.

Note how this theme contrasts with the romantic "Julia" by the same author! Poets are not always consistent.

William Congreve (seventeenth–eighteenth centuries)
Pious Celinda

Pious Celinda goes to prayers,
  If I but ask the favour;
And yet the tender fool's in tears,
  When she believes I'll leave her.

Would I were free from this restraint,
  Or else had hopes to win her;
Would she could make of me a saint,
  Or I of her a sinner.

Dorothy Parker (contemporary)
Unfortunate Coincidence

By the time you swear you're his,
  Shivering and sighing,
And he vows his passion is
  Infinite, undying—
Lady, make a note of this:
  One of you is lying.

You have seen how lyricism, narration, drama, classicism, romanticism, humor, and seriousness are not necessarily exclusive of one another in the same work. The degree of dominance of one or more of these characteristics determines the category in which one places the material. And with a master such as Shakespeare, one frequently finds all these natures and traits expertly combined.

SURREALISM / REALISM

The surrealists sought to reveal more than the surface image of life. The concept may be tentatively defined as follows: If realism is "to hold . . . the mirror up to nature," as Shakespeare preferred art to do, then surrealism holds its mirror up to the fantastic juxtapositions of a dream world—and defines this as "a higher reality."

Whether any work of art can be truly surreal—that is,

over and above reality as we think of it—is a moot point. But this genre introduced into the art of poetry some exciting approaches and possibilities. Material produced by the subconscious contains amazing qualities and strengths; it can be rich in imagery, mysterious in connections and relationships between elements, and bursting with feeling—all factors that not only succeed in fascinating audience and writer alike but also can enrich and nourish the body of poetry as well as its spirit.

The subconscious tends to be well in advance of the conscious in having access to the ties between juxtapositions of the parts of an idea and the place of those parts to the emerging work as a whole. Too often, to our conscious selves, the components in such juxtapositions seem to have no tenable connections whatsoever. We have to train ourselves so that we learn to what degree we can rely on the subconscious to make viable contributions without descending into verbal anarchy.

The thesis that surrealist art is art raised from the subconscious and unhampered by the intrusion of the conscious is valid, of course. Whether such work is worthwhile and real art may depend on other factors as well. After all, material just surfacing is still raw material. Parts of the material are bound to be less striking, less pertinent than others. So some mechanism that decides what shall be retained and what must be discarded has to be in operation, however sublimated it may be. And no matter how free the form, some shaping must occur. The handling of this kind of material is as much a process as is the handling of material furnished in any other manner. Process implies selection, evaluation, and other judgmental procedures, as well as movement toward a result—in this case, the organization of elements into a poem. Merely because such an organization process may be different from what we're accustomed to does not mean it isn't present. What may be happening is that the subconscious has been working more diligently than usual and may have already accomplished much of the poet's procedural tasks in connection with the poem. The selection and organization processes may be operating at such an intuitive level as to seem automatic. Intuition of this sort is likely to be the fruition of prior study and practice combined with a strong natural sensitivity. These are still speculations, of course; no one knows just what is going on in this particular process nor why it happens as it does. But there's no question that it does happen, and with amazing and moving results when it happens to poetic talent.

The roots of the surealist movement are attributed by the surrealists themselves to Baudelaire and Rimbaud. Some French poets in the 1920s organized themselves into a group dedicated to worship in art the subconscious, without service to any other discipline. Those most closely identified with the movement are André Breton, Guillaume Apollinaire, Louis Aragon, Antonin Artaud, David Gascoyne, and Paul Éluard. The works of these poets and others of their group are usually very lyrical and vivid, achieving at times a compelling incantatory effect that is reminiscent of biblical poetry.

In studying the work of the surrealists, think about triggers. In this genre perhaps more than in any other, the suggestive leaps that occur between elements are usually triggered from something real and literal into something fanciful and otherworldly, attaining a magic seldom equaled in other kinds of poetry. A striking example is "L'Union Libre" by André Breton (in Breton's *Young Cherry Trees Secured Against Hares* translations by Edouard Roditi. Ann Arbor, Mich.: University of Michigan Press, Ann Arbor Paperbacks, 1969), a sensual presentation of parallel structure invested with a multiplicity of images.

The following poem by the author illustrates a different surrealistic approach:

Quartet in One Movement

the door opens another five inches
another stranger enters
sits beside her
touches her knee
she smiles permission
in the kitchen the husband opens the window
climbs over the sill
vanishes in the trees

the stranger nods a bald head
prods her flesh with a fork
nods again
good he mumbles good
tenderly she pushes him
you came just in time she says I was almost alone again
the door rattles
the stranger jerks upright
it's nothing it's the wind
she pulls his head back to her lap
what if someone comes
no one will come
out on the road the husband flags a car
hurry take me to the movies I've cut my wrists
the blood won't stop
the driver floats through the windshield
over the hood of the car
and flattens to a shadow
the husband drives the car to the edge of the cliff
they'll think I've had an accident
he watches the car roll down
she screams something's happened
about time the stranger mutters
his face is dark with blood
she opens her fingers
wedding rings roll to the floor
the stranger picks them up puts them in a blue envelope
just in case he says
the door rattles
she turns her head
the stranger laughs it's nothing it's the wind
no something's happened
the stranger opens the sideboard takes out a cellophane-
  wrapped chicken
the chicken breaks free flies around the room
she screams again catch it it drives me crazy it's a bad omen

he looks at her
puts the blue envelope in the sideboard
cuts a hole under the stairs
disappears
she trembles
afraid the husband is lost
taunted by a hunger just beyond her fingertips
she screams again
the window in the kitchen slides shut
leaving the husband out there somewhere
the stranger prowls in the cellar
paints nudes on the walls
eats cold food from the vegetable-bin
the husband walks backward from the cliff
looking for words to explain to the driver
she opens the door another five inches
calls the husband
the driver walks in
touches her
you can add me to the list
no more she cries no more
she calls the husband's name
the husband pulls feathers from the chicken on the table
the chicken clucks angrily
she stands near the husband
the driver takes the chicken
goes out
the husband shakes his head
I had to do it
I'm sorry for the driver
there was no other way

    An excellent example of a conscious exploitation of the subconscious is *The Castle,* the book-length "poem" by Franz Kafka. James Joyce similarly exploits the subconscious, more deliberately in *Ulysses* and more mysteriously in *Finnegans Wake.*

We've had a look at the principal natures of poetry, at poetry's appearances. Beyond the visual, which we explore in greater detail next, we have sampled the flavors poetry offers, the inner workings that can come to life in our own imaginations when spurred by a well-made poem.

The importance of the presentation of poetry must be emphasized. Poetry is still basically an art of sounds. The page on which the poem appears is the score for the reader, directions as to how the poem is to be sounded. Whether the form is fixed or free, the visual presentation is the only guide available to the reader that will enable him or her to translate printed words and lines properly into articulated sound existing in time, a structure that speaks not only through the sense of the words but also through form.

It is time to probe deeper into the structural specifics of form.

4. Bone and Muscle

In this chapter, we consider form as the visual or outer shape of the poem, made possible by particular arrangements of structural components. These include the physical skeleton of a poem and the pattern occasioned by the organization of sounds and rhythms.

Poetic form is divided into two main categories: *fixed forms*, such as the sonnet, sestina, and villanelle; and *organic forms*, which evolve from within the poem itself. Fixed forms have a recognizable tradition to support them. Organic forms, however, are not necessarily an outgrowth of fixed forms. Although we tend to think of them as something quite recent, organic forms have existed side by side with fixed forms for centuries. In the larger, enveloping sense, form is organic for all lyrical poems, epics, medieval tales and romances cast in verse, and verse drama. The contours, lengths, and shapes of many of these works have been dictated by the content, although of the longer works, some sections contained internally may have been produced in observance of the stricter conventions of fixed forms. There *are* exceptions, as in the case of the ode, which shifted from a fixed form in Pindar's hands to a looser organization in the hands of later poets.

The evolution of traditional forms has come about through experimental variations of existing features and from the relaxation of formal criteria. In free verse, an organic form is developed during the actual creative process. Form and theme are developed in tandem, the result being a unique structure. Each poem in free verse has its own shape.

Nonmetric fixed forms (forms not organized on accent or measure) are not unknown in our own time, as evidenced by the contents of the more experimental journals. Such forms generally rely on a sculptured or "picture" shape. These visual poems have a long continuing history. Apollinaire suggested the term *calligramme* to describe a poem in which the typographical arrangement is designed to reinforce the theme or sense. In one of his own poems ("It Rains"), the lines have been printed in wavering verticals. Even the mere indentations (stepping inward or outward of lines) may be related to the same technique. George Herbert's "Easter Wings" is wing shaped. The shape of "Vision and Prayer" by Dylan Thomas has been variously interpreted as that of a chalice, a womb, or a pyramid. Poems in the shapes of altars and crosses exist in the poetry of the past as well as in contemporary work, which also includes such shapes as umbrellas and pears. Stéphane Mallarmé, in his poem "Un Coup de Des Jamais N'Abolira le Hasard" ("A Throw of the Dice Never Will Abolish Chance"), published in the magazine *Cosmopolis* in 1897, did amazing and intriguing things with typography and white space. And thumb through any volume of the work of E. E. Cummings to discover more typographic innovations.

Poetry is an art that wears many costumes, each in its own way exciting. But for now, back to the investigation of the physical elements that hold poems together.

STRUCTURAL ELEMENTS

These are the skeleton and sinews of the poem over which the visual appearance takes shape. The physical parts of the structure—which include meter and rhythm, lines, stanzas or verse paragraphs, rhyme or sound patterns—are easier to detect than the elements of the poem's contents, which are idea and its development, metaphor, mood, tonality, emotion, intensification, climax, and resolution or denouement.

The physical components rely on design and plan, and they are revealed upon the analysis of organization at a schematic level. The content elements are understood through interpretation of detail and the degree of such detail's tactility, the development of imagery, diction, syntax, color, atmosphere, action, dialogue (if present), situation, exposition, and characterization.

In traditional forms, the poet has a given diagram with which to work. In free verse, the shape is generated by the material as it goes through the process of being designed into a poem.

In its largest sense, form embraces more than erectile structure and external shape; it represents the integration of expression (the *totality* of expression) and sense. In the true poem, form and content are inextricably one.

TRADITIONAL FORMS

For our purposes, we examine the more popular forms, with perhaps an oddity here and there to add spice. Let's begin by having a look at some self-contained units that make up the poem and that have, on occasion, functioned as complete poems in themselves.

Couplet
A unit in poetry made up of two lines that usually rhyme and that are composed in the same meter (strict rhythmic design). If both lines are end-stopped (have a natural pause at the end), the unit is complete and is called a *closed couplet*. Enjambment (where the first line is not end-stopped but continues its thought or idea into the next line to become complete) does occur now and then in a closed couplet. An *open couplet* is a unit in which the *second* line is a run-on line and completes its thought in the following couplet.

Vladimir Nabokov's humorous *Pale Fire* abounds in splendid examples:

CLOSED COUPLET
The more I weigh, the less secure my skin;
In places it's ridiculously thin;

CLOSED COUPLET WITH ENJAMBMENT
I was the smudge of ashen fluff—and I
Lived on, flew on, in the reflected sky.

OPEN COUPLETS
I was an infant when my parents died.
They both were ornithologists. I've tried
So often to evoke them that today
I have a thousand parents. Sadly they
Dissolve in their own virtues and recede,

The classical form of the couplet usually includes lines of five feet (pentameter). (Think of a foot in poetry as somewhat equivalent to a measure in music.) When a couplet is cast in four-foot lines (tetrameter), the unit is called a *short couplet*. Couplets that follow classical criteria are sometimes given special names, like *heroic couplet*. Such terms are usually imprecise because they refer to the mechanical design of the lines but no longer to the quality of the text. A couplet may be organized in the same way the ancient heroic couplet was without having a thing to do with anything heroic. It's best to avoid unnecessary confusion.

Couplets may function as stanzas or as parts of stanzas; at times, in very short poems, they may very well be the entire poems in themselves. Epigrams and epitaphs, for instance, often are no more than a couple of lines.

Tercet / Terza Rima

A stanza (a group of lines related in idea and metrics and forming a pattern usually repeated throughout the poem) made up of three lines, sometimes referred to as a *terzain* or a *triplet*. The poem "Julia" by Robert Herrick, given in the preceding chapter, is formed of two tercets, and each tercet has its own rhyme sound. (In other words, the poem's rhyme scheme is *aaa bbb*.) "Ode to the West Wind" by Percy Bysshe Shelley is a poem of five sections; each section is composed of four tercets and closes with a couplet. The outside lines of each tercet rhyme with each other, and the middle line establishes the rhyme sound for the outside lines of the succeeding tercet. The rhyme sound of the closing couplet in each section is taken from the middle line of the preceding tercet. The couplet was often used by poets to interrupt the persistence of tercets, when the intention was to show a break between sections or *cantos* (a special term for a section). The linking effect occasioned by the way Shelley used the rhymes in his poem is called *terza rima*, and the greatest practitioner of terza rima was Dante in *The Divine Comedy*. Here, in the Dorothy Sayers translation, are the opening tercets of the second canto from the "Inferno" section of Dante's masterpiece:

> Day was departing and the dusk drew on, (*a*)
> Loosing from labour every living thing (*b*)
> Save me, in all the world; I—I alone— (*a*)
>
> Must gird me to the wars—rough travelling, (*b*)
> And pit's sharp assault upon the heart— (*c*)
> Which memory shall record, unfaltering; (*b*)
>
> Now, Muses, now, high Genius, do your part! (*c*)
> And Memory, faithful scrivener to the eyes, (*d*)
> Here show thy virtue, noble as thou art! (*c*)

Quatrain

A four-line stanza or poem, the most popular organizing unit in English poetry. As the *ballad stanza* and the *hymnal stanza*, the quatrain is composed in lines of four and three feet alternating and is rhymed *abcb*; that is, the second and fourth lines rhyme, but the first and third do not.

The hymnal stanza is sometimes varied to rhyme *abab*, meaning that the first and third lines rhyme as well as the second and fourth, and each line is tetrameter (four feet)—in which instance it's known as *long measure*. Hardy provides an enjoyable example. The sole metrical relief in this hymnal stanza poem occurs in the third line of the second stanza. See if you can detect the rhythmic variation.

> Thomas Hardy (nineteenth–twentieth centuries)
> *Let Me Enjoy*
> Minor key.
>
> Let me enjoy the earth, no less
> Because the all-enacting Might
> That fashioned forth its loveliness
> Had other aims than my delight.
>
> About my path there flits a Fair,
> Who throws me not a word or sign;
> I'll charm me with her ignoring air,
> And laud the lips not meant for mine.
>
> From manuscripts of moving song
> Inspired by scenes and dreams unknown,
> I'll pour out raptures that belong
> To others, as they were my own.
>
> And some day hence, towards Paradise
> And all its blest—if such should be—
> I will lift glad, afar-off eyes,
> Though it contain no place for me.

Another quatrain variant, the *envelope stanza*, has enclosing rhymes, as in this example from Alfred Tennyson's *In Memoriam:*

> I hold it true, whate'er befall,   (a)
>   I feel it when I sorrow most,   (b)
>   'Tis better to have loved and lost, (b)
>   Than never to have loved at all.   (a)

You will also discover quatrains (made up of three-, four-, five-, or

68 Body and Soul

six-foot lines) that are rhymed *aabb* or *aaba*. Examples of both rhyme patterns are found in John Dryden's *The Secular Masque* (seventeenth century):

> Since Momus comes to laugh below,   (*a*)
> Old Time, begin the show,   (*a*)
> That he may see, in every scene,   (*b*)
> What changes in this age have been   (*b*)
>
> . . . .
>
> Then our age was in its prime,   (*a*)
> Free from rage, and free from crime: (*a*)
> A very merry, dancing, drinking,   (*b*)
> Laughing, quaffing, and unthinking time (*a*)

In the second stanza, the rhyming is even more complex than the end rhymes alone would indicate. Note the internal rhyming of *age* and *rage*. The fourth line is a tumble of rhyme: *Laughing-quaffing, unthinking* reaching back to the end of the preceding line to match *drinking*, and of course the final *time* pulling the whole thing together with the two opening lines of the stanza.

Another favorite measure for the quatrain among English-language poets is iambic pentameter. (See Chapter 5 for a detailed analysis of iambic pentameter.) Let's look at the second stanza of "Discordants" by Conrad Aiken:

> Your hánds once toúched this táble ánd this sílver, (*a*)
> And Í have séen your fíngers hóld this gláss.   (*b*)
> These thíngs do nót remémber yóu, belóvèd,—   (*c*)
> And yét your toúch upón them wíll not páss.   (*b*)

Aiken varies the meter slightly by including an extra unstressed syllable at the ends of the first and third lines; all the other feet in the stanza are straight iambic. By counting the stresses (indicated by the accent marks, except for the accent over *-ed* at the end of the third line that functions as a direction to pronunciation—the syllable is sounded), you will find that each line is made up of five feet. This is a splendid example of traditional iambic pentameter from a contemporary poet. By the way, those extra ending syllables contribute a subtle and gentle softness to the meter that is in harmony with the somber tone.

Quintain
Shelley, the Brownings, Tennyson, Longfellow, and many other poets have used five-line stanzas, employing a variety of line lengths and rhyme patterns. Let's look at some samples:

Robert Browning
Two in the Campagna (first two stanzas)

I wonder do you feel to-day	(a)
As I have felt since, hand in hand,	(b)
We sat down on the grass, to stray	(a)
In spirit better through the land,	(b)
This morn of Rome and May?	(a)
For me, I touched a thought, I know,	(c)
Has tantalized me many times,	(d)
(Like turns of thread the spiders throw	(c)
Mocking across our path) for rhymes	(d)
To catch at and let go.	(c)

Here are the first three stanzas of Tennyson's "On a Mourner." This time, *you* determine what the rhyme pattern is.

Nature, so far in her lies,
    Imitates God, and turns her face
To every land beneath the skies,
    Counts nothing that she meets with base,
    But lives and loves in every place;

Fills out the homely quickset-screens,
    And makes the purple lilac ripe,
Steps from her airy hill, and greens

>   The swamp, where humm'd the dropping snipe,
>   With moss and braided marish-pipe;
>
>   And on thy heart a finger lays,
>   Saying 'Beat quicker, for the time
>   Is pleasant, and the woods and ways
>   Are pleasant, and the beech and lime
>   Put forth and feel a gladder clime.'

Two samples from Shelley follow—the first, a stanza from "Invocation to Misery" and the other, the final stanza from the ode "To a Skylark":

> Hasten to the bridal bed—
> Underneath the grave 'tis spread:
> In darkness may our love be hid,
> Oblivion be our coverlid—
> We may rest, and none forbid.

>   Teach me half the gladness
>   That thy brain must know,
>   Such harmonious madness
>   From my lips would flow
>   The world should listen then, as I am listening now!

Henry Wadsworth Longfellow (nineteenth century) wrote "Midnight Mass for the Dying Year" (stanzas 1 and 2). Note how this poet uses the fifth line of his stanzas.

>   Yes, the Year is growing old,
>   And his eye is pale and bleared!
>   Death, with frosty hand and cold,
>   Plucks the old man by the beard,
>   Sorely,—sorely!
>
>   The leaves are falling, falling,
>   Solemnly and slow;
>   "Caw, caw!" the rooks are calling,

It is a sound of woe,
A sound of woe!

Here is one example of the use of the quintain stanza that is impossible to resist, including the way the poet uses that fifth line in the first and third stanzas, almost as though he's spitefully emphasizing his point—emotionally dramatic and expressive.

Thomas Carew (seventeenth century)
To My Inconstant Mistress

When thou, poor excommunicate
  From all the joys of love, shalt see
The full reward and glorious fate
  Which my strong faith shall purchase me,
  Then curse thine own inconstancy.

A fairer hand than thine shall cure
  That heart, which thy false oaths did wound;
And to my soul a soul more pure
  Than thine shall by Love's hand be bound,
  And both with equal glory crown'd.

Then shalt thou weep, entreat, complain
  To Love, as I did once to thee;
When all thy tears shall be as vain
  As mine were then, for thou shalt be
  Damned for thy false apostasy.

Sestet

A six-line stanza, usually rhymed. The sestet is also a component in the sestina and in some of the sonnet forms that we discuss later in this chapter. In his poem "A Ballad of François Villon," Algernon Charles Swinburne (nineteenth century) used the sestet as the *envoi* (or *envoy*)—a climactic summary or a dedication or address to an important individual or personification. Though this one has six lines, an envoi may include any number of lines; it is frequently made up of half the number of lines the other stanzas of the poem have. Swinburne's envoi, here, is rhymed *aabaab*.

> Prince of sweet songs made out of tears and fire
> A harlot was thy nurse, a God thy sire;
>   Shame soiled thy song, and song assoiled thy shame.
> But from thy feet now death has washed the mire,
> Love reads out first at head of all our quire,
>   Villon, our sad bad glad mad brother's name.

Septet

A seven-line stanza composed on a variety of rhyme patterns. Here's a stanza from Wordsworth's "Resolution and Independence." Pay special attention to the dramatic effect of the extended seventh line:

> He with a smile did then his words repeat;
> And said, that, gathering Leeches, far and wide
> He travelled; stirring thus about his feet
> The waters of the Pools where they abide.
> "Once I could meet with them on every side;
> But they have dwindled long by slow decay;
> Yet still I persevere, and find them where I may."

As you can see, the rhyme scheme of Wordsworth's septet is *ababbcc*. The stanza is in iambic rhythm. If Wordsworth's septet had been made up all of five-foot lines, we would have what's called a *rhyme royal*. Chaucer, Spenser, and other early poets, as well as—more recently—John Masefield, favored use of the rhyme royal stanza. Shakespeare employed it throughout *The Rape of Lucrece;* here is a sample stanza from that work:

> 'What win I, if I gain the thing I seek?   (*a*)
> A dream, a breath, a froth of fleeting joy.   (*b*)
> Who buys a minute's mirth to wail a week?   (*a*)
> Or sells eternity to get a toy?   (*b*)

> For one sweet grape who will the vine destroy? (*b*)
> Or what fond beggar, but to touch the crown, (*c*)
> Would with the sceptre straight be strucken down? (*c*)

Octave
The term identifies a poem or stanza of eight lines. It is also applied to the first eight lines of the sonnet form. "Night" is one of many poems in which Blake employs the octave stanza form. The opening stanza illustrates:

> The sun descending in the west,
> The evening star does shine;
> The birds are silent in their nest,
> And I must seek for mine.
> The moon, like a flower
> In heaven's high bower,
> With silent delight
> Sits and smiles on the night.

Note that Blake varied the lengths of his lines here. In your opinion, is such length variation in keeping with the meaning of the poet's lines?

When the lines of the octave are all in iambic pentameter and the rhyme pattern is *ababa bcc*, the stanza is known as *ottava rima*, a favorite stanza form of Italian, Spanish, and Portuguese poets. Among the English poets, Byron made excellent use of it in *Don Juan*, as this sample shows:

> And thén with teárs, and síghs, and sóme slight kísses,
>   They párted fot the présent—thése to awaít,
> Accórding tó the artíllery's híts or mísses,
>   What ságes call Chánce, Próvidénce, or Fáte—
> (Uncertaíntý is oné of mány blísses,
>   A mórtgage oń Humaníty's estáte)—
> While their belovéd friénds begań to arm,
> To burń a town which néver did them harm.

73

Nine-line stanza

One arrangement of the nine-line stanza (eight lines of iambic pentameter followed by an Alexandrine—a six-foot iambic line; the combination is constructed on the rhyme pattern *ababbcbcc*) is known as the *Spenserian stanza*, devised by Edmund Spenser (Elizabethan period) for use in his *Faerie Queene*. The stanza form was also taken up by others, including James Thomson in "The Castle of Indolence," Robert Burns in "The Cotter's Saturday Night," Byron in *Childe Harold's Pilgrimage*, Keats in "The Eve of St. Agnes," Tennyson in "The Lotus Eaters," and Shelley in "Adonais" and "Revolt of Islam." Here is a stanza from Spenser's masterpiece:

A gentle Knight was pricking on the plaine,[1]
Ycladd in mightie armes and silver shielde,
Wherein old dints of deepe woundes did remaine,
The cruéll markes of many' a bloódy fielde;
Yet armes till that time did he never wield.
His angry steéde did chide his foming bitt,
As much disdayning to the curbe to yield:
Full jolly knight he seemd, and faire did sitt,[2]
As one for knightly giusts and fierce encounters fitt.[3]

Other styles of nine-line stanzas are found in the works of Shelley, Robert Browning, and John Donne. Presented here is a familiar example from one of Donne's songs:

Go and catch a falling star,
    Get with child a mandrake root,
Tell me where all times past are,
    Or who cleft the Devil's foot;
Teach me to hear mermaids singing,

---

[1]*Pricking:* spurring.
[2]*Jolly:* handsome.
[3]*Giusts:* jousts.

> Or to keep off envy's stinging,
> And find
> What wind
> Serves to advance an honest mind.

(Do you experience a difference in the metrical rhymes here compared with the examples we've had so far?)

Very likely, by now, you've discovered that the basic formative components of stanzas, besides the makeup of the lines themselves, are couplets, tercets, and quatrains. It's true that sometimes quatrains consist of two couplets combined, but more frequently the four lines contain a complete thought or idea too long for a couplet, or a concept presented in the first two lines is completed in the next two. Poets have relied on the quatrain as a basic stanza form for so long that its acceptance as a compositional unit has been assured. As for the other stanza forms, analysis will indeed reveal that a quintain is generally a combination of a tercet and a couplet or two couplets and a spare line or a quatrain and a spare line, that a sestet is made up of two tercets or a quatrain and a couplet, and so on.

Stanzas may be of any length when they aren't part of an established form. The traditional concept of form requires that stanzas within any one poem be of equal length, with occasional variations permitted, especially in final stanzas.

Among the exceptions, we'd like to mention that many odes in English are composed of irregular stanzas in which rhyme, meter, and line length may be an intricate pattern, and the stanza may range from four to over twenty lines. (See the odes of Milton, Dryden, Pope, Thomas Gray, William Collins, and Shelley.)

In prose, we understand that the paragraph is a separate section, the use of which enables the author to divide material into sequential but distinct units. In poetry's traditional forms, the stanza performs the same function as the paragraph does in prose. Content development should proceed from stanza to stanza.

There are any number of poems, especially in more recent

times, in which one stanza may run into the next, creating a linked effect much as enjambment does between lines. Here, too, technique should be justified by the way the idea or image is being developed. Note how the thought continues by crossing over the stanza space between the first and second rhyme-enclosed quatrains in "Heart's Needle" by the contemporary poet W. D. Snodgrass. This same technique is used for almost every stanza break throughout the poem (which, by the way, uses a different stanza form for each of its ten sections).

> Child of my winter, born
> When the new fallen soldiers froze
> In Asia's steep ravines and fouled the snows,
> When I was torn
>
> By love I could not still,
> By fear that silenced my cramped mind
> To that cold war where, lost, I could not find
> My peace in my will,

In *free verse*, we often refer to textual divisions as "stanzas," but properly, these groups of lines forming rhetorical units not restricted in line length or rhythm are called *verse paragraphs*. They may be as long as content requires, or they may form components in patterns of the writer's designs.

Blank verse is a traditional form of poetry made up of lines of unrhymed iambic pentameter. Most of the text of Shakespeare's plays is in blank verse form. James Thomson, Wordsworth, Keats, Tennyson, and Edwin Arlington Robinson, to name a few, often used blank verse, as did Milton; here are some lines from his *Paradise Lost:*

> The plánets iń their státions lístening stoód,
> While thé bright pómp asceńded jubiláńt.
> 'Ópen, ye éverlásting gátes,' they súng;
> 'Ópen, ye Héavens, your líving doórs! let iń
> The gréat Creátor, fróm his wórk retúrned
> Magníficeńt, his síx days' wórk, a wórld!

The running of the five-beat meter is powerful in Milton's work; even though the lines don't rhyme and there are some variations in the iambic pattern, the total effect is compelling, and the poem's sense and dramatic nature leave no doubt that the lines carry the music of poetry.

Robert Frost is another poet who turned to blank verse for his narrative and dramatic poems quite often. You might read his "In the Home Stretch" (*The Complete Poems of Robert Frost.* New York: Henry Holt and Company, 1936, 1942, 1949) to get the feel of how he makes use of it.

Before moving on to the forms themselves, here are a few structural units that are encountered less frequently but are worthwhile knowing.

A *canto* is a section of a poem, usually made up of stanzas or verse paragraphs. As noted earlier, Dante's *The Divine Comedy* is divided into cantos. Ezra Pound produced *The Cantos,* a work in which the number of cantos is equal to the number in Dante's masterpiece.

Sapphics refers to a four-line stanza written in the meter we associate with Sappho's work. The Romans made use of it; in English, Swinburne turned out a work entitled *Sapphics* in which he imitates the meter of the Greek poet. We take a closer look at the meter itself in the next chapter.

A *rune* has come to signify a magic formula or a poem or saying with mystical meaning. Originally, runes were the letters of the earliest Teutonic alphabet. Runes have also been described as riddles, spells, ritualistic incantations, and aphorisms. Early examples are not dissimilar in nature and style to the Greek oracular verses. Here is an example taken from *The White Goddess* by Robert Graves that serves as an illustration of runic verse—a witch formula for turning oneself into a hare; "come home again" means to return to human shape.

> I shall go into a hare
> With sorrow and sighing and mickle care,
> And I shall go in the Devil's name
> Aye, till I come home again.

In our day, W. S. Merwin has composed a set of stanzas,

"Runes for a Round Table," in which each stanza focuses on one of the signs of the zodiac.

A fine example of *parallelism* is André Breton's "L'Union Libre," mentioned earlier. Parallelism is found in early Hebrew poetry, and there are many instances of its presence in biblical passages. When expertly combined with subject matter, parallelism—with its technique of repetition and the balancing of ideas, images, phrases, and lines—is capable of achieving an incantatory effect and a rhetorical and rhythmic power of great intensity. The structural phenomenon has a universal appeal and is also found in Oriental and Finnish poetry and in the songs of the American Indians, where the accumulation of parallel sequences reinforces the strongly imagistic content of the lyrical texts. William Blake, Alexander Pope, Walt Whitman, T. S. Eliot, and Ezra Pound are among English-language poets who have made use of the technique.

> Ezra Pound (contemporary)
> *Salutation*
>
> O generation of the thoroughly smug and thoroughly uncomfortable,
> I have seen fishermen picknicking in the sun,
> I have seen them with untidy families,
> I have seen their smiles full of teeth and heard ungainly laughter.
> And I am happier than you are,
> And they were happier than I am;
> And the fish swim in the lake and do not even own clothing.

This is a good example of the pattern in both structure and idea. Note how the sequence of structural parallels in the lines' openings matches the sequence of idea development. The repetition factor of the text affords us an intensification that is supported visually and aurally. At the same time, the two sides of the idea developed in the lines after the first one are producing a dynamic that appears to drive in a direction opposite the structure's drive but, paradoxically, results in a parallel intensification. The poem is lyrical in nature, whereas its character is didactic. What is the "lesson" that Pound is trying to make us understand?

BALLAD

In the previous chapter, we noted that the major divisions of the nature of poems are lyric, narrative, and dramatic. The ballad touches all bases: it is lyrical, and it tells a story in a dramatic way. In the ballad, the pattern is generally clear: stanzas and metrical lines occur at regular intervals, and there is most often a heavy, almost thumping interplay of rhyme. These very singable compositions were frequently accompanied by tunes invented specifically for them. We define a ballad, therefore, as a narrative poem that is lyrical in tonality, that includes dramatic elements (character and dialogue are mainstays of the form), and that reveals a situation (again, dramatic) already existing and follows it to its conclusion. Quite often, a ballad begins by implying the previous action and incidents. The language is uncomplicated, and the pacing, despite repetitions, is quite rapid.

Folk ballads were passed on orally in the beginning, with embellishments and changes to suit occasion or time. They developed as storytelling devices to describe events of general interest. Although the tone may be tragic, comic, or pathetic, the ballad is always lyrical and its lines, pronouncedly rhythmical. Here is an old favorite. Note how the story is revealed through the dialogue.

Anonymous
Lord Randal

"O where ha you been, Lord Randal, my son?
And where ha you been, my handsome young man?"
"I ha been at the greenwood; mother, mak my bed soon,
For I'm wearied wi huntin, and fain wad lie down."

"And wha met you there, Lord Randal, my son?
And wha met you there, my handsome young man?"
"I met wi my true-love; mother, mak my bed soon,
For I'm wearied wi huntin, and fain wad lie down."

"And what did she give you, Lord Randal, my son?
And what did she give you, my handsome young man?"

"Eels fried in a pan; mother, mak my bed soon,
For I'm wearied wi huntin, and fain wad lie down."

"And wha gat your leavins, Lord Randal, my son?
And wha gat your leavins, my handsome young man?"
"My hawks and my hounds; mother, mak my bed soon,
For I'm wearied wi huntin, and fain wad lie down."

"And what becam of them, Lord Randal, my son?
And what becam of them, my handsome young man?"
"They stretched their legs out and died; mother, mak my bed soon,
For I'm wearied wi huntin, and fain wad lie down."

"O I fear you are poisoned, Lord Randal, my son!
I fear you are poisoned, my handsome young man!"
"O yes, I am poisoned; mother, mak my bed soon,
For I'm sick at the heart, and I fain wad lie down."

"What d ' ye leave to your mother, Lord Randal, my son?
What d ' ye leave to your mother, my handsome young man?"
"Four and twenty milk kye; mother, mak my bed soon,
For I'm sick at the heart, and I fain wad lie down."

"What d ' ye leave to your sister, Lord Randal, my son?
What d ' ye leave to your sister, my handsome young man?"
"My gold and my silver; mother, mak my bed soon,
For I'm sick at the heart, and I fain wad lie down."

"What d ' ye leave to your brother, Lord Randal, my son?
What d ' ye leave to your brother, my handsome young man?"
"My house and my lands, mother, mak my bed soon,
For I'm sick at the heart, and I fain wad lie down."

"What d ' ye leave to your true-love, Lord Randal, my son?
What d ' ye leave to your true-love, my handsome young man?"
"I leave her hell and fire; mother, mak my bed soon,
For I'm sick at the heart, and I fain wad lie down."

The ballad measure has appealed to many poets down

through the centuries. Here is a loosely rhymed example occurring in the latter part of the nineteenth century:

Emily Dickinson
#712

Because I could not stop for Death—
He kindly stopped for me—
The Carriage held but just Ourselves—
And Immortality.

We slowly drove—He knew no haste
And I had put away
My labor and my leisure too,
For His Civility—

We passed the School, where Children strove
At Recess—in the Ring—
We passed the Fields of Gazing Grain—
We passed the Setting Sun—

Or rather—He passed Us—
The Dews drew quivering and chill—
For only Gossamer, my Gown—
My Tippet—only Tulle—

We paused before a House that seemed
A Swelling of the Ground—
The Roof was scarcely visible—
The Cornice—in the Ground—

Since then— 'tis Centuries—and yet
Feels shorter than the Day
I first surmised the Horses' Heads
Were toward Eternity—

This is in the regular ballad stanza form of four-beat and three-beat lines alternating, except for the fourth stanza (which is sometimes omitted from the poem, as are Dickinson's habit of punctuating almost entirely with dashes and her arbitrary capitalization), in which the poet reverses the metric measure of the first and second lines.

ODE

The ode has a stately and soberly elevated quality. The form is used most often to express the poet's intense personal feeling concerning an event or a person. In dealing with the death of a public figure or close friend, it usually is elegiac in spirit.

The form originated in the Greek choric songs. Early odes were composed of themes and responses sung by choirs: half the group sang the strophe (the opening stanza); the other half of the group followed with the antistrophe (the middle stanza); then the group recombined to sing the epode (the last stanza). The performance included a stately, dancelike movement around the altar—in one direction during the strophe, in the opposite direction during the antistrophe, and standing still for the epode.

The greek terms *strophe, antistrophe,* and *epode* are, in English, also called the *turn,* the *counter-turn,* and the *stand* or *after-song.*

Perhaps the greatest odists of classical times were Pindar and Horace. Pindar's odes are made up of one or more triads (sections composed of three parts, as named earlier), and the strophe and antistrophe are metrically and formally identical, the rhythms in keeping with the dance movements, whereas the epode, usually shorter, is arranged to suit the cessation of movement. Because of the difficulty in trying to emulate Pindar's form of the ode in English, Horace emerged as a less forbidding model. Most English odes are rather irregular, and now and then a poem referred to as an ode is, in reality, an extended lyrical poem unconcerned with the conventions of the ode form. Some of William Collin's odes, for instance, might be so described; "The Passions" or "Ode Written in the Beginning of the Year 1746," beginning, "How sleep the brave, who sink to rest," are good examples.

Pindar was born in 522 B.C. and died in 443 B.C. Here, as a sample, is the first triad of his "Pythian 2," translated by Frank J. Nisetich:

TURN 1
Great city of Syracuse,
   the war god's sacred ground,
      divine support of men
         and horses flashing iron,
            to you I come, bringing a song,
         an announcement from shining Thebes:
   the chariot Hieron drove
over the echoing earth has won.
He has crowned Ortygia,
      where Artemis has her throne,
     the goddess
      who joined him
   when he tamed those mares,
she and the man together,
   gently lifting the intricate reins.

COUNTER
TURN 1
For the maiden of showering arrows
   and Hermes, god of contests,
      together make a radiance
        glisten about him
           when he yokes his powerful team
        to the burnished chariot,
      takes the reins in hand,
   and calls on Poseidon,
the trident-wielding, wide-dominioned god.
                          Men have praised
      other kings, too, for their virtues,
     and the voices
    of the Kyprians
often sing of Kinyras—
           whom Apollo gladly cherished

STAND 1
    and Aphrodite loved, her favored priest,
    hymned by his people, surely, in return
    for his kindness.
              So the West Lokrian maiden
    sings of you before her house, O son of Deinomenes!
    Thanks to your power, she looks forth, free
    from the hopeless stress of war.
               But they say that Ixion,
    spun every way upon a winged wheel, proclaims,
    under command of the gods,
               his lesson to mankind:
    Repay your benefactor honor's kind return!

In the Horatian ode, each stanza follows the same metrical pattern, which must have provoked in English poets a sigh of relief. In fact, Abraham Cowley, in the seventeenth century, misunderstood Pindar's form completely and decided the stanzas were not metrically related at all. The form's structure as Cowley interpreted it was irregular, with uneven numbers of lines, and many later poets have written odes in the Cowleyan mode—among them, Dryden, Wordsworth, and Allen Tate. Many odes were written in English during the eighteenth and nineteenth centuries, most of them irregular in one fashion or another, some after the style of Horace. Here, as a sample, is one of Horace's own, translated by Milton, from Book I of the *Odes*. Horace lived from 65 B.C. to 8 B.C.

    To Pyrrha

    What slender youth, bedew'd with liquid odors,
    Courts thee on roses in some pleasant cave,
        Pyrrha? For whom bind'st thou
        In wreaths thy golden hair,
    Plain in thy neatness? O how oft shall he
    Of faith and changed gods complain, and seas
        Rough with black winds, and storms
        Unwonted shall admire!

Who now enjoys thee credulous, all gold,
Who, always vacant, always amiable
    Hopes thee, of flattering gales
        Unmindful. Hapless they
To whom thou untried seem'st fair. Me, in my vow'd
Picture, the sacred wall declares to have hung
    My dank and dropping weeds
        To the stern god of sea.

SONNET

A poem expressing a single complete thought, idea, or sentiment. Its fourteen lines are divided into either an octave and a sestet or three quatrains and a couplet. The sonnet may be used to illuminate a simple paradox rather than to treat a theme of multilayered complexity—as might a sestina. The sonnet's meter is regularly iambic pentameter, and it is rhymed according to a specific pattern.

The different kinds of sonnets are distinguished not only by the rhyme scheme but also by how the "turn" is introduced. The turn refers to the point at which the thought shifts from the statement of the idea or sentiment to its resolution or summation. In the Petrarchan (or Italian) sonnet, which normally rhymes *abbaabba cdecde*, this turn occurs as you enter the sestet. The Spenserian sonnet, in which the quatrains are rhyme linked—*abab bcbc cdcd ee*—the turn usually is introduced between the third quatrain and the closing couplet. The Shakespearean (or English) sonnet is not rhyme linked; the form is rhymed *abab cdcd efef gg*. But here, too, the turn occurs at the closing couplet.

There is another sonnet, the Miltonic sonnet, which has for its octave the same rhyme scheme as the Petrarchan (*abbaabba*), but it adopts a new pattern for the sestet—*cdcdcd*—creating, in effect, a series of three couplets rather than two tercets or a quatrain and a couplet.

There have been examples of the sonnet form built on quatrains and couplets where the turn came in between the second and third quatrains—in effect, between octave and sestet. In the kinds of sonnets other than the Petrarchan, there seemed to be some sentiment to deny or at least to minimize the importance of the turn. But the turn is an inherent feature of the sonnet form, and however much the poet may try to subdue it, it will invariably reveal its presence upon examination unless the poem is a sonnet in structure only.

Although the sonnet focuses on a single thought or idea and although it may deal with a simple paradox, do not assume that it's a simplistic form. It makes severe demands on its practitioners, and its high popularity with poets may be exactly because it constitutes such a challenge. In concentrating on the focus of the subject, the poet is involved in a highly complex expression of his or her theme, organizing and clarifying a multiplicity of feelings and attitudes into a unified comprehension. The approach to the theme tends to be somewhat philosophical. The sonnet is primarily lyric in nature; the form may encompass a brief narrative, especially in a sonnet sequence, although the narrative may be implied rather than explicit. Neither the narrative nor the dramatic is essential to the form, however.

A *sonnet sequence* is a series of related sonnets or sonnets that develop a particular theme or express a narrative. Examples include D. G. Rossetti's *The House of Life*, Sir Philip Sidney's *Astrophel and Stella*, *Sonnets from the Portuguese* by Elizabeth Barrett Browning, and W. H. Auden's *The Quest* (with section II an extended modification of the sonnet form). Petrarch himself wrote a series of sonnets to the woman he called Laura; and Shakespeare's sonnets, since they appear to be addressed all to the same person, would be classed as a sequence.

The sonnet form was a favorite of Dante's, too, and much Renaissance love poetry is in the sonnet form. The sonnet continues to enjoy a prestigious vogue among poets, and a sonnet well made is considered an impressive achievement. You are encouraged to practice this form extensively—all the different kinds; it will sharpen your thinking about poetry. Let's look at some examples.

Francesco Petrarca (fourteenth century)
Love's Inconsistency
Petrarchan—Italian—sonnet form.
Translated by Sir Thomas Wyatt.

I find no peace, and all my war is done;
  I fear and hope, I burn and freeze likewise;
  I fly above the wind, yet cannot rise;
  And nought I have, yet all the world I seize on;
That looseth, nor locketh, holdeth me in prison
  And holds me not, yet I can 'scape no wise;
  Not lets me live, nor die, at my devise,
  And yet of death it giveth none occasion.
Without eyes I see, and without tongue I plain;
  I wish to perish, yet I ask for health;
  I love another, and yet I hate myself,
I feed in sorrow, and laugh in all my pain;
  Lo, thus displeaseth me both death and life,
  And my delight is causer of my grief.

Note that in the first eight lines (the octave), the poet expresses the sentiment that he is assailed by paradoxes *from without*. With the sestet (at the turn), it is revealed to us that the disturbing paradoxes are *from within* the poet, that his quandary is of his own design—the result of a romantic stance toward love, no doubt. *Malaise d'amour* was fashionable even in those days.

    This sonnet provides us with an intriguing example. Even Sir Wyatt's near rhymes of *health–self* and *life–grief* in the sestet—quite a modern touch for the time—add interest. In the original, the rhymes are all exact (but rhyming is much easier in Italian than it is in English). But there is another peculiarity in connection with this particular poem. The original uses a rhyme scheme that varies from the Petrarchan design. Instead of the normal *abbaabba* rhymes for the octave, Petrarch decided on *abababab*. The translator saw fit to pattern his version of the octave after the accepted model of the Petrarchan sonnet form; but he, in turn, altered the rhyme scheme of the sestet to *cddcee*. The variations introduced by Petrarch, however, continued to appear in various later sonnets in English by later poets, as did numerous modifications of the sonnet form in general.

Edmund Spenser (sixteenth century—Elizabethan period)
From *Amoretti (LXXV)*
Spenserian Sonnet form.
Note linking effect of the rhymes.

One day I wrote her name upon the strand,
but came the waves and washed it away:
   again I wrote it with a second hand,
   but came the tide, and made my pains his prey.
Vain man, said she, that doest in vain assay,
   a mortal thing so to immortalize,
   for I my self shall like to this decay,
   and eke my name be wiped out likewise.
Not so, (quoth I) let baser things devise
   to die in dust, but you shall live by fame:
   my verse your virtues rare shall eternize,
   and in the heavens write your glorious name.
Where whenas death shall all the world subdue,
   our love shall live, and later life renew.

The turn here occurs in the couplet at the end.

William Shakespeare (Elizabethan period)
Ninety-Eighth Sonnet
Shakespearean—English—sonnet form.

From you have I been absent in the spring,
When proud-pied April, dress'd in all his trim,
Hath put a spirit of youth in everything,
That heavy Saturn laugh'd and leap'd with him.
Yet nor the lays of birds, nor the sweet smell
Of different flowers in odour and in hue,
Could make me any summer's story tell,
Or from their proud lap pluck them where they grew;
Nor did I wonder at the Lily's white,

Nor praise the deep vermilion in the Rose;
They were but sweet, but figures of delight,
Drawn after you, you pattern of all those.
  Yet seem'd it Winter still, and, you away,
  As with your shadow I with these did play.

In this one, can you detect how the couplet introduces the turn?

> John Keats (nineteenth century)
> *On First Looking into Chapman's Homer*
> Miltonic sonnet form.
>
> Much have I traveled in the realms of gold
> And many goodly states and kingdoms seen;
> Round many western islands have I been
> Which bards in fealty to Apollo hold.
> Oft of one wide expanse had I been told
> That deep-browed Homer ruled as his demesne:
> Yet did I never breathe its pure serene
> Till I heard Chapman speak out loud and bold.
> Then I felt like some watcher of the skies
> When a new planet swims into his ken:
> Or like stout Cortez, when with eagle eyes
> He stared at the Pacific—and all his men
> Looked at each other with a mild surmise—
> Silent, upon a peak in Darien.

Keats has confused Cortez with Balboa. "Darien" refers to the Isthmus of Darién, now known as the Isthmus of Panama. In this poem, the turn occurs at the start of the sestet.

    Upon occasion, Milton adopted Petrarch's form more closely. Here the rhyme scheme is Petrarchan, but the turn occurs in the paradox at the end.

> *On His Blindness*
>
> When I consider how my light is spent
>   Ere half my days in this dark world and wide,

    And that one talent, which is death to hide,
      Lodged with me useless, though my soul more bent
    To serve therewith my Maker, and present
      My true account, lest He returning chide,
      "Doth God exact day-labour, light denied?"
    I fondly ask. But patience, to prevent
That murmur, soon replies, "God doth not need
    Either man's work or his own gifts. Who best
Bears his mild yoke, they serve him best. His state
Is kingly: thousands at his bidding speed,
    And post o'er land and ocean without rest;
    They also serve who only stand and wait."

By the time he was forty-four, Milton's blindness had become total. The word *talent* is a reference to the Parable of the Talents; Matthew, 25:14–32.

How does Milton equate *talent* with reference to his condition?

The sonnet has played a major role in the development of poetry. Additional examples illustrating differences in style, tone, and subject and variations in technique will broaden our understanding of the form.

    John Donne (seventeenth century)
    From the *Holy Sonnets* (X)

Death be not proud, though some have called thee
Mighty and dreadfull, for, thou art not soe,
For, those, whom thou think'st, thou dost overthrow,
Die not, poore death, nor yet canst thou kill mee.
From rest and sleepe, which but thy pictures bee,
Much pleasure, then from thee, much more must flow,
And soonest our best men with thee doe goe,
Rest of their bones, and soules deliverie.
Thou art slave to Fate, Chance, kings, and desperate men,
And dost with poyson, warre, and sicknesse dwell,
And poppie, or charmes can make us sleepe as well,
And better than thy stroake; why swell'st thou then?

One short sleepe past, wee wake eternally,
And death shall be no more; death, thou shalt die.

This poem also has the paradox-turn in the ending.

Elizabeth Barrett Browning (nineteenth century)
From *Sonnets from the Portuguese (XXVI)*

I lived with visions for my company
Instead of men and women, years ago,
And found them gentle mates, nor thought to know
A sweeter music than they played to me.
But soon their trailing purple was not free
Of this world's dust, their lutes did silent grow,
And I myself grew faint and blind below
Their vanishing eyes. Then THOU didst come—to be,
Belovèd, what they seemed. Their shining fronts,
Their songs, their splendors (better, yet the same,
As river-water hallowed into fonts),
Met in thee, and from out thee overcame
My soul with satisfaction of all wants:
Because God's gifts put man's best dreams to shame.

This sonnet has two turns; one begins in the last half of the eighth line, and the other is in the paradox at the ending.

Gerard Manley Hopkins (nineteenth century)
The Beginning of the End: 2

I must feed fancy. Show me any one
That reads or holds astrologic lore,
And I'll pretend the credit given of yore;
And let him prove my passion was begun
In the worst hour that's measured by the sun,
With such malign conjunctions that before
No influential heaven ever wore;
That no recorded devilish thing was done
With such a seconding, nor Saturn took
Such opposition to the Lady-star

In the most murderous passage of his book;
And I'll love my distinction: Near or far
He says his science helps him not to look
At hopes so evil-heaven'd as mine are.

The turn in this one occurs in the twelfth line.

John Crowe Ransom (contemporary)
Parting at Dawn

If there was a broken whispering by night,
It was an image of the coward heart
But the white dawn assures them how to part—
Stoics are born on the cold glitter of light,
And with the morning star lovers take flight.
Say, then, your partings; and most dry should you drain
Your lips of their wine, your eyes of the frantic rain,
Till these be as the barren Cenobite.

And then? O dear Sir, stumbling down the street,
Continue, till you come to wars and wounds;
Beat the air, Madam, till your house-clock sounds;
And if no Lethe flows beneath your casement,
And when ten years have brought to full effacement,
Philosophy was wrong, and you may meet.

George Barker (contemporary)
Sonnet of Fishes

Bright drips the morning from its trophied nets
Looped along a sky flickering fish and wing,
Cobbles like salmon crowd up waterfalling
Streets where life dies thrashing as the sea forgets,
True widow, what she has lost; and, ravished, lets
The knuckledustered sun shake bullying
A fist of glory over her. Every thing,
Even the sly night, gives up its lunar secrets.

And I with pilchards cold in my pocket make

Red-eyed a way to the bed. But in my blood
Crying I hear, still, the leap of the silver diver
Caught in four cords after his fatal strake:
And then, the immense imminence not understood,
Death, in a dark, in a deep, in a dream, for ever.

John Donne created a lovely sequence of sonnets that he titled *La Corona*—which gave rise to the term *a crown of sonnets*. The last line of each sonnet is identical with the first line of the succeeding sonnet, and the last line of the last sonnet in the sequence—there are seven sonnets in all—is the same as the first line of the first sonnet, thereby closing the linked circle.

There is also a sonnet form, called the composite sonnet, that combines the different sonnet forms' features. Perhaps the most telling example is Wordsworth's "Sonnet on the Sonnet," a mixture of the Shakespearean and Miltonic forms.

Milton established the *tailed sonnet*, a twenty-line piece with the rhyme scheme of the usual sestet running *cdedec* and the added-on sestet *cfffgg;* the fifteenth and eighteenth lines are generally half lines. It's the last six lines that comprise the *tail* of the form. Milton's own "On the New Forcers of Conscience Under the Long Parliament" is a good illustration.

The *curtal sonnet* is a shortened sonnet created by Gerard Manley Hopkins. It has ten and one-half lines instead of fourteen, and the form is divided into a first stanza of six lines and a second stanza of four plus the added half line. The opening sestet rhymes *abcabc;* the concluding quatrain and short line rhyme *dbcdc* or *dcbdc.* "Pied Beauty" by Hopkins illustrates the form well:

> Glory be to God for dappled things—
>   For skies of couple-colour as a brinded cow;
>   For rose-moles all in stipple upon trout that swim;
> Fresh-firecoal chestnut-falls; finches' wings;
>   Landscape plotted and pieced—fold, fallow, and plough;
>   And all trades, their gear and tackle and trim.

All things counter, original, spare, strange;
  Whatever is fickle, freckled (who knows how?)
  With swift, slow; sweet, sour; adazzle, dim;
He fathers-forth whose beauty is past change:
  Praise him.

To the beginner, *syllabic verse* may sound like a mysterious new technique, but it is neither mysterious nor new. Rather than measuring by stress, accent, or quantity (time), the line is measured by the number of syllables it contains. In the most rudimentary form of syllabic verse, the poet chooses a measure—five syllables per line or six or twelve or whatever is appropriate for the way he or she is going to develop the theme—and works out the lines so that measure and sense are in harmony. A short line will quicken the pacing; a long line will encourage a more stately progress. But the number of intricate patterns that can be devised is limitless. For instance, the poet may decide on six-line units and elect to use the following syllabic pattern: first line—three syllables; second line—seven; third line—six; fourth line—eight; fifth line—three; sixth line—five. Any arrangement is possible. If the poet repeats the pattern in each unit, the structure will give unity to the form. And in the pattern imposition, too, there is room for variations. The interest that may be introduced is limited only by the imagination of the writer.

Syllabics is the technique used in early Hebrew poetry, in Oriental forms, in Welsh forms, and in some French poetry. Currently, it enjoys the support of many poets writing in English. Marianne Moore was strongly identified with it; Auden used it; Milton and Pope experimented with it. The cinquain, a five-line form said to be the equivalent of the Japanese haiku or tanka, is a syllabic form with a distinct quality of density.

Because English is such a heavily accented language, there's some doubt that any poem in English can ever be truly syllabic. It's much easier to produce poems that are plainly syllabic in a language like Japanese or French, both of which are practically without stress or accent. Nevertheless, the challenge to the poet writing in English is the opportunity to effect a counterpoint between the syllabic measure and the normal word accents.

CINQUAIN

A syllabic five-line poem (not to be confused with the five-line stanza called *quintain*). The first line of the cinquain is made up of two syllables; the second, third, and fourth increase the number of syllables by increments of two, and the fifth line returns to two syllables.

The cinquain form was invented by Adelaide Crapsey (1878–1914), and her poem "Triad" is the most popular and perhaps the best example of the form's use.

> These be
> Three silent things
> The falling snow... the hour
> Before the dawn... the mouth of one
> Just dead.

The form offers more than a simple syllabic arrangement. There's an elastic effect to it. The first four lines stretch; the final line snaps and releases. This startling factor throws the poem into harsh relief, as it does in this next one:

> Mary Terrell (contemporary)
> (untitled)
>
> Wrinkles,
> gray hair, dry bones,
> arthritic knees, crumbled
> stick fingers, blown away by death's
> cold wind.

FOREIGN-LANGUAGE FORMS

In dealing with poetry from other languages, an almost insurmountable problem in translation is the medium itself, the languages involved. Once again, the best that may be achieved is *an approach*. Too literal a translation will convey the sense at the sacrifice of the original poetics. Too poetic a rendition usually betrays or distorts the original sense, departing from *translation* to become another "poem" in the second language. Yet the reader is still unable to savor the poetics of the original.

Oriental Forms

The problems of translation are compounded in dealing with Oriental poetry translated into English. The Oriental script characters, although now artistically refined, are ideograms and at one time were actual pictograms, so that the radiational effect we strive so hard to achieve in our poetry is a natural characteristic of Oriental poetry. Adverbs are hardly ever used. Chinese and Japanese vocabularies used in poetry are largely concrete noun-vocabularies. The use of verbs and adjectives, along with the syntax, involves a high order of complexity.

Oriental poetry reveals a sharpened awareness and acceptance of the physical universe that harmonizes with a reverently restrained appeal to a hidden otherworld. Oriental poets express their ideas and feelings in their poetry by employing characters in juxtapositions that sometimes are strange to our notion of syntax.

The concern of the Oriental poet with a concrete particularity has been overlooked by Western poets until fairly recent times. Oriental poets avoid abstractions. Their poetic diction is direct and literal. Metaphors are merely suggested by a stylistic and intuitive touch, the result of long years of apprenticeship and training in the classical mode of the art. The valuable space of their lines is not cluttered with prepositions, personal pronouns, articles, connectives, and the like. The reader must understand these from the context.

To point out an obvious instance of the translation difficulties involved, consider the *Book of Songs* (perhaps China's earliest recorded poetry). The entire collection is made up of four-syllable lines. Attempts at translation have invariably required the use of many more syllables in English for each line in order to communicate the sense of the poems. In several cases, the equivalent line in English has taken up to fourteen syllables.

A great deal of traditional Chinese poetry is composed of five-syllable or seven-syllable lines, but variations are not uncommon. In some poems, the number of syllables varies widely from line to line.

Of the many poets China has nurtured, Li Po is the one whose name is most familiar to Western students of the art. But the Chinese have always considered poetry their greatest art, and its practitioners are many. It would be valuable to you to review the work of Arthur Waley, perhaps the most ardent translator of Chinese poetry into English, and to scan Kenneth Rexroth's *One Hundred Poems from the Chinese*.

It is the Japanese forms, however, that have caught the Westerners' fancy—mainly the *haiku* and, to a more modest extent, the *tanka*. The tanka is the court, or official, form—the preference of the classicists. The haiku, however, enjoys a wider popularity. Earlier forms such as the *renga* ("linked verse"—a serious form of important length), the *chōka*, also called *nagauta*, ("long poem"—an indefinite number of pairs of five-syllable and seven-syllable lines with an additional seven-syllable line at the end), and the *sedōka* ("head-repeated poem"—two stanzas, each with three lines, five, seven, and seven syllables, respectively) are used much less frequently in Japan and seem to arouse little interest in the West.

The tanka is the form most important to the development of Japan's poetic tradition and, as we said, the one recognized as the norm for Japanese poetry. It is a thirty-one-syllable poem arranged in five lines with the following distribution of syllables: five, seven, five, seven, seven. An English tanka is usually attempted in thirty-one syllables, following the Japanese requirement. Admitting the difficulties of translation while striving to suggest the syllabic structure, many translators have concentrated on capturing the spirit of the form.

Here is a translation of a tanka by the poet Fujiwara Teika (twelfth-thirteenth centuries):

> For her straw-mat bedding,
> The Lady of the Bridge of Uji now
> Spreads the moonlight out,
> And in the waiting autumn night
> Still lies there in the darkening wind.

The most popular form of poetry in Japan is the *haiku*, a short, self-contained seventeen-syllable form that evolved from the *hokku* (the first three lines of the tanka), which in turn comprised the first stanza of the renga. The syllables of the haiku are arranged in three lines with the following distribution: five, seven, five.

In the haiku, the aim is to express delicate insight or emotion through a concrete image. The established conventions of the form are as follows:

1. The poem must involve one central image.

2. The imagery is related to nature in some way, and the time of year is either stated or implied.

3. The first twelve syllables (the first two lines) present the details referring to the central image, but it is not unusual for a haiku to present details that seem to suggest one thing and turn out to be something else entirely in the last line.

4. That all-important last line, the *insight line*, in the ideal haiku reveals the intent and *meaning*—a term that has a special application here. It involves understanding of the sense of the text from within the reader's psyche, a way of knowing that is dependent not primarily on a process of discursive reasoning, but on an intuitive, sudden grasp of the sum of the witnessed details. It is as if the reader's eyes have been trying to penetrate a curtain when, at the right moment, the curtain is ripped aside, and the struggle to understand is over. Not all haiku achieve this effect, of course—many do not even attempt it—but we're talking about the perfectly executed haiku here. An examination of haiku written by Westerners will reveal

that few English-language attempts are true haiku. Most of them are statements cast in the correct number of syllables that lack the punch and vividness of the Oriental form.

In Japanese poetry, Basho (seventeenth century) is the poet most readily identified with the haiku form; next in popularity and fame is Buson (eighteenth century). The examples that follow evoke spring, summer, fall, and winter, respectively.

BUSON
Hazy ponded moon
   And pale night sky are broken...
Bungling black frog

TAIGI
As I picked it up
   To cage it... the firefly
Lit my finger-tips

BASHO
We stand still to hear
   Tinkle of far temple bell...
Willow-leaves falling

BONCHO
Snow-swallowed valley:
   Only the winding river...
Black fluent brushstroke

In trying to cope with the brief Japanese form, the Western writer tends to become concerned with the verse structure (number of syllables and arrangement of lines) and seldom pays sufficient attention to the spirit of the haiku. The Japanese poet has been trained to concentrate on the image's potential and evolving sense instead. None of the limited, valuable space of the form is wasted on nonessentials; therefore, space is used most advantageously. For the Western writer, the choice would be either to de-emphasize syntax in the way the Japanese poet does or, as Pound, Amy Lowell, and the Imagists did, to concentrate on the central image and not try to duplicate the structure.

Welsh Forms

Included here because they are also forms organized and measured syllabically, Welsh forms use rhymes of greater complexity and subtlety than most English poetry rhyme patterns. Welsh forms also use *light rhyme* (which is discussed in Chapter 7) and *cross-rhyme*—rhyming that pairs the rhyme sounds of the syllable ending one line and the syllable in the middle of the following line, usually at a pause in the line. (Cross-rhyme should not be confused with *crossed rhyme*, which is also discussed in Chapter 7.)

In general, Welsh poetry is governed by consideration of the relation between word accent and pauses within the lines. *Cynghanedd* ("harmony") is the term for certain patterns of rhyme, alliteration, assonance, and consonance occurring within the line.

Englyn is a term that designates a specific syllabic form and rhyme scheme of the poet's choice and may be a stanza of three lines or four. Each line of the simplest englyn, called the *soldier's englyn*, has seven syllables. Other englyns have different syllabic arrangements. The repetition of elements in successive stanzas is reminiscent of some of the early ballads, and for all we know, there may have been a connection where cross-influencing took place. It is almost impossible to duplicate rhyme schemes and syllable measure of original englyns in translation, but here are two, taken from Robert Graves's *The White Goddess*, to allow you to experience the flavor and style of the form. These are englyns that were sung at the Battle of Achren; they involve discovering the secret names of enemies in order to practice destructive magic against them.

'Sure-hoofed is my steed impelled by the spur;
The high sprigs of alder are on thy shield;
Bran art thou called, of the glittering branches.

Sure-hoofed is my steed in the day of battle:
The high sprigs of alder are in thy hand:
Bran thou art, by the branch thou bearest—
Amathaon the Good has prevailed.'

French Forms

Here we come to poems that aim at a display of virtuosity, tours de force. But we shall also find examples that transcend mere ornamentation and attain a noble dignity and elevated tone. Do not minimize the *fun* of poetry, however; if your first endeavors in trying these forms center on light or humorous subjects, so be it. The practice and understanding of the structure concern you at this point. You will, no doubt, compose more serious pieces in these forms when you have mastered the techniques involved.

The French forms are a set of complex, ornate, lyrical, metrical poetic structures that originated with the troubadours of Provence and that, during Chaucer's time, were eagerly embraced by English poets. One of the greatest masters of these forms, who served as model for many poets including the English, was François Villon (fifteenth century). His greatest imitators were among the Victorian poets, who used French forms largely for light verse. In our century, however, these forms have been used with serious intent, and this has changed the forms' character, fortifying it with deep emotional involvement. Some twentieth-century examples include *sestinas* by W. H. Auden, Ezra Pound, and Elizabeth Bishop; *villanelles* by William Empson, Dylan Thomas, W. H. Auden, and Theodore Roethke; *triolets* by Barbara Howes; and variations of these forms by many other poets.

Besides the sestina, villanelle, and triolet, the French forms include the *ballade* (different from the ballad), *rondeau* and *roundel, virelay, chant royal,* and *pantoum* (which isn't French at all, but a Malaysian form that is usually grouped with the French forms). The villanelle, triolet, rondeau, and ballade have the following characteristic in common: no rhyme sound used once may be used again anywhere in the poem, not even if the word has a different meaning or spelling. A strict pattern rules that every rhyming syllable must be a new sound. If the word *bred* is used as a rhyme sound, for example, a word such as *inbred* or *bread* cannot be used anywhere in the poem. The meter for these forms should be tetrameter or pentameter, but you'll find that convention is violated as often as it is observed.

The *ballade* has a strict form. It is composed of three stanzas of eight lines each (occasionally the stanzas have ten lines) and an envoi or ending half stanza; the entire poem uses only three rhyme sounds. Each stanza, including the envoi, ends with the identical refrain line. As we noted before, no rhyme sound can be repeated in any other place in the poem. The rhyme scheme is *ababbcbc* for each stanza, and the envoi is rhymed *bcbc*.

There is a ballade with a double refrain, in which one refrain line occurs in the middle of the stanza (usually the fourth line) in addition to the customary refrain at the end of each stanza. Then there's the double ballade, made up of stanzas that have eight, ten, or eleven lines; the poem contains six stanzas instead of three, and the envoi is usually omitted.

In the ballade, the rhyme scheme must be maintained in the same order for each stanza, whether it's a straight ballade or one of the variations or larger versions. The metrical rhythm is most often iambic or anapestic (two unstressed syllables followed by a stressed one for each foot) tetrameter.

The following example of the normal ballade is by Algernon Charles Swinburne (nineteenth century):

Ballad of Dreamland

I hid my heart in a nest of roses,
  Out of the sun's way, hidden apart;
In a softer bed than the soft white snow's is,
  Under the roses I hid my heart.
Why should it sleep not? why should it start
  When never a leaf of the rose tree stirred?
What made sleep flutter its wings and part?
  Only the song of a secret bird.

Lie still, I said, for the wind's wing closes,
  And mild leaves muffle the keen sun's dart;
Lie still, for the wind on the warm sea dozes,
  And the wind is unquieter yet than thou art.
Does a thought in thee still as a thorn's wound smart?
  Does the fang still fret thee of hope deferred?

What bids the lids of thy sleep dispart?
   Only the song of a secret bird.

The green land's name that a charm encloses,
   It never was writ in the traveller's chart,
And sweet on its trees as the fruit that grows is,
   It never was sold in the merchant's mart.
The swallows of dreams through its dim fields dart,
   And sleep's are the tunes in its tree-tops heard;
No hound's note wakens the wildwood hart,
   Only the song of a secret bird.

ENVOI

In the world of dreams I have chosen my part,
   To sleep for a season and hear no word
Of true love's truth or of light love's art,
   Only the song of a secret bird.

   The *rondeau* evolved gradually from the older *rondel* and consists of thirteen full lines of four beats each, arranged in three stanzas of five, three, and five lines. Only two rhyme sounds are permitted. At the end of the second and third stanzas, there is a tail—a half line taken from the first half of the first line. It's a nonrhyming tail and is frequently turned as a pun. Using R as the symbol for the tail, the rhyme pattern is *aabba aabR aabbaR*.

   Voltaire produced numerous rondeaux. During the nineteenth century, Austin Dobson, Sir Edmund Gosse, and William Ernest Henley delighted in the French forms, and they also contributed rondeaux to the treasury of formal verse. Here is a popular rondeau by Henley:

Rondeau

Let us be drunk, and for a while forget,
Forget, and, ceasing even from regret,
Live without reason and despite of rhyme,
As in a dream preposterous and sublime,
Where place and hour and means for once are met.

Where is the use of effort? Love and debt
And disappointment have us in a net.
Let us break out, and taste the morning prime . . .
    Let us be drunk.

In vain our little hour we strut and fret,
And mouth our wretched parts as for a bet:
We cannot please the tragicaster Time.
To gain the crystal sphere, the silver clime,
Where Sympathy sits dimpling on us yet,
    Let us be drunk!

    More complicated than the rondeau is the *rondeau redoublé*, which includes six quatrains on two rhymes. The final lines of the second, third, fourth, and fifth quatrains are the four lines of the first quatrain, occurring in the same order. Whereas the last line of the sixth quatrain is a new line, it is followed by a half line that is identical with the first phrase of the first line of the poem. The rhymes are alternating, but the pattern is reversed from stanza to stanza—*abab baba abab baba abab baba* plus the half line attached to the last stanza.

    The *roundel*, as recognized today, is a version created by Swinburne and is composed of three three-line stanzas on two rhymes and a refrain taken from the opening line and rhyming with the second line. The pattern runs *abaR bab abaR*. (Keep in mind that *b* and *R* rhyme.)

    Two other forms are simply variants of the same concept. They are the *rondelet*—a short poem composed of five lines on two rhymes in one stanza, with the half-line refrain occurring after the second and fifth lines (*abRabbR*)—and the *roundelay*, which merely refers to a short lyric poem with a refrain. (*Roundelay* is also used to mean any of the fixed forms using a refrain, such as those we've been examining in this section.) These forms all include the root *rond-* or *round-*, implying a circle—which the refrain supports.

    The rondeau is the French form that has found the easiest niche in English fixed-form poetry. Next to the rondeau in popular acceptance is the *triolet*. This form is a genuine challenge, with little room to develop an idea. In a total of eight lines, the first two are identical to the last two, and the fourth is the same as the first. That accounts for five lines out of eight, leaving the poet three lines in which to add new material. Using capitals for identical lines, the rhyme pattern is as follows: *ABaAabAB*. The example that follows is an amazing execution by Robert Bridges (nineteenth–twentieth centuries):

Triolet

When first we met we did not guess
    That Love would prove so hard a master;
Of more than common friendliness
When first we met we did not guess.
Who could foretell the sore distress,
    This inevitable disaster
When first we met? we did not guess
    That Love would prove so hard a master.

Although the ballade, rondeau, triolet, and their variants provide today's poet with opportunities to display technique and mastery of form, their themes and subjects are generally light in tone and treatment. The two French forms that have demanded more serious attention and content from the poet in our time are the *villanelle* and the *sestina*.

Originally, the villanelle was as light as other French forms. A pastoral poem at first, dealing only with rural themes, the villanelle is one of the most musical of the French forms, and it waited for contemporary writers to raise its music from dreamy meadows to dark and stately symphonies.

The form appears easy until a writer tries to make it come to life in a natural and unstilted way. Its stylized tradition is one of the factors to be overcome. With fixed forms, especially those with refrains or repeat lines, the novice tends to place the text in the prescribed sequence mechanically. The volume of villanelles is filled with such awkward attempts. An examination of the form's structure will reveal the difficulties.

The first five stanzas are tercets; the final (sixth) stanza is a quatrain. The entire poem is constructed on two rhyme sounds. The stanzas are linked by the rhyme pattern and by repeat lines. The first line of the first stanza doubles as the last line of the second and fourth stanzas; the last line of the first stanza reappears as the final line in the third and fifth stanzas. And both these repeat lines form a concluding couplet in the sixth stanza. The rhyme formula, in essence, is A^1bA^2 abA^1 abA^2 abA^1 abA^2 abA^1A^2.

From a strictly pastoral treatment, the villanelle went through a transition period when it was considered a vehicle for humorous or perhaps precious subjects before it attained its current stature as a serious art form. Out of all those efforts to make the poem keep moving across the repeat lines and to avoid the feeling of mechanical insertions, some very striking and powerful results have emerged. Before we examine some of the difficulties the less experienced poet may run into, let us look at one of the noblest successes of all, "Do not go gentle into that good night" by Dylan Thomas:

> Do not go gentle into that good night,
> Old age should burn and rave at close of day;
> Rage, rage against the dying of the light.
>
> Though wise men at their end know dark is right,
> Because their words had forked no lightning they
> Do not go gentle into that good night.
>
> Good men, the last wave by, crying how bright
> Their frail deeds might have danced in a green bay,
> Rage, rage against the dying of the light.
>
> Wild men who caught and sang the sun in flight,
> And learn, too late, they grieved it on its way,
> Do not go gentle into that good night.
>
> Grave men, near death, who see with blinding sight
> Blind eyes could blaze like meteors and be gay,
> Rage, rage against the dying of the light.
>
> And you, my father, there on the sad height,
> Curse, bless, me now with your fierce tears, I pray.

> Do not go gentle into that good night.
> Rage, rage against the dying of the light.

Notice how the repeat lines, rather than serving as mere ornamentation, actually intensify the poem's theme with every repetition. For those trying the form for the first time, this is the area of greatest difficulty. Too often, not enough thought is given to the movement of the theme as the lines are placed automatically where the form's schematic dictates. The result is a poem whose progression falters or halts at the end of each stanza.

Dylan Thomas avoided such pitfalls while adhering strictly to the form's conventions. In his handling of the villanelle, the form works in concert with the poem's substance without obtruding; in fact, the form is a perfect choice for his theme, allowing exactly the development he planned.

Although it is unclear, in the first stanza, who is being addressed, the "advice" given is easy enough to understand. The addressee's identity is masked deliberately, affording the poet the opportunity—in stanzas 2 through 5—to broaden the poem's application, to generalize to the extent that the reader can move with the poet through a series of personalities and experience how they react to the phenomenon of dying. And in each of these stanzas, the line being repeated always completes a part of the developing idea and helps to push the poem forward. In the final stanza, the addressee is finally recognized and revealed, and the poem moves back from its generalized considerations to its intended particularization. The two specific stanzas (the first and the last) bracket the more expansive internal ones.

Why does the poet go through this round robin with the "wise men" and the "good men" and so forth? Why doesn't he deal directly with his own father and let it go at that? Dylan Thomas was a master craftsman who took great pains with his poems. In this villanelle, he attained a perfect blend of form and substance. We are standing close to the heart of poetry here.

The villanelle, by its structure, affords the poet a *delay*. His subject is personal and painful, yet he is aware that it must be confronted. But the confrontation is held at mind's length while the narrator (the poet himself, in this case) can gather his forces for the confrontation. Although the stanzas afford the needed delay, they also develop an inevitable progression toward facing the truth of mortality—the poet's as well as his father's. Subject and form are working together to make each other possible. So the poem, by its execution, appeases the needs of its author.

But it does much more than that. The tension occasioned by the expansion of the inner stanzas and then the contraction occurring in the last stanza have the effect of gathering us, as readers, into the poem to share with the poet his concerns and feelings. We recognize the universality of what the poet is showing us, and we too are given time to assimilate these thoughts. Then we are drawn into the event and cannot retreat from it. We understand the emotions involved; we identify with the experience, sharing in its effect along with the narrator. The poet has taken a personal experience, one that is certainly not unique, and has expressed it in such a way that the experience has become unique while retaining its inclusiveness. The poem's experience is now ours, and we have it forever.

Like most fixed forms, the villanelle refuses to remain "fixed" and experiences variations and experimentation from time to time. Quite often, rather than hamper the poem's progression by using strictly repeated lines, a skilled poet will take liberties with those lines, allowing the repeated lines to retain only enough principal elements to convey the sense of repetition. For instance, if the original version of a repeat line is: "And all the men who lived in Thebes are gone," when it next appears, it may be altered to a slight but meaningful degree: "And every man who loved in Thebes is gone."; a later appearance might be: "No more is Thebes; its loves and lives are gone."

Another liberty taken is a greater reliance on enjambment (run-on lines) into the repeat lines, as Thomas does, or from the repeat lines across the stanza break to the next stanza. This aids the writer in achieving smoothness and syntactical purpose *through* the repeat lines.

The contemporary poet Barbara L. Greenberg has written a villanelle that takes even more liberties. Her poem is constructed on one rhyme sound instead of two, and the poem's involvement in today's technology represents quite a departure from the form's original pastoral character. The antiphonal technique employed in the final stanza is the inevitable consequence of the idea's development. Here, too, repeat lines are woven into the movement of the material; there is no faltering between stanzas. And the last two lines are not a repetition of the first and third lines of the first stanza but a double repetition of the first line of the poem.

To use a repetitive form like the villanelle to portray a contemporary answering machine with its mechanical repetitions is an inspired (and ironic) marriage of form and subject.

Barbara L. Greenberg (contemporary)
227-2272*

This voice is a recording in the wilderness.
The circuits are all in use now. Nevertheless,
thank you for calling Barbara in your hour of stress.

You wish to report disaster at your address?
Fire? Flood? Earthquake? Avalanche? Small craft in distress?
This voice is a recording in the wilderness

and can not reach the Coast Guard. Let this voice express
a sense of deep involvement in your SOS.
Thank you for calling Barbara in your hour of stress.

You wish to report a crime? You wish to confess?
Don't blame yourself. We are all guilty, more or less.
This voice is a recording in the wilderness

and will not reach a verdict. What it says, it says
by careful prearrangement with your consciousness.
Thank you for calling Barbara in your hour of stress.

---

*The letters of the name *Barbara* coincide with the numerals of the title as they appear on a telephone dial.

Hello. Hello. Are you there? Are you there? Yes. Yes.
Will you help me? Will you help me? Godbless. Godbless.
This voice is a recording in the wilderness.
This voice is a recording in the wilderness.

  The sestina form may seem forbidding to the beginner. It *is* an intricate form, but its complexities are structural and can be made clear. The satisfaction you will experience when you take on its challenge will be worth every bit of effort it requires. The form originated in Provence, along with the other French forms, and was imported into English poetry through Italy. The structure is six stanzas of six lines each followed by a concluding tercet or half stanza. As a rule, the sestina is unrhymed (although Swinburne tampered with that feature), but the pattern of repeated line-end words creates the effect of rhyme. The difficulty arises because those end words must be repeated in accordance with a strict pattern. This pattern may appear completely arbitrary, but if you study the following diagram, you will find that there is indeed a logical progression. Be aware that the words that end the lines of your first stanza are going to be your tools throughout; choose them carefully.

  To arrange the end words in order in the second stanza, start taking the end words from the first stanza in the following manner: the one from the end of the sixth line in the first stanza will become the end word of the first line of your second stanza; the one from the end of the first line of the first stanza will go at the end of the second line of the second stanza. Having used the outside end words (sixth and first lines) of the first stanza, continue working inward as you take the other words you'll need. Take the end words (in this order) of the fifth, second, fourth, and third lines of your first stanza, and add them to the ends of the third, fourth, fifth, and sixth lines of your second stanza. Repeat the process in the same way between the second and third stanzas and so on until you come to the tercet.

  All six end words are used in the tercet, but the order is often left to the poet's discretion. The normal order is taken from the sixth stanza: the first three end words are used midline in the tercet; the remaining end words are used as the end words in the tercet also (in that order—see the diagram).

In the diagram, think of each column of numbers as representing the ends of the stanzas' lines, the figures themselves standing for the end words. The numbers 1 through 6 in the first column represent the normal order of end words for the first stanza.

(stanza)	(one)	(two)	(three)	(four)	(five)	(six)	(tercet)	
							(middle)	(end)
1	6	3	5	4	2			
2	1	6	3	5	4	2		5
3	5	4	2	1	6	4		3
4	2	1	6	3	5	6		1
5	4	2	1	6	3			
6	3	5	4	2	1			

If you can master the principle involved in the progression of the pattern of end words (remember, you can take some liberties with the word arrangement in the tercet), you should be able to write a sestina—at least, erect the form—without having to dig out your poetry manual. You will, however, find many exceptions to the strict rules governing the form. Poets are seldom willing to accept things as they are. But you should be able to distinguish how a poet has strayed from the traditional sestina, and your enjoyment will be increased for being able to do so.

The Italians, especially during the thirteenth century, were very fond of the sestina. Here is one by Dante, as translated by the author:

Dante Alighieri (thirteenth–fourteenth centuries)
Sestina

To twilight and the great circling shadows,
I've climbed, and to the bleaching of the hills
where all the color's faded from the grass.
But still my yearning does not lose its green,
so firmly has it rooted in hard stone
which speaks and listens as though it were a woman.

A statue made of ice, this slim young woman,

as cold as snow which lies within the shadows,
for she is no more moved than is a stone
by that sweet warmth the season feeds the hills
to bring them back again from white to green,
dressing their slopes once more with flowers and grass.

When on her head she wears a crown of grass,
my mind can give no thought to other women,
because she weaves the golden with the green
so well that Love is forced to hide in shadows,
this Love that has me trapped among low hills
and more securely than in walls of stone.

Her beauty has more fire than precious stones,
the scars she leaves cannot be healed by grass,
so I have fled to distant plains and hills
for refuge from so dangerous a woman;
yet in her sunshine there's no room for shadows,
nor any hill, nor walls, nor season's green.

Not long ago I saw her dressed in green
so fair she might have wakened in a stone
this love which I feel even for her shadow.
And so I wooed her in a field of grass
which is as lovely as any lovely woman
and is embraced by many lofty hills.

Yet shall the rivers turn and climb the hills
before Love's flame in this damp wood still green
shall catch and burn as in the heart of woman
for me, who'd sleep my life away on stone
or graze, an animal upon the grass,
just to see her clothing cast a shadow.

However dark the hills cast out their shadows
upon the season's green, this shining woman
covers them like stones concealed in grass.

   In the next sestina, note that the poet has abandoned

some of the end words in the tercet and includes at the beginning an explanatory note to the text.

Ezra Pound (contemporary)
Sestina: Altaforte

Loquitur: En Bertrans de Born.
  Dante Alighieri put this man in hell for that he was a stirrer up of strife. Eccovi!
  Judge ye!
  Have I dug him up again?
  The scene is at his castle, Altaforte. "Papiols" is his jongleur.
  "The Leopard," the device of Richard Coeur de Lion.

Damn it all! all this our South stinks peace.
You whoreson dog, Papiols, come! Let's to music!
I have no life save when the swords clash.
But ah! When I see the standards gold, vair, purple, opposing
And the broad fields beneath them turn crimson,
Then howl I my heart nigh mad with rejoicing.

In hot summer have I great rejoicing
When the tempests kill the earth's foul peace,
And the lightnings from black heav'n flash crimson,
And the fierce thunders roar me their music
And the winds shriek through the clouds mad, opposing,
And through the riven skies God's swords clash.

Hell grant soon we hear again the swords clash!
And the shrill neighs of destriers in battle rejoicing,
Spiked breast to spiked breast opposing!
Better one hour's stour than a year's peace
With fat boards, bawds, wine and frail music!
Bah! there's no wine like the blood's crimson!

And I love to see the sun rise blood-crimson.
And I watch his spears through the dark clash
And it fills all my heart with rejoicing
And pries wide my mouth with fast music
When I see him so scorn and defy peace,

His lone might 'gainst all darkness opposing.

The man who fears war and squats opposing
My words for stour, hath no blood of crimson
But is fit only to rot in womanish peace
Far from where worth's won and the swords clash
For the death of such sluts I go rejoicing;
Yea, I fill all the air with my music.

Papiols, Papiols, to the music!
There's no sound like to swords swords opposing,
No cry like the battle's rejoicing
When our elbows and swords drip the crimson
And our charges 'gainst "The Leopard's" rush clash.
May God damn for ever all who cry "Peace!"

And let the music of the swords make them crimson!
Hell grant soon we hear again the swords clash!
Hell blot black for alway the thought "Peace"!

You can see that the sestina's construction lends itself very well to a subject that the poet wants to examine from different viewpoints. It suits the contemplative reflections upon a theme as well as it allows Dante to let his lover know (indirectly, as he must have assumed) about his feelings regarding her lack of response, and as well as it permits the wildly exhortative daring of Pound to couch an unpopular theme in metaphor. A more internalized and subdued example is this sestina by W. H. Auden, which contains a narrative thread:

Paysage Moralise ("Landscape Moralized") (1936)

Hearing of harvests rotting in the valleys,
Seeing at end of street the barren mountains,
Round corners coming suddenly on water,
Knowing them shipwrecked who were launched for islands,
We honour founders of these starving cities
Whose honour is the image of our sorrow,

Which cannot see its likeness in their sorrow
That brought them desperate to the brink of valleys;
Dreaming of evening walks through learned cities
They reined their violent horses on the mountains,
Those fields like ships to castaways on islands,
Visions of green to them who craved for water.

They built by rivers and at night the water
Running past windows comforted their sorrow;
Each in his little bed conceived of islands
Where every day was dancing in the valleys
And all the green trees blossomed on the mountains
Where love was innocent, being far from cities.

But dawn came back and they were still in cities;
No marvellous creature rose up from the water;
There was still gold and silver in the mountains
But hunger was a more immediate sorrow,
Although to moping villagers in valleys
Some waving pilgrims were describing islands...

"The gods," they promised, "visit us from islands,
Are stalking, head-up, lovely, through our cities;
Now is the time to leave your wretched valleys
And sail with them across the lime-green water,
Sitting at their white sides, forget your sorrow,
The shadow cast across your lives by mountains."

So many, doubtful, perished in the mountains,
Climbing up crags to get a view of islands,
So many, fearful, took with them their sorrow
Which stayed them when they reached unhappy cities,
So many, careless, dived and drowned in water,
So many, wretched, would not leave their valleys.

It is our sorrow. Shall it melt? Ah, water
Would gush, flush, green these mountains and these valleys,
And we rebuild our cities, not dream of islands.

Variants of the sestina form are appearing here and there. For example, in *Yankee* magazine for July 1967, Dolores Stewart has a sestina ("I and Thou, a New England Translation") in which she has used modified versions of her original end words in the stanzas after the first. The end words of the first stanza are *idle, July, hour, country, delight,* and *ruins.* The word *idle* becomes *idyl* in the second stanza and in the tercet; *July* is changed to *Julius* in the third stanza; *hourly* in the third sestet is the variation on the original *hour; country* is altered in the fourth stanza to *countryside; delight* becomes *undelightedly* in the third stanza and, internally in the last line of the poem, is given as *delightful*; and *ruined* is used in place of *ruins* in the third stanza and as the last word of the tercet. Another contemporary poet, Terry Kennedy, has substituted synonyms as end words in place of the usual repetitions.

Inventiveness and daring are what revitalize these familiar forms and prevent them from becoming mummified curios. Once you've mastered the technique of the traditional sestina, do not be afraid to try out some of your own experimental ideas with the form.

FREE VERSE

Free verse is the form that has occupied most of the attention of many poets during recent decades. The term is a translation from the French *vers libre*, but French poets meant something quite different than we do by it. For them, it was only a relaxation of the rigors of strict meter. We've adopted it to mean an abandonment of meter and a turning to cadences of natural speech. Of course, the two languages are dissimilar; French has almost no accents with which to contend, but for English, the opposite is true. Not that we've abandoned accents—we can't; they're part of our language. What we have done is to break free from the demands of fixed metric construction. Metric feet are no longer important in free verse, but accents are. We cannot avoid the *feeling* of alternation between strong and weak beats. But in free verse, these are allowed to occur naturally. An accent is not forced onto some normally weak syllable, for instance, in order to obey the meter, because that would not be natural to the language as we use it. (Still—and it is a strange phenomenon—if you've studied or been brought up in the tradition of poetry, you will hear or, rather, sense the presence of a metrical pulse even in free verse—especially in exquisitely crafted free verse. Some things never let go.) There will be lines of free verse that are only a few words long combined with longer lines. The words themselves, their meanings, and the emotions they intimate will suggest appropriate line lengths.

This use of language in a natural way in poetry is not unlike Hopkins's aim in advocating the use of his *sprung rhythm* (which is discussed in the next chapter).

In free verse, we're not working with outlined form but with form in an organic sense—evolving, emergent. Free does not mean formless, although at times one might wonder. A unit of words, phrases, and lines cannot be formless and be a poem at the same time.

The principal measuring unit in free verse is not the line but the verse paragraph (an equivalent to the stanza, as noted earlier). Some prosodists prefer to call this unit a *strophe*, which can be justified on the basis of the meaning behind the Greek term: the verse paragraph is, in a way, a complete round that turns back into itself. We have compared it in function not only to the stanza but to the prose paragraph as well. But the term *strophe* suggests some measure of metrical control, which would be at odds with the concept of free verse; and, too, the word is associated with the Pindaric ode form, which may make things confusing. Until someone invents something better, it may be wise for us to go on using *verse paragraph* as the working term. With this unit as our measurement, we can see more clearly that Walt Whitman's extremely long lines were indeed free verse. And they were long lines of poetry, not prose. We must not confuse the limits of paper and printing methods with the unlimited imagination of the poet.

Using the term *free verse* did not establish a new kind of poetry, since poetry of that sort long preceded the appearance of the term. The Psalms, Job, and The Song of Songs are all in free verse form in the King James version of the Bible. Poets such as Milton, Dryden, Blake, Matthew Arnold, Heinrich Heine, and others wrote poems that, if written today, would be described as free verse.

Although not making use of metrical pattern and lines of even lengths and generally avoiding patterned rhyme (random rhyme does appear now and then), free verse does avail itself of other poetic devices. Metaphor, image, regional diction, dialogue, lyricism, narrative, drama, and description are as much parts of free verse as they are of any other kind of poetry. The technical devices of alliteration and consonance (the matching of consonant and vowel sounds) are relied upon to achieve the music poetry offers in free verse; and in many ways, music serves as a guide for this type of poetry. Pound said: "Compose in the sequence of the musical phrase, not in the measure of the metronome."

The attraction of free verse is that it affords the poet greater freedom in expressing emotion and theme, unhampered by the requirements imposed by traditional metrical forms. Free verse does allow more latitude, of course, but it is certainly not an easier form with which to work. Since there are less specifically outlined guides, the work must proceed on an intuitive level. Each poem generates its own rules of form. A great deal of practice is required to develop effective intuitions for free verse. And it is doubtful that any poet can be sure of perfect pacing in every poem he or she writes. So free verse poses a greater gamble than other forms. Still, it offers greater potential in several ways. The writer creates form along with the rest of the poem, and this may lead to a luxury of variation that would not be available to us in any other way.

In writing free verse, imposing a pattern may very well be your most efficient organizational device. This can range from the obvious—recognizable verse paragraph lengths, refrain lines at regular intervals, a certain style of indentation, a play on a particular set of sounds—to a more subtle pattern, one that depends on elements not readily discernible to the unpracticed eye—larger configurations based on verse paragraph structure rather than on lines, paragraphs that echo each other in sequence or skip back and forth, or ones that mirror each other so that lines appearing to be random lengths within one paragraph will be matched in other paragraphs. Or the pattern may involve sections or larger divisions of the poem, or it may depend on content material, the way images are repeated, altered, played against each other; a recurring set of symbols; or anything of that nature. The effectiveness of these subtle devices will rely on the poem's length and breadth, of course, but the element of pattern will be a strongly unifying feature of any free verse poem.

The most important free verse pattern of all is that one expressed through the cadence of the poem's language. In fact, Amy Lowell suggested "cadenced verse" as a more appropriate term for this kind of poetry. *Cadence* refers to the natural rhythm of the language, determined by the innate alternation of accented and unaccented syllables. The poet's artistry comes into play when these accents are appreciated as rhythmic beats and are organized into rhythmic patterns—not into meter but into patterns, the more original designs that free verse allows.

The intent behind the use of free verse is not to toss out the rule books and create an anarchy of words and phrases, but to enrich the features of form; not to destroy, but to expand the borders and to give poetry room to grow in new directions. In the examples that follow, you will discover that the term *free verse* does not imply the absence of lyricism any more than it implies the lack of rhythm and pattern.

Although the following poem is free verse, the poet has retained the traditional quatrain form and uses repetition in a traditional style—the first two lines occurring again as the last two, bringing the poem full circle:

Samuel L. Albert (contemporary)
After a Game of Squash

And I thought of how impossibly alone we were,
Up in the room where the lockers are and the showers.
He with wiping the sweat from his face and head
And I bending over, loosening the laces from my sneakers.

We had just finished this long game of squash.

Then, we were much closer; smashing the same ball;
Lurching forward, out-maneuvering each other
Hard down the sidelines, death to the opponent.

It was a battle, the killer's eye in the middle
Of the round black ball. Two men struggling
To find each other out. What made each one's mind work
And with what heart each fell to the long odds.

And when the game was over we thanked each other generously;
Complimented one the other on his skill, his finesse.
And I thought of how impossibly alone we were,
Up in the room where the lockers are and the showers.

John Holmes (contemporary)
Hearing Margaret, Aged Four

"I dare to walk in this water, but not when I am angry."
It hurries across my ankles. The checkerboard bottom shines
Raggedly when I drop my eyes, but I do not try not to think.
I am singing a long unlikely story, a ripple of surprises,
Things I never knew to happen. Though I have read storybooks
And looked out castle-windows, I do not like to be laughed at.

I speak interrupting my own delight, and break my prose
With the song, skimming and foolish, sometimes so beautiful
I do not know who I am, what curling of air is like waterflow
Across blue glass, then green, then green-yellow glass.
The story must not end, but it splashes into my head always
From somewhere, and I float out on my voice with its words,
With its pictures I can't draw yet when I am drawing pictures,
People's names, bobbing end-up in the shallow clear flood,
Drifts of clothes and shoes I outgrew, all weightless, all
Whirling like glass bowls in a glass bowl too big to have a rim.

I am at the other side now, and did not stumble on anger
And drown screaming in that hole where it is too deep to sing.
It is the end of the day, carpet-edge, the other side of the hall,
A field with barns and buttercups, and I can let the story end,

Except for some of the singing, as if I am remembering it,
When I sit down on this grass to rest from walking in water.

Anne Sexton (contemporary)
Ghosts

Some ghosts are women,
neither abstract nor pale,
their breasts as limp as killed fish.
Not witches, but ghosts
who come, moving their useless arms
like forsaken servants.

Not all ghosts are women,
I have seen others;
fat, white-bellied men,
wearing their genitals like old rags.
Not devils, but ghosts.
This one thumps barefoot, lurching
above my bed.

But that isn't all.
Some ghosts are children.
Not angels, but ghosts;
curling like pink tea cups
on any pillow, or kicking,
showing their innocent bottoms, wailing
for Lucifer.

LeRoi Jones (contemporary)
The Invention of Comics

I am a soul in the world: in
the world of my soul the whirled
light / from the day
the sacked land
of my father.

In the world, the sad

nature of
myself. In myself
nature is sad. Small
prints of the day. Its
small dull fires. Its
sun, like a greyness
smeared on the dark.

The day of my soul, is
the nature of that
place. It is a landscape. Seen
from the top of a hill. A
grey expanse; dull fires
throbbing on its seas.

The man's soul, the complexion
of his life. The menace
of its greyness. The
fire, throbs, the sea
moves. Birds shoot
from the dark. The edge
of the waters lit
darkly for the moon.

And the moon, from the soul. Is
the world, of the man. The man
and his sea, and its moon, and
the soft fire throbbing. Kind
death. O,
my dark and sultry
love.

CONCRETE POETRY

Concrete poetry enjoyed a degree of attention during the fifties and sixties but seems now to have been relegated to library corners. Why it is called "concrete" is a mystery. It has been pointed out that concrete poetry is abstract rather than concrete. For our purposes, we shall have to deal with the poems that illustrate what the term has come to mean, in spite of its imprecision. Perhaps it has been called concrete because it demands the eye's attention, much as a drawing or painting does. There are examples that actually combine line drawings with text. But most concrete poetry relies on a special use of the language medium: typography. This may manifest itself either as a mix of different typefaces and sizes and intuitive designs arranged with a typographic virtuosity or as a block of text (in some cases, a design profile produced by the text) from which some startling effect evolves. There is a tenuous parallel in the way a concrete poem is perceived by the viewer and the way a Japanese haiku is grasped by the reader. The impact should be sudden, the result of instant realization rather than of studied deduction. The contemporary poet Aram Saroyan has a concrete poem that is composed in a column with the single word *crickets* constituting line after line. Nothing else but that one word creating the long column. One does not "read" such a poem; one *looks* at it and *absorbs* it. If you look at that poem long enough, you will actually experience ("hear") crickets.

The concrete poetry movement got under way semiofficially in 1955, when the Swiss poet Eugen Gomringer met with Brazilian poet Decio Pignatari in Ulm, West Germany. In 1955, Gomringer coined the term *Konkrete Poesie* for a projected anthology that never saw publication. However, other poets were encouraged to try the technique: among them, four other Brazilians, Augusto de Campos, Haraldo de Campos, Pedro Xisto, and Edgard Braga; Ian Finlay in Scotland; the French poet Pierre Garnier; two Austrians, Ernst Jandl and Gerhard Rühm; Robert Lax and Aram Saroyan in the United States; Claus Bremer of Germany; another Scot, Edwin Morgan; Dom Sylvester Houédard from Guernsey; and Seiichi Niikuni of Japan. Unquestionably, this was an international movement.

There are solid connections between concretists and the poets who arranged calligrammes, "picture" poems, poems resembling crosses, altars, wings, and so forth and with the surrealists. The quality of surrealist poetry invites the manipulation of typographic quantities.

In concrete poetry, the emphasis is always on the visual impact the poem offers. The intelligible communication factor is submerged or subordinated. It seems reasonable to assume that the origins of the concept of concrete poetry may be traceable to hieroglyphics, Chinese characters, and ideograms. We are intended to grasp the poem and to sense its overtones, meanings, and emotional impact all at once. A concrete poem is described by the concretists as an object in and by itself, with dynamics that force the viewer to look *at*, rather than through, the poem—a confrontation between viewer and artwork.

Concrete poetry is identified with a "spatial or visual syntax," or "composition based on direct (analogical—not logical–discursive) juxtaposition of elements." Meaning becomes inseparable from the manner of its notation. Concrete poetry is an art of signs. Metaphor, rather than arising from any discursive framework, evolves from the variations that can be exercised on the printed word or phrase.

Several of the more experimental periodicals, like *The Beloit Poetry Journal* and *The Wormwood Review*, feature such poetry in their pages, and occasionally these magazines devote entire issues to it. There is also a publication issued in 1967 by Something Else Press *(An Anthology of Concrete Poetry)* that illustrates several variations. Here (opposite) are two examples of concrete poetry that appeared in *Pyramid* #4 in 1969. The first one (spiral) is by the contemporary poet and artist Valerie Jayne. The second one is by the author.

FOUND POETRY/COLLAGE

A strong link exists between these two forms. They've been compared to op or pop art, and there's justification for that if the process involves mere appropriation without transformation.

Found poetry, which has had difficulty being taken seri-

```
                    compartmented
            horn-                    determined
        crust-                       from its original
        the shell                    grain of DNA
      ly /                           and by random
    ous                    First     action of tide
  u                       immacu-    color of sand
tin                    late pearl-   mineral content
                        brimming     surrounding
  con                  sound / a stem
                                     its growth /
      twisting
                                     turning
                                    not a helix
                                   but spiraling

                              outward

                            from the

                          beginning

              perfection
```

ously, may range from text excerpted from some other source (advertisements or news stories, for instance) and arranged as a poem to the blending of such "found" material with text of the poet's composition to form a new entity that may become a poem. Collage involves a cutting and pasting technique, a juxtaposition of disparate elements to form a new meaning. Examples of collage show sections of text obtained from magazines, newspapers, or brochures pasted over each other at various angles, at times accompanied by cuttings of photographs or drawings that are also pasted over pieces of text as well as over each other, with the poet intending the whole to meld into a poem.

Whereas collage poetry is decidedly visual, found poetry is intended to be accepted in the way traditional poetry is, because the poet tries to make the combination of found and original materials coalesce into new insights.

A sophisticated use of found poetry appears in *Thou Shalt Not Overkill: peace poems* by Walter Lowenfels (Hellric Chapbook No. 1. Jamaica Plain, Mass.: Hellric Publications, 1968). In this work, the poet has integrated into his original text quotations from books, newspaper headlines and releases, item paragraphs, parts of radio broadcasts, and so on. The result is a sequence that makes its point forcefully and defensibly.

This example of found poetry is by Dolores Stewart and was first published in *Pyramid* #8, 1970:

Personals

latest European tech

AC/DC BLONDE avail

no kooks no dopers

gay guy fun&games
discreet sincere

really beautiful
couple to join us
we are really

beautiful too
write full details

GEORGE TRILBY
please call home
you can pick
your own school

bi-girl educ uninhib

white woman to 55
for boating and fishing
send photo

do you cry yourself
to sleep? I will
hold you any sex

desires black or
oriental any age

GEORGE call collect
we understand
money can buy
everything we gave you

French will satisfy
you & yr roommate too

Laverne, where are you
we want you to see
last movie we made

HOT DADDY 60 WANTS
HOT MAMA to share apt

affect tiny girls
with long dark hair

GEORGE you don't
have to finish school

The same issue of *Pyramid* featured Gary Elder's "The Compleat MOON LANDER," a collage of text, drawings, parts of photographs, all organized visual references to the first moon landing, other current issues, reports of protests, and bits of Hollywood advertisements—the whole restless poem implicitly inquiring if we've got our priorities mixed up. Elder's collage runs twelve pages, and it's a convincing bit of sustaining the poet has achieved.

Many of these various experiments, in their rudimentary forms, seldom attain the level of art. Only when the process is more than assemblage, when the new juxtapositions result in a transcendence of the limitations of the original character and function of the parts, will the assemblage become poetry. As an example, look at the separate entries in "Personals" by Stewart again. When you read them with a continuity that you accept from the poet, those separate parts meld into something else, into an insight that not only informs us of the lives of separate people but of the status of life in general. The parts of the poem have been made part of a new poem.

When this evolving amalgam fails to manifest itself, the poem itself fails, just as it does when the poet has put together in a sonnet or rondeau a group of images that are vivid in themselves but not sufficiently related or unable to coalesce into a new entity. This additional dimension in a work of art is a prime requisite. Otherwise, the result may be moving or momentarily attractive, but it won't have the enduring quality of true art.

PROJECTIVE VERSE

(Projective verse is called variously *open verse, composition by field, poetry by field*.) Projective verse leans heavily on tactile detail. The poet is consciously and deliberately concerned with the dynamics of language, breath intervals, the "rests"—expanses of white space on the page—and the visual impact of text organization. In projective verse, the text is not arranged in lines but in *word clusters*, which are the power stations that produce the energy required for the poem's kinetics. Unity of sense and sound is approached with more conscious attention. According to Charles Olson, one of the promotional advocates of projective verse, "one perception must immediately and directly lead to a further perception," and this effect gives the poem its pacing. To an even greater extent than in other forms of poetry, the visual arrangement is regarded in terms of a musical score. Emotion is often deemphasized, and diction is kept to the natural (at times, journalistic) level.

The word clusters actually generate a specific energy, one designed to propel the reader's eye over white space to the next cluster. The placement of these word clusters is largely intuitive, as it must be, since the form is inevitably organic. In practice, the process can be honed only through trial and error. Thinking of word clusters in terms of traditional poetic lines ending on a suspension may help make the concept a bit clearer.

Projective verse is not anarchic or antipoetry, as some of its critics claim. It's a new approach. The techniques involved represent the evolution of the poetic process: the line becomes the word cluster; the line ending becomes the space between clusters.

Not all projective verse excludes emotion and depends on journalistic diction. Here is an example of one kind of projective verse, written by the author:

Thin Ice

I walk
in   the ice
a dead man's skin   cracks spiderly
                       the sun
today   bounces   yesterday
spent   light   to tomorrow
in solitude

             I wink
         from
             a dead man's eye   the window
    remind me   opens stiffly
    to leap
    on this dead star   the fence
                                         that keeps my secret
                 the ice
                 makes
                 the star alive   my fingers tremble
                                              I breathe white air
    whisper me to sleep   at the wind
    your angled vision
    spears the lunge   glancing at the ice
    which spills to air   which cracks to sound
                                             its nervous music
                                         I walk
                                         in
                                             a dead man's skin
    you wait
    for   the whirl of blue in
    my eyes to shine life   the air confuses me
             I think
                     my mind
                     is the knowledge
                     of my body
                 you ask
                     what is a mind
                     but a few entire thoughts
                     and a host
                     of unrelated fragments?
                 the ice
                 breaks
                 its skin
                         the water
                         bends
                         barely bends
                         to the wind

130

                    the skin I wear
                    feels too tight

Several of the word clusters in "Thin Ice" radiate rather than aim, and the result is that you may read the poem in more than one way in several of its parts. You can read, for example, the first cluster as just that: "I walk / in / a dead man's skin." Then you can read the cluster immediately below it; or the "sun" one to its lower right; or the first one across to the right. In effect, your choices so far are as follows: (1) "I walk / in / a dead man's skin // today / spent / in solitude"; (2) "I walk / in / a dead man's skin // the sun / bounces / light"; (3) "I walk / in / a dead man's skin // the ice / cracks spiderly." There is also another way of reading that same section, one that fragments the clusters: "I walk / in / the ice // a dead man's skin / cracks spiderly // the sun // today / bounces / yesterday // spent / light / to tomorrow // in solitude."

These various dynamics are harnessed together during the poem's progression and are brought into tight unity as the poem ends, technique and sense achieving the same conclusion but in suspension, implying a further breakout.

In this kind of poetry, the word clusters invade other word clusters, and both invaders and invadees become altered. It involves a technique that is not simple, but it offers much potential for development and should be encouraged.

Surrealism, concrete poetry, found poetry, collage poetry, and projective verse present us with techniques we're not, as a rule, accustomed to, and it is to be expected that there will be a certain amount of fumbling. But this is no reason to deny the validity of these new approaches. It is in the nature of experiment that it makes its way through trial and error. The time will come when some of these techniques, if not all, will find a deserved niche in the cathedral of poetry.

We must remember that as dear a prosodist as R. F. Brewer grouped the sestina, villanelle, and the other French forms under a chapter heading "Poetic Trifles" in his book *The Art of Versification and the Technicalities of Poetry*. The "trifles" of today may very well find the masters tomorrow who will elevate them to serious attention, those poets who will use the best of the present experiments to form a vital new addition to poetry. As a student, allow your mind to be open to these different approaches. Who knows? You may turn out to be one of tomorrow's masters.

Those poets whose genius and effort have carried the tradition of poetic expression forward for us to enjoy were expert artists, and their dedication was total. There is indeed much to learn about poetry if one is to become a poet. It takes patience, time, and work to achieve the best expression in language that one is capable of and to turn that expression into a completed work of art. Yes, writing poems is work, but it is joyous work. And to give it less than your best, to give it less than masters of the past gave it in their time, is to fall short of your commitment.

Up to this point is prologue. We have acquired a familiarity with poetry—no more than that. It's still a long way to the complete knowing poetry demands of us. There is, in our bodies and minds, movement—movement that will not cease while we live, for it is the movement of life, the rejuvenating dance. We are an arc from one stillness to another, and it is in the arc that we find our dance. We are warned of darknesses inside us, of dangers we face if we dismiss the censors that keep our demons hidden. But there is also song within us—jubilant, vibrant melody that holds our lives together. We must face inherent risks if we are to reveal the rhythm and song within us, if we are to transpose such basic compulsions into poems.

Our aim in the next three chapters is to comprehend the roles of the movement, the sound, and the masks of poetry. We shall use a figurative microscope, for we must conduct a detailed examination.

5. The Nervous System and the Middle Ear

Rhythm is measured flow. From the pulse in the heart of the sun to the pulse in the heart of the body, all is rhythm. Before early humans were capable of comprehending the natural phenomena around them, they responded to their rhythms. In their imaginations they appeared to be god directed, and they adopted a reverence toward those gods. Once they acquired the beginnings of language, they offered suppliant chants and invocations and rude dance steps they had improvised as appeasement to these unknown gods. Although they would have been unable to explain why it should be so, the employment of rhythm seemed right and proper. The gods would be expected to listen only if prayers were intensified by repetition. Even while language was still only a series of grunts and cries and dance no more than a tentative shuffling, people performed such acts rhythmically, repeating the voiced sounds over and over and clapping their hands to the movements of their bare feet. The patterns initially were crude and awkward; with practice, they became smoother and, over a period of time, began to acquire sophistication. As they began to understand the rhythms in the environment, people sensed the intimations of being in harmony with the universe.

Their bodies revealed their natures as composites of complementary rhythms, and these appeared to be influenced by the cycles of appetites and bodily functions, by the alternation of night and day, and—in a larger pattern—by the change of seasons. Too primitive to analyze or rationalize the bases for feelings, early human beings were satisfied to express their gratitude and to request the fulfillment of their needs through prayer offered in rhythm and song—humankind's first poetry.

Rhythm is a matter both physical and psychological. According to Plato, the lives of people in every part have need of rhythm. It is this need that influences the way we walk, run, work, play, and move in any number of activities. Rhythm is in our breathing, in the beat of the blood in our veins, in the fluctuations of our emotional state, in the cycles of our bodily functions, in every facet of our living. When everything is in order, we experience a feeling of well-being. We find pleasure in these bodily rhythms. And we transfer this experiencing of pleasure to rhythmic evidence outside our bodies, to the movement of tides, the repetitions in nature, the beating of drums, and the sounds of engines—joying in the anticipated regularity of them. These external rhythms make us feel in tune with our environment, for they make themselves felt in our bodies. And the rhythms of our bodies themselves convince us that we are alive and well.

This need for rhythm, this realization of its fundamental place in our lives, has been responsible for the spontaneous generation of folk songs and work songs, for singing games, lullabies, nursery rhymes, and sailors' songs. Rhythm makes effort less tiring, reassures us against our fears, and cajoles us to learn and remember.

The patterns of rhythm, the fantastic creations of nature and the careful constructions of humankind, impose order on chaos. But without meaningful variation, pattern remains a dull reiteration, lacking the stimulating intensification of emotion. Universal rhythms operate on a wave-sense, whether elemental, sound, or light. We respond to these waves, and our behavior is guided by the tension between such influences and the dictates of our conscious desires. Although we have a strong need for the basic rhythms of our lives, we also cherish the variations that prevent monotony and lend interest and excitement to existence. These variations (we may call them counter-rhythms) result in a syncopation played against the basic rhythms, and the complexities thus engendered enrich our psyches. The basic rhythms provide a sense of security, whereas the variations provide stimulus. We need both.

The body's nervous system is a network of "information feeders" to the brain, feeders that transmit not only external rhythms but internal rhythms as well. The middle ear is the body's balance-maintaining (and -registering) device. It records the basic rhythm as being stable. If this rhythm becomes disturbed, we have difficulty in keeping our balance.

Poetry is possible without meter and without rhyme. Poetry is not possible without rhythm. Whether you prefer the metrical designs of traditional forms or the freer natural speech rhythms, there is no avoiding the inherent rhythm of language. Making the best use of language rhythms is a matter vital to poetry.

Speaking of the wave-sense of rhythms, words—in context—set waves of their own in motion. If we take steps to restrain the wave so that it is forced to travel in one discursive direction, we are allowing the words to exercise a prose rhythm. If we permit the wave more flexibility, exploiting its radiational qualities, we are encouraging a freer play, syncopating counter-rhythms against that more basic beat that unifies; and the words begin to attain the province of poetry. Construct several such word-waves, create a textual environment for them, instill a momentum, and you have started a rhythmic action. Introduce variations, arranging them in an emotionally interesting fashion, and you are on the verge of poetic pattern. Repeat such patterns, again varying and intensifying to avoid monotony and (always) to reinforce the sense of the words, and you have a unifying rhythmic structure. You have, in essence, achieved one necessary element in the composition of the poem.

Naturally, you are not expected to sit at your desk and analyze rhythmic concepts at the moment the Muse inspires. But you should be familiar enough with these aspects of rhythm so that while you compose, you rely on their assitance at an intuitive level. You learn to use rhythm on a conscious level through practice. After the heat of composition has cooled, your work is just beginning. You must have the patience, then, to analyze what you have written. It is through such self-study, and through as many revisions as are required, that you train yourself. Eventually, you will reach the point where you will spend less conscious thought on such matters, but you will never be completely free of them. They are the instruments of your art.

The elements of rhythm in poetry include stress or accent, quantity (the duration of a particular syllable), and pitch. In classical meter, quantity is regarded as demanding more attention than the other elements. In the Romantic period, stress was the dominant factor. Today, there seems little regard for either in a great deal of published poetry; the preference is largely for the rhythms of natural speech. All these elements have always coexisted, of course, and will continue to do so in meaningful and well-executed poetry.

Quantity, which is the length of time it takes actually to mouth each syllable, defines syllables as *long* or *short*. Long ones are those that consist of a short vowel followed by two or more consonants, as in the word *c*atch, or in a syllable containing a long vowel, as in the words *smoke* and *be*. Short syllables are those that contain a short vowel followed by one consonant, as in *sit*, or by none, as in *the*. Polysyllabic words would be divided into long and short beats accordingly. Two short syllables are considered the equivalent of one long one; the work *minute*, for example, is the equivalent of one long beat, since both syllables fall into the short category.

Metrical stress is the emphasis of weight imposed arbitrarily in the line, dictated by the design of the meter. In classical verse, the beats are identified by the ‾ sign for long ones and the ˘ sign for short ones, rather than by the accent mark ´ with which we're familiar from later English poetry scanning. In other words, such beats are measured *in time* rather than by pitch and intensity in volume.

Scansion is the analysis of the metrical rhythm of the line. This is another of those "inexact sciences." Take any line of poetry, and chances are, opinions on how it should be scanned will vary. However, scansion is part of the process of learning the craft of poetry, so it cannot be ignored. Bear in mind that it *is* a subjective undertaking and that one person's opinion may be as defensible as another's.

You may already have had some experience in scansion in your courses at school. You've also been exposed to it somewhat in the previous chapter, when we were considering the beats in some of the stanza constructions we examined. When we scan a line of English poetry, remember that we count by syllable and stress and that how many syllables and what kind of stress there are reveal the configuration of the foot, which enables us to measure the line. The foot in poetry is similar to the measure (or bar) in music. In scansion, the *virgule*—shown as / or | —divides one foot from the next, much as the bar-line does between measures in a music score. The terminology of poetry's structure bears a resemblance to music's terminology.

When we scan to determine the measure of the classical line, we still count by syllables, but we take into account their longness and shortness, their temporal value, to determine the kinds of feet involved. *Sapphics* refers to a four-line stanza written in the classical meter that we associate with Sappho's own work. English poets tried their hand at it from time to time, as did the Romans before them. Swinburne turned out a work entitled "Sapphics" in which he imitates the original meter of the Greek poet. His opening stanza affords us an opportunity to see how it is constructed:

All the night sleep came   not upon my eyelids,
Shed not dew, nor shook   nor unclosed a feather,
Yet with lips shut close   and with eyes of iron
    Stood and be   held me.

Horace was the one who attempted to establish the metrical breakdown of Sapphic meter. There are variations, introduced by Sappho herself, but generally the scansion is as already indicated except that the fourth and eleventh syllables in the first three lines may be either short or long (*sleep* in the first line is long, whereas the fourth syllables of the next two lines are short), and the final syllable of the last line may also be either short or long.

The vertical lines (virgules) separate the feet that make up the line, and the spaces near the middle of the lines indicate only the way a pause unaffecting the measuring of the meter would divide the line. The Swinburne stanza illustrates some of the problems involved in trying to adapt a system that works well in one language to the idiosyncrasies of another language.

In English poetry, there is a tendency, where stress or accent occur, to raise the tonal level as well as to increase the loudness of the syllable, however slightly, whereas unstressed or unaccented syllables tend to be sounded in a more muted fashion. This involves pitch and volume. Because the English and the Americans, although in different styles, have acquired the habit of slurring certain unaccented syllables, the poet must be even more diligently aware of being true to life in constructing rhythmic patterns. The complementary dynamics of all these various elements result in rhythms that appeal to us and that move us when we listen to a poem.

Rhythm and meter are related, but they aren't the same thing. Rhythm is the natural beat as it exists in the words themselves; meter is a number of beats organized into a pattern. One can plot a chart representing a poem's metrical design and recognize the progression of metrical beats. But the rhythms of natural speech are too random and too connected with meaning, which moves in several directions at once, to lend themselves to that precise an analysis.

Meter, of course, should also have a strong relationship to the sense of the text. The most difficult commandment of poetry is: The sense and the technical features of a poem must be congruous, presenting a unity and an integrity that is beyond challenge. Obviously, the poet must select the meter that is most appropriate to the subject matter.

The days of wrenching accents and torturing syntax for the sake of meter and rhyme are past. But even in eras gone by, the best poets did not rely on contortions of the language. In our time, awkward syntax is criticized. The language itself, as well as its rhythms, must move naturally through the lines. The rhythm on the treble level must move in the cadences of natural speech while the metrical scheme provides the bass against which the counterpointing of the speech rhythms takes place.

In classical meter (Greek and Latin poetry), although the chief factor governing rhythm is quantity, the inexactitude of the "long" and "short" measurements saves even the strictest classical meter from becoming metronomic. Long vowels vary in duration one to the next, and their lengths are also conditioned by the number and the *quality* of the surrounding consonants—not just the ones that follow the vowel. And the same is true for the short vowels. This is one of the charms of the art: There are no absolutes. Robert Frost said that meter enabled the poet to move easily in harness.

The most commonly used feet in metrical verse are the *iamb,* the *anapest,* the *trochee,* and the *dactyl;* and for special effects, there's the *spondee.* (It would be hard to imagine a poem constructed entirely of spondees except as a tour de force.) Most of the metrical poetry we encounter will be constructed on the types of feet already mentioned.

As we learned in Chapter 4, the iambic foot is made up of an unstressed syllable followed by a stressed one. Its scansion symbol is ˘ ´ . An iambic foot may be formed by one word *(appróach),* by two words *(tŏ gét),* or by syllables that bridge the virgules *(mak / ĭng món / ey).* Because iambic rhythm moves from unstressed to stressed syllables, it is often referred to as *rising rhythm.*

Anapestic rhythm, scanned by the sign ˘ ˘ ´, includes feet made up of two unstressed syllables followed by a stressed one and is also considered a rising rhythm. Examples of anapests are *interrúpt, ĭf thĕ bóy, love / lў ĭn spár / kling.*

The trochaic foot is composed of two syllables, the reverse of the iambic in order, and is called a *falling rhythm* (´˘). *Sóns ăr / rĭve bĕ / fóre thĕir / fáthĕrs* is a line composed entirely of trochaic feet.

Another example of falling rhythm is produced by the dactyl, which—reversing the order of the anapest—is made up of a stressed syllable followed by two unstressed ones (´˘˘). These dactylic feet provide illustrations: *slóvĕnlў, ásking thĕ, en / ráptŭred bĕ / yond.*

The spondee, shown as ´´ , includes two stressed syllables only. It occurs when the poet uses a word compounded of two one-syllable words (*slípshód*), two monosyllabic words, each requiring a stress (*sét týpe*), or uses the stressed syllables in juxtaposition from parts of two adjacent words (*a / gáin ták / ing*). Although the stress is said to be equal on each part of the spondee, this can be so only in theory. In practice, the language being what it is, one stress is invariably a bit heavier than the other. The spondee enables the poet to introduce a pause, induce a slower reading, or indicate a special emphasis. It is another means of achieving variety in the meter.

The following examples illustrate uses of the iambic, anapestic, trochaic, dactylic, and spondiac feet, respectively.

J. M. Synge (nineteenth–twentieth centuries)
Epitaph (Iambic)

A silent sinner, nights and days,
No human heart to him drew nigh,
Alone he wound his wonted ways,
Alone and little loved did die.

And autumn Death for him did choose,
A season dank with mists and rain,
And took him, while the evening dews
Were settling o'er the fields again.

Egan O'Rahilly (eighteenth century)
Lament for Banba (second stanza) (Anapestic)
Rendered into English by James Clarence Mangan.

As a tree in its prime,
  Which the ax layeth low,
Didst thou fall, O unfortunate land!
  Not by time, nor thy crime,
  Came the shock and the blow.
They were given by a false felon hand!

Alas, alas, and alas!
　　For the once proud people of Banba!

William Blake
The Piper (first two stanzas) (Trochaic)

Piping down the valleys wild,
　　Piping songs of pleasant glee,
On a cloud I saw a child,
　　And he laughing said to me:

"Pipe a song about a lamb!"
　　So I piped with merry cheer.
"Piper, pipe that song again;"
　　So I piped: he wept to hear.

Thomas Hood (nineteenth century)
The Bridge of Sighs (first three stanzas) (Dactylic)

One more Unfortunate,
　　Weary of breath,
Rashly importunate,
　　Gone to her death!

Take her up tenderly,
　　Lift her with care;
Fashioned so slenderly,
　　Young, and so fair!

Look at her garments
Clinging like cerements;
Whilst the wave constantly
　　Drips from her clothing;

Táke hĕr ŭp / ínstănt̄y,
   Lóvĭng, nŏt / lóathĭng.

Henry David Thoreau (nineteenth century)
Mist (Spondaic)

Lów-ánchored cloud,
Newfoundland air,
Fountain-head and source of rivers,
Déw-clóth, dréam-drápery,
And napkin spread by fays;
Drifting meadow of the air,
Where bloom the daisied banks and violets,
And in whose fenny labyrinth
The bittern booms and heron wades;
Spirit of lakes and seas and rivers,
Bear only perfumes and the scent
Of healing herbs to just men's fields.

   The iamb, anapest, trochee, dactyl, and spondee are the poetic feet encountered most often in metric poetry. Some less familiar feet are of interest because they will provide those of you who choose traditional forms with a flexibility for special effects and for variety within the line.
   The *amphibrach*, composed of a stressed syllable between two unstressed ones (˘ ´ ˘), makes possible a *rocking rhythm*:

The rĭvĕr / ĭs flówĭng; / cŏme báptĭze / my chíldrĕn.

   The opposite configuration, an unstressed syllable between two stressed ones, is called the *amphimacer* or *cretic* (´ ˘ ´):

Táke my hánds, / lét thĕm gúide / hómewărd nów.

   The *choriamb*, a four-syllable foot, is actually a combination of a trochee followed by an iamb (´ ˘ ˘ ´). In a true choriambic line, the opening foot *is* a trochee and the closing one an iamb:

Spéak thĕ / phrásĕs ŏf lóve / caúght ĭn yŏur héart / lĕt thĕm dispél / my dréad.

Two other little-used feet are the *dibrach* (or *pyrrhic*) and the *tribach*, composed of two and three unstressed syllables respectively (˘ ˘)(˘ ˘ ˘). Formerly, these were used sparingly because of their limitations, being reserved for phrases that generally required no stresses (ĭn thĕ). Today, they're hardly considered legitimate feet in scansion, their elements more often being absorbed in more substantial neighboring feet—altering, in effect, our concept of proper scanning.

The *paeon* is a four-syllable foot with a unique feature: it boasts a variable stress. Its full name is determined by which of the syllables claims the stress; hence, *first paeon*—´˘˘˘; *second paeon*—˘´˘˘ ; *third paeon*—˘˘´˘ ; *fourth paeon*—˘˘˘´. Gerard Manley Hopkins used the first paeon extensively in his work, and it's an important part of his *sprung rhythm*. (We come to that shortly.) In this first line of his poem "Hurrahing in Harvest," the first paeons are italicized:

Súmmĕr ĕnds nŏw; / now, / *bárbărŏus ĭn* / beauty, the stooks arise.

There is another classical foot that also employs variable stresses, the *Ionic*. It is made up of a spondee and a dibrach. When the spondee precedes the dibrach (´´˘˘), it is known as the *greater Ionic* or the *major Ionic*; when the spondee follows the dibrach, it is called the *lesser Ionic* or the *minor Ionic*.

(The greater Ionic): Gúide shíps ĭn frŏm / bláck ócĕans ănd
(The lesser Ionic): Ŏn thĕ whíte pláte / ĭs ă shárp knífe.

However complex the metrical foot may appear, meter is

always either duple (two-beat) or triple (three-beat) rhythm. Those feet that contain more than three syllables are, as in music, combinations of twos and threes.

Even the strictest meter can avoid monotony if the poet pays adequate attention to the natural speech rhythms of the lines. Imagine, if you will, a bass drum muted almost to silence. Against it, a snare drum executes intricate rhythmic figures. Although on an immediate level, your attention will be attracted by the variables of the figures the snare drum produces, at a deeper level, you will be aware of—you will feel—the regular, controlled anchoring of that bass beat. Those insistent vibrations will not be denied.

When a poem is described as being, say, *iambic pentameter*, that means that the basic metrical foot is iambic and there are five such feet to each line. It does not mean, however, that every foot in the poem must be iambic. *Substitution* permits the introduction of other kinds of feet to provide relief from what would be a jingling or, especially in iambic, singsong effect. A trochee may be substituted for an iamb, or an iamb for a trochee. The commonest type of substitution in English verse is a trochee for an iamb at the beginning of the line, as in this line from Dylan Thomas's "The Hand That Signed the Paper":

Doúblĕd / thĕ́ globe / ŏ́f deád / aňd halvéd / ă coúntry;

Note, too, that the line's final foot is an amphibrach. Such variations do not alter the general application of the term *iambic* to the line. The iambic rhythm is established sufficiently to be felt *through* the varying feet—the bass drum effect. Dactyls, anapests, spondees, amphibrachs, and amphimacers may also be substituted for one another.

Substitution also allows a stress omitted from one line or foot to be included in the preceding line or foot. But this practice is infrequently encountered; it is more usual to find the kind of substitution involving different kinds of feet, as already shown.

A metrical verse or line—technically speaking, the term

The Nervous System and the Middle Ear 145

verse means *line* in poetry—is named according to the number of feet composing it. A line with only one foot is called *monometer*; two feet, *dimeter*; three feet, *trimeter*; four feet, *tetrameter*; five feet, *pentameter*; six feet, *hexameter* (if the six feet are all iambs, the line is known as an *Alexandrine*); seven feet, *heptameter* (also called *septenary* and, because the line usually has fourteen syllables, *fourteener*); eight feet, *octameter*. From classical verse, we have, in addition, a tensyllable line known as *decasyllabic* and one with eleven syllables called *hendecasyllabic*. When lines extend to six or more feet, they tend to divide themselves into trimeters, tetrameters, and so on.

A syllable or syllables left out of one foot may be added to another to equalize things; this is called *compensation*. The usual method is to include the compensation in the same line as the omission, but sometimes the compensation occurs in the following line. Compensation may also be achieved through the use of a *pause* that counts in the timing. It may be, as in music, a *rest* or a *hold*, a silence that has a temporal value in the metrical design, making it a part of the measure.

SOME SPECIAL TERMS
DEALING WITH LINES

A line that has its full complement of syllables is *acatalectic*. If unstressed syllables have been dropped from the final foot of a line, the line is *catalectic*, or *truncated*. When unstressed syllables are dropped from the beginning of the line (to allow the poet to open a line with a strong beat for emphasis when the basic meter is a rising rhythm), the line is called *headless*. A one-syllable word at the end of the line enables the poet to end on a strong or stressed beat, so the final syllable of a trochaic foot is frequently dropped in a trochaic line.

To achieve a staccato effect in a line, the poet employs pauses or breaks that—unlike the pause used for compensation—do not affect the metrical count but divide the line into more or less equal parts:

God makes stones;   God makes trees;   man makes promises.

Although multiple pauses within the line were not common in the poetry of the past, they occur more frequently in contemporary work. There are occasions when the poet will manipulate pauses to enhance the rhythm he or she wishes to dominate the line. A skilled artist will take care not to have such pauses occur in the same position in line after line, especially in lines that are constructed on a grammatically parallel pattern, to avoid structural monotony or the effect of having put two or more lines on one line's space. In his blank verse, Milton varied his pause technique to avoid risking this rhythmic dullness. Shakespeare went to even greater lengths in varying the pauses in his lines.

EXAMPLES OF THE USE OF THE
PAUSE

Milton's *Lycidas* is made up of basically iambic feet, although he uses substitution freely. Most of the lines are pentameter, but there are several tetrameter and trimeter lines and even some six-foot lines, like the opening one:

Yet once more, O ye Laurels, and once more,

The line could conceivably be forced into pentameter if we stressed only *Yet, more, Laur-, and,* and *more*, but that would require us to pay less attention to the realities of the language than we should. If we examine the line closely, we find that it is *headless* (it does not open with a trochee but with the second half of an iamb; the unstressed syllable is omitted). The line does fit the iambic mold; there's a rest between the first *more* and the *O*. The rest is the compensating pause for another omitted, unstressed syllable. The pause has, in this case, metric value—it is part of the counting. So the line would scan solidly as a headless iambic line:

    ˘ Yét ´once ´more, ˘ O´ ye Láurels, ănd ´once móre,

But then the line (starting with a spondee)

    Blı́nd moúths! thǎt scárce themsélves knŏw hŏw tŏ hóld

has a pause that is not part of the scanning count. Emphasized by the exclamation point, the hesitation before *that scarce* is purely for emotional effect. And again, in a markedly divided line, pauses intended not to infringe on the meter but to heighten the dramatic meaning:

    Whăt recks ĭt thém? Whăt neéd they? They áre spéd;

Two internal pauses divide the line in thirds without violating the metric pattern.

    In a freer form, these lines from the second section of "Hands," by the twentieth-century poet Siv Cedering Fox, illustrate how deliberately using pauses as part of a parallel pattern produces an especially dramatic effect. The variations here are supplied by the lines following the pause in each case. The pauses set off the first two verse paragraphs to provoke an almost liturgical response. The last line brings the matter up short with a finality that is both intellectual and emotional.

    They say: "We are the giver,"
    and tell of oranges
    growing on trees.

    They say: "We are the vessel,"
    and tell of journeys
    through water.

    They say: "We are the cup."

    Final pauses, those that come at the ends of lines, are varied by the use of enjambment (run-on lines). The ends of all lines should be noted as metrical pauses to some degree, however, since this subtle interruption to the flow of language protects the music of the lines.

We can understand, then, that we have at our disposal several mechanisms for avoiding monotony in metrical verse. On the subject of metrical variety, I. A. Richards wrote: "Verse in which we constantly get exactly what we are ready for and no more is merely toilsome and tedious." Samuel T. Coleridge said: "For any poetic purpose, meter resembles (if the patness of the simile may excuse the meanness) yeast, worthless or disagreeable by itself, but giving vivacity and spirit to the liquor with which it is proportionately combined." And from C. Day Lewis: "One of the things that please the ear when we listen to a poem being read aloud is the contrast, the sort of friendly wrestle between its meter and its speech rhythm. The meter is like a tide pulsing regularly underneath, the speech-rhythm is a less regular movement, like ripples on the surface." Meter is regular; rhythm is variable. We scan according to meter, but we hear according to rhythm.

For the more daring among you, there is another means of avoiding monotony in this matter of metrical verse. It's called *mixed meters*, which in Greek and Latin prosody meant a meter composed of either a blend of iambs and anapests or one of trochees and dactyls. In later times, however, any combination of meters may be called mixed meter.

Gerard Manley Hopkins revived a rhythm neglected since Spenser's time and coined the term *sprung rhythm* to describe it. He claimed that this rhythm more closely conformed to natural speech. In his time, Hopkins's sprung rhythm was regarded by some as a genuine challenge to the rules of orthodox prosody, whereas others considered it an aberration, interesting as a term but unworkable as a technique. By its apparent abruptness, sprung rhythm contrasted to the smoother flow of the running rhythm common to English poetry of the day. Hopkins's stresses seem to crowd upon one another. Running rhythm forbade the juxtaposing of stresses except for special effect, as when a spondee was used.

It has been said of Hopkins that he relied too heavily on the spondee. This appears to be a misunderstanding of his rhythmic system. In sprung rhythm, no foot may include more than one stress; therefore, the spondee cannot be part of such a system. Sprung rhythm has any number of feet of mixed variety to the line, as long as the stress of each foot *always* occurs on the *first* syllable, which automatically excludes the iamb and the anapest. There may be anywhere from no unstressed syllables to three in each foot. Extra syllables are sometimes included for special effects. Except for the occasional *uncounted* syllable that may be used to begin a stanza or line (Hopkins called such syllables *hangers* or *outrides*), Hopkins's system limits itself to the use of monosyllable, trochee, dactyl, and first paeon.

In scansion of sprung rhythm, the lines are "rove over"; that is, one must scan the entire stanza rather than each line separately. Feet that remain incomplete at the end of a line are completed at the start of the following line. When we encounter a series of juxtaposed stresses, we are encountering not spondees but a series of monosyllabic feet.

Gerard Manley Hopkins
In honour of St. Alphonsus Rodriguez, Laybrother of the Society of Jesus

Honour is flashed off exploit, so we say; +
And those strokes once that gashed flesh or galled shield +
Should tongue that time now, trumpet now that field,
And, on the fighter, forge his glorious day. +
On Christ they do and on the martyr may; +
But be the war within, the brand we wield +
Unseen, the heroic breast not outward-steeled,
Earth hears no hurtle then from fiercest fray.

*Yet God (that hews mountain and continent,
Earth, all, out; who, with trickling increment, +
Veins violets and tall trees makes more and more) +

Cŏuld | crówd | cāreér | wĭth | cónquĕst | whíle | thĕre | wént   +
Thŏse | yeárs | aňd | yeárs | bў | ŏf | wórld | wĭthóut | ĕvént   +
Thăt | ĭn | Măjŏrcā | Ālfónsŏ | wátched | the | dóor.

The plus signs (+) on the right signify incomplete feet that are completed on the following lines. The * designates an uncounted syllable.

In *syllabic verse*, the measuring element is not quantity, stress, or word accent but, as noted earlier, the number of syllables in the line. Pattern plays a large role in syllabic verse. Complexity increases with the increase in sophistication of the rhythmic pattern unit. The simplest would be to repeat exactly the same number of syllables in each line of the poem. Patterns of alternating numbers of syllables from line to line begin to add rhythmic interest. The more subtle such patterns become, the less they interfere with the effect of the poem as a whole; otherwise, they tend to call undue attention to themselves as virtuosities.

To give you a feel for syllabics, here's a poem by Marianne Moore in which the pattern of syllables to the line runs 1–3–9–6–8:

Marianne Moore (contemporary)
The Fish

wade
through black jade.
    Of the crow-blue mussel-shells, one keeps
    adjusting the ash-heaps;
        opening and shutting itself like

an
injured fan.
    The barnacles which encrust the side
    of the wave, cannot hide
        there for the submerged shafts of the

sun
split like spun

        glass, move themselves with spotlight swiftness
        into the crevices—
           in and out illuminating
the
turquoise sea
   of bodies. The water drives a wedge
   of iron through the iron edge
      of the cliff; whereupon the stars,
pink
rice-grains, ink-
   bespattered jelly-fish, crabs like green
   lilies, and submarine
      toadstools, slide each on the other.
All
external
   marks of abuse are present on this
   defiant edifice—
      all the physical features of
ac-
cident—lack
   of cornice, dynamite grooves, burns, and
   hatchet strokes, these things stand
      out on it; the chasm-side is
dead.
Repeated
   evidence has proved that it can live
   on what can not revive
      its youth. The sea grows old in it.

    The most effective free verse achieves its poetry through subtle variations of changing rhythms and carefully wrought balance. Rhyme is not a usual feature of free verse, but it is not excluded entirely. At times, it occurs in random fashion; at other times, it forms part of a designed pattern. Cadence is the most effective tool in the development of free verse. When speech rhythms are highly organized, the cadences will fall into symmetrical patterns that are sensed or recognized. Note how in the first of the following examples, the natural rhythms (along with the speech sounds) establish one pacing for the first verse paragraph, a slower one for the second, and a still slower one for the third. Does this reduction in pacing seem to you appropriate to the subject matter?

Stanwood K. Bolton (contemporary)
The Place of the Carp

I have grown old enough
to fear the fear of death.
It is told
how mongols stabled their horses
in mosques of Bukhara,
killed sixty thousand in Herat
and believed they were sent by God
to punish men for their sins.
It is as easy to find death now.

I once saw a long blue shark
cruise around my boat
easily and faster than a gull.
I gazed with my hands held high
and the fin walked the waves
perhaps cutting a skim of ashes
dropped from an urn from a plane.

I seek the fountain of age,
that breaking of mirrors
into fractions of goldfish;
the body is mind.
But this brown corner
beyond scattered reflections
is the place of the carp.
He feeds on himself.

Richard Gillman (contemporary)
Aiming

Before, I picked up the crumb and the peel,
The snarl of dust and the dirty towel
And saw her hanging daylong upside down.

Now I bend, hating rather what I move;
Not fully hating either. If mind is pleased to order them
There may be something to be said for crumbs, etcetera.

Which is not to say I've been taking secret walks
To a secret grotto, that love has washed me,
Given me touch with souls and a perfect heart.

I am aiming,
I am aiming more slowly,
I am aiming with painful selectivity

My sights and insights
To try to kill as little as I can
Of what is left to love.

In the poem by Gillman, what effect does the length of the lines have in reference to the momentum and the natural rhythms? How would you explain the function of the third stanza, with its parallel construction, in relation to the rest of the poem?

In the following poem by Carl Sandburg, do you feel that the lines convey the feel of a jazz rhythm? Study the piece line by line. Each line is in itself a course in the manipulation of speech rhythmic pattern to transform the word phrases into musical phrases. This is rhythm freed to an extreme degree from the traditional concepts of prosody, pushing even beyond the frontiers established by Whitman. Yet can one deny that it is poetry? It is a different way of handling language in the service of poetry, and it relies on a tight bond between subject, image, detail, rhythm, and sound. Enjoy.

Jazz Fantasia

> Drum on your drums, batter on your banjos, sob on the long cool winding saxophones. Go to it, O jazzmen.
>
> Sling your knuckles on the bottoms of the happy tin pans, let your trombones ooze, and go husha-husha-hush with the slippery sandpaper.
>
> Moan like an autumn wind high in the lonesome treetops, moan soft like you wanted somebody terrible, cry like a racing car slipping away from a motorcycle-cop, bang-bang! you jazzmen, bang altogether drums, traps, banjos, horns, tin cans—make two people fight on the top of a stairway and scratch each other's eyes in a clinch tumbling down the stairs.
>
> Can the rough stuff... Now a Mississippi steamboat pushes up the night river with a hoo-hoo-hoo-oo... and the green lanterns calling to the high soft stars... a red moon rides on the humps of the low river hills.... Go to it, O jazzmen.

Rhythm, then, is an essential element to the creation of the poem's immediate music. The second element necessary to achieve this music is sound. In the next chapter we see how sound joins with rhythm not only to provide the music but also to reinforce the sense of the text.

6. The Voice

Christopher Marlowe (Elizabethan period)
The Passionate Shepherd to His Love

Come live with me and be my Love,
And we will all the pleasures prove
That hills and valleys, dale and field,
And all the craggy mountains yield.

There will we sit upon the rocks
And see the shepherds feed their flocks,
By shallow rivers, to whose falls
Melodious birds sing madrigals.

There will I make thee beds of roses
And a thousand fragrant posies,
A cap of flowers, and a kirtle
Embroider'd all with leaves of myrtle.

A gown made of the finest wool,
Which from our pretty lambs we pull,
Fair linèd slippers for the cold,
With buckles of the purest gold.

A belt of straw and ivy buds
With coral clasps and amber studs:
And if these pleasures may thee move,
Come live with me and be my Love.

Thy silver dishes for thy meat
As precious as the gods do eat,
Shall on an ivory table be
Prepared each day for thee and me.

The shepherd swains shall dance and sing
For thy delight each May-morning:
If these delights thy mind may move,
Then live with me and be my Love.

(Treat yourself as well to a reading of "Her Reply" [also known as "Reply to Marlowe's Passionate Shepherd], written by Sir Walter Raleigh.)
Christopher Marlowe, in the preceding poem, and Dylan Thomas, in the next, have orchestrated their works admirably. The Marlowe piece is melodious and pleasing to the ear; Thomas assaults the ear with harsh, percussive dissonances. Study how the words are organized into sound patterns to convey the emotional content and *to complete the meaning* of each line.

Dylan Thomas
Poem on His Birthday

In the mustardseed sun,
By full tilt river and switchback sea
    Where the cormorants scud,
In his house on stilts high among beaks
    And palavers of birds
This sandgrain day in the bent bay's grave
    He celebrates and spurns

His driftwood thirty-fifth wind turned age;
   Herons spire and spear.

   Under and round him go
Flounders, gulls, on their cold, dying trails,
   Doing what they are told,
Curlews aloud in the congered waves
   Work at their ways to death,
And the rhymer in the long tongued room,
   Who tolls his birthday bell,
Toils towards the ambush of his wounds;
   Herons, steeple stemmed, bless.

   In the thistledown fall,
He sings towards anguish; finches fly
   In the claw tracks of hawks
On a seizing sky; small fishes glide
   Through wynds and shells of drowned
Ship towns to pastures of otters. He
   In his slant, racking house
And the hewn coils of his trade perceives
   Herons walk in their shroud,

   The livelong river's robe
Of minnows wreathing around their prayer;
   And far at sea he knows,
Who slaves to his crouched, eternal end
   Under a serpent cloud,
Dolphins dive in their turnturtle dust,
   The rippled seals streak down
To kill and their own tide daubing blood
   Slides good in the sleek mouth.

   In a cavernous, swung
Wave's silence, wept white angelus knells.
   Thirty-five bells sing struck

On skull and scar where his loves lie wrecked,
   Steered by the falling stars.
And to-morrow weeps in a blind cage
   Terror will rage apart
Before chains break to a hammer flame
   And love unbolts the dark

   And freely he goes lost
In the unknown, famous light of great
   And fabulous, dear God.
Dark is a way and light is a place,
   Heaven that never was
Nor will be ever is always true,
   And, in that brambled void,
Plenty as blackberries in the woods
   The dead grow for His joy.

   There he might wander bare
With the spirits of the horseshoe bay
   Or the stars' seashore dead,
Marrow of eagles, the roots of whales
   And wishbones of wild geese,
With blessed, unborn God and His Ghost,
   And every soul His priest,
Gulled and chanter in young Heaven's fold
   Be at cloud quaking peace,

   But dark is a long way.
He, on the earth of the night, alone
   With all the living, prays,
Who knows the rocketing wind will blow
   The bones out of the hills,
And the scythed boulders bleed, and the last
   Rage shattered waters kick
Masts and fishes to the still quick stars,
   Faithlessly unto Him

   Who is the light of old

And air shaped Heaven where souls grow wild
   As horses in the foam:
Oh, let me midlife mourn by the shrined
   And druid herons' vows
The voyage to ruin I must run,
   Dawn ships clouted aground,
Yet, though I cry with tumbledown tongue,
   Count my blessings aloud:

   Four elements and five
Senses, and man a spirit in love
   Tangling through this spun slime
To his nimbus bell cool kingdom come
   And the lost, moonshine domes,
And the sea that hides his secret selves
   Deep in its black, base bones,
Lulling of spheres in the seashell flesh,
   And this last blessing most,

   That the closer I move
To death, one man through his sundered hulks,
   The louder the sun blooms
And the tusked, ramshackling sea exults;
   And every wave of the way
And gale I tackle, the whole world then,
   With more triumphant faith
Than ever was since the world was said,
   Spins its morning of praise,

   I hear the bouncing hills
Grow larked and greener at berry brown
   Fall and the dew larks sing
Taller this thunderclap spring, and how
   More spanned with angels ride
The mansouled fiery island! Oh,
   Holier than their eyes,
And my shining men no more alone
   As I sail out to die.

The voice of poetry does not speak to us only through the meanings of words. It creates an accompaniment to meaning in music, and we feel the experience on an emotional level while perceiving it on an intellectual one. As much consideration must be given to the sounds of the words as to their meanings. E. B. White has said that "too little attention is paid by most writers to sound, and too many writers are completely tone-deaf."

LANGUAGE

The syllable plays an important role in connection with the rhythms of poetry, as do the letters themselves in their work of creating syllables. For most people, it is enough to know that the English alphabet has twenty-six letters that make up the words of the language. They also know with a vague kind of comprehension that these letters are capable of producing more than twenty-six sounds; they're willing to accept this process without bothering to examine closely the procedures creating such magic.

For you, as a student of the writing of poetry, this is not sufficient. You need much more information about letters and their workings in syllables and words. If you are to use language near its maximum potential, you must understand how the sounds of words are achieved and what is required to make them serve your poem. A poem is as limited in expression as the poet is limited in his or her understanding of the language.

Of the alphabet's twenty-six letters, three (*q*, *c*, and *x* may be considered redundancies in sound, which reduces the number of available sounds to twenty-three. The letter *k* furnishes the sound for the letter *q; quick* is pronounced as if it were spelled *kwik*. The letter *c* is also pronounced *k*, so phonetically, it too is superfluous. Note that it is omitted before the final *k* in *kwik*, because if kept, it would be soundless. When followed by *e*, *c* assumes the sound of *s*. Basically, *c* has no sound of its own. The word *accept* is sounded *aksept*. The third letter, *x*, is served by the sounds of *k*, *g*, or *z: except*, X-*ray* (*eks*); *exist*, *example* (*egs*); *xerography* (*zer*-). Twenty-three letters do not represent a bountiful inventory. Yet the language must produce some sixty-odd sounds to serve its purposes.

We compensate by requiring each working letter to do extra duty and by grouping letters to form additional sounds. The versatility of our vowels is increased tremendously by our assigning to them a wide range of pronunciations and by our coupling them in diphthongs (*diphthong* means "two-sounding"). Consonants, too, lend themselves to association, resulting in consonantal diphthongs (combinations of inseparable consonants). These techniques greatly extend the range of sounds available.

Language is a living entity and has a variable as well as a developing nature. Since poetry is an art intended to be heard, language as it is spoken plays a major part in the composition of poetry. Spoken language varies regionally; it is also subjected to colloquialism. Except for those times when poets deliberately portray regional use, they will want to use English in its standard form to overcome such variations.

CONSONANTS

Our spoken alphabet offers us eighteen basic consonant sounds:

b	g	k	n	s	w
d	h	l	p	t	y
f	j	m	r	v	z

By adding to our total the following *consonantal diphthongs,* we extend this number to twenty-five:

(sound)	(example)	(sound)	(example)
ch	church	th (soft)	bath, thin, breath
hw	when	th (hard)	breathe, then
ng	sing	zh	azure
sh	sure, mission		

Further subtle variations in sound are possible by creating additional combinations of consonants, as in triple consonants like *nst (against)*, *rst (thirst)*, and *rth (worthy)* or quadruples like *ngth (strength)*—really a combination of two sounds, *ng* and *th*. Something similar occurs when a letter like *r, s, l.*, or *n* is placed before *d, t, m.*, or *p;* the quality of each consonant is altered to a slight degree. This technique of combining expands the range of our consonant resources considerably.

VOWELS

We're all familiar with the basic five vowels in our language: *a, e, i, o, u.* (Although as a consonant, *y* cannot be considered a redundant sound, it is such when pressed into service as an alternate *i* sound.) We gain more working vowel sounds from the different ways a vowel may be voiced as it is influenced by consonantal environment. There are at least eight sounds for the letter *a*, six for *e*, three for *i*, eight for *o*, and six for *u*. The following chart shows these sounds, their symbols, and examples to convey their pronunciations.

Vowel sounds: *s/e: symbol/example*

(*name*)	*a* (*s/e*)	*e* (*s/e*)	*i* (*s/e*)	*o* (*s/e*)	*u* (*s/e*)
long	pāle	mēter	inspīre	ōde	flūte
hooked long		mḛre			
half-long	fȧtal	create		ôbey	ůnion
circumflex	câre			lôrd	fûrl
				law	her
				all	fir
short	găg	mĕt	pĭty	nŏt	stŭdy
short circumflex				clŏth	
italic short	guidănce	novĕl	possĭble	ŏccur	circŭs
					demon
two-dot	bär				
one-dot	dȧnce				

italic one-dot	ideȧ	
long double		no͞on
		ru͞de
short double		goo̯d
		wo man
		pu̯t
tilde	metē̃r	
umlaut		kümmel (German)
		menu̇ (French)

The sounds produced by vowels are increased in number by the use of *proper* or *full diphthongs* (a speech sound changing continuously from one vowel to another in the same syllable). This list includes only those vowel diphthongs that do not repeat sounds already furnished by other letters.

(diphthong)	*(sounded)*	*(example)*
oi, oy	oi	oil, boy
ou, ow	au	house, cow
ī	ai	ice, high (different from the long *i* in words like l*i*ne, t*i*me)

OTHER SOUNDS

Two consonants borrowed from other languages have a slightly different sound than their equivalents in English: the German sound *ich* represented in our pronunciation guides by a small capital *k*, and the *n* sound from the French, as in *bon*, represented by a small capital *n*. Other sounds result from special combinations; the *dg* of the word *judge*, for example, varies slightly from both the initial *j* in the same word or from the similar sounds *z* or *zh*. In addition, there are two somewhat related sounds in which consonants rely on a half-long *u* for a partner: verd*u*re and nat*u*re. D*u* and t*u* are not diphthongs, strictly speaking, but they do contribute to our store of sounds.

The extraordinary demands that English makes upon its resources are served by these linguistic techniques, and we can see that sixty or so sounds are indeed available to us, even though only twenty-three letters are involved.

THE QUALITY OF SOUNDS

Our professional interest in these letters and sounds is with the textures they make possible in lines of poetry—the smoothness, the harshness, the conflict and sibilance, the harmony and dissonance.

The consonants *l, m, n,* and *r* are smooth and flowing and are referred to as *liquids.* Their fluidity is increased when they're doubled (*lu*ll, *summer, banner, mirror*). Letters that have a degree of hiss to them—*s, z, j,* and the combinations *ch, sh,* and *zh*—are called *sibilants.* Doubling the *s* or *z* intensifies the hissing quality (*sissy, sizzling*).

The *mutes* are divided into three groups: the *labials* are those consonants that require that the lips be brought together for their sounding—*p, b, f, v* (*m* is a labial, but because of its smoothness, it is classed with the liquids); the harsher *dentals,* sounds made by bringing the teeth together, include *t, d, th,* and *ch;* and the raspiest of all, the *gutturals k* and *g,* are sounded in the throat. Consider the effect in sound of such words as *brute, gut, chop,* and *drink.*

Each letter is capable of supplying subtle variations of basic sounds. A vowel will alter its sound, based on whether or not it is accented; in an unaccented syllable, the vowel may take any of a number of sounds, depending on neighboring letters. The presence of silent letters may influence the voicing of sounded letters. Expanded combinations will also condition the normal sounds of letters. Consider these sound factors as so many tools you will be able to use.

These are the letters and letter combinations at your disposal. Set aside your knowledge of words, and look at them as if for the first time. Examine how the syllables are used to form the words. A syllable is "something held together" and can be defined as a group of letters taken together to form one sound, an uninterrupted unit of utterance, a complete word or part of a word. You will notice as you speak that your voice mechanism adjusts itself to enunciate syllables rather than either letters or words (except, of course, when the word is one syllable).

If you were merely reciting the alphabet, you'd pronounce individual letters in a certain way. That pronunciation won't do when you pronounce syllables. In voicing syllables, you are pronouncing the combinations of letters, which is something for you to take into account as you plan the sounds that best support the meanings of your poems. As the syllables combine to become a word, the aggregate is yet another entity. You will still pronounce syllables—a three-syllable word requires three stages of voicing—but you'll assign different accent and volume values to the syllables, depending on their arrangement to form the word. Monosyllabic words offer no variables, but two-syllable words will include one accented syllable plus an unaccented one. In the unaccented syllable, the vowel may change its tonal quality from what it would be if it occurred in an accented syllable. In words of more than two syllables, you may also have a secondary or lesser accent as well as the main one. In a word like *probable*, the main accent falls on the first syllable, but there is also a hint of a quieter accent on the second syllable, made noticeable by the falling away of the last syllable. In multisyllabic words, the speed of voicing is conditioned by accented syllables' receiving a slightly slower pronunciation time, whereas unaccented ones may be raced over or almost skipped. Geographic location may play a role. For example, the word *secretary* in American English, has its principal accent on the first syllable (*sec*); the secondary or lighter accent falls on the third syllable (*tar*). These two syllables receive more volume when enunciated than the other two (*re* and *y*), through which the voice moves faster. In the British pronunciation, however, the third syllable is practically omitted. The word is sounded as if it contained three syllables (*secretry*).

Although the letters change the nature of their sounds when assembled into syllables, the syllables when organized into words do not. We are putting syllables rather than words into a particular relationship when we construct the poetic line. It is the sound of the syllables to which we must pay close attention in the process.

More than having the sounds of the syllables-formed-into-words echo the sense, we must take care that the movement from syllable to syllable and word to word also bears a relationship to the sense, at least to the ambience of the poem. Harsh juxtapositions, juxtapositions that clash and thump, are proper to reflect a disturbed or energetic atmosphere and/or thematic attitude. But it certainly would not do to have such treatment applied where the mood is intended to be restful and pleasant. The movement from one word to the other in voicing the line should be controlled by the theme and atmosphere. Care must be exercised to avoid creating combinations or phrases that are impossible to enunciate with any degree of rhythm and clarity. To stumble over a couple of words (*special message* will trip some reciters) is to destroy the line if not the whole poem. It is equivalent to writing a musical score and including notes that instruments aren't able to play.

So syllables take letters and transform them into unified sounds that organize themselves into words. And if everything goes right, the words become a line of articulated word music.

IMITATIVE HARMONY

This term is applied to the resemblance that the sounds of words bear to the descriptive meaning or action that those words convey. In these matters, a finely tuned sense of taste is essential.

The most familiar type of imitative harmony is *onomatopoeia*—words that actually imitate their meanings in sound (*buzz, snap, hiss, coo, murmur, thud, crash, gurgle*). In poetry, the term is broadened to mean a general harmony between the sounds as *suggested* by the action in the lines. The more subtle this harmony, the more persuasive the tonal unity of the composition. A naive treatment will attract too much notice to itself and defeat the balance of the poem. A pair of lines like the following would damage any serious poem in which they occurred:

> The drip, drip, drip of water drops
> Plopping in the sink won't stop.

A more successful use of onomatopoeia is revealed in these lines by Tennyson:

> The moan of doves in immemorial elms
> And murmuring of innumerable bees

The truly onomatopoeic sounds are *moan* and *murmuring*, but the effusive use of the consonants *m, n, r,* and the short vowels allow the onomatopoeic effect to embrace the lines totally because of the suggested accord between these sounds and the scene, details, and action residing in the lines. One can feel a restful shimmering in the elms and hear the soft humming of the bees, and the pulling into the two *b*'s at the end barely hints at a starting stir. It's a good touch. Still, it's a matter of personal preference. Tennyson's lines *are* a bit self-conscious. Compare them with these lines from *Hamlet*:

> If ever thou didst hold me in thine heart,
> Absent thee from felicity awhile,
> And in this harsh world draw thy breath in pain,
> To tell my story.

The first line is rather smooth iambics. There's not an overabundance of long vowels, and the consonants are about evenly divided between liquids and dentals. The words don't clash; they come close to a slight bump in the word *didst*, but the harshness is self-contained, and the next word eases the tension immediately. The line is quiet, on the brink of emotion, hinting—in that one place with the hissing sound—of harsher prospects. This is as it should be. The poet is not investing the line with heavy feeling; such investment would conflict with the purpose of the line. It is an attracting line, a device to catch the attention so that listening is assured. And it is an arresting line. Having caught the attention, it holds it in suspension until the line has completed its task and propelled the listener into the next line.

The plaintive tone of the second line is sweetened by the internal pairs of rhymes very close to each other: *thee* and *felicity* embracing the two short *i*'s (*felicity*), and the nearness to those sounds of the *e*'s in *Absent* and *felicity*. Again, there's a sort of equal distribution of consonants. But there's another factor, too. Some readers insist on reading such a line iambically. Although the line can be made to scan entirely that way, to do so is to imply that Shakespeare was both undramatic and tone-deaf. The line cannot be read by metronomic control; it must be read rhythmically. Therefore, we find that the pacing has been altered. This headless line starts with a stressed beat, which is a bit of a rush in itself; then the anapest in the middle (*frŏm fĕli*) trips the meter just enough to jar the rhythm and the tempo. Looking at the sense behind the words, we discover that sound and rhythm are reinforcing the touches of regret and self-pity that the line suggests. The sibilants indicate the direction of the sense; they are a foreshadowing. At the same time, the line has extended the suspension by further delaying the main substance of the speech.

And then that magnificent third line resolves the suspension; emotion and tension are brought to their climax. Again, avoid a metrical reading. Scan, instead, as follows:

Ănd ĭn thís hărsh wořld draw thў breáth ĭn páin,

Retain the pentameter measure; the pause before *draw* is a compensation. But examine the rhythm! Had you scanned the whole line as iambics, you would have heeded the meter while ignoring the sense and the drama of the line. If we scan the line as it should be scanned, we find that the opening anapest provides a pivot for the mood to shift from the previous line over to this one. And the attention is drawn from the listener to the speaker. The compensating pause, breaking the line, is an emotional rest. And the sounds of the words themselves are rough and hard, as though those sounds were being dragged out of Hamlet's mouth. The saying of them is, in itself, painful. The sounds in the last line lapse into a moribund neutrality.

This passage is an example of imitative harmony of the highest order. It doesn't rely on direct onomatopoeia nor on sounds strongly describing action. With great subtlety, the poet *reveals* attitude, mood, tension, conflict, sadness, regret, and subdued anger. While we were busy listening to the meanings, Shakespeare was busy punching us in the gut.

Did you realize that we were able to make our observations without referring to the context in which the lines appear—Hamlet's death scene? *The magic is in the lines themselves and in how they are organized.* In grasping how these lines accomplish their ends, you will gain as much as you would by considering a score of examples.

The language available to poetry in our time is enhanced by the addition to it of various new vocabularies. Subject matter has been broadened—in addition to agrarian, political, military, celestial, divine, and amorous themes, poets are now permitted to address themselves to themes dealing with urban life, science, technology, everyday happenings, and objects—anything they please. They draw on the vocabularies and jargons of these newly admitted disciplines, thereby increasing their terminology resources. And there have been innovations and changes transfused into the language that would have amazed our poet ancestors.

Many of today's poets don't hesitate to manipulate grammar and syntax in new and exciting ways (still, of course, avoiding the inversions of yesteryear) in order to achieve the effects they envision. That such still-young freedom is frequently abused is admitted, but there are those among the experimenters who are creating daring techniques that can, if handled wisely, advance the development of poetry. It's up to us to distinguish between the legitimate approaches and slick trickery. We must nurture the soundest of these fresh techniques so that they can increase the future resources of poetry.

DICTION

In its simplest definition, *diction* is the selection and arrangement of words in a literary work. The diction you choose for your poem will be decided by the nature and characteristics of the subject matter; by the quality of mood, tone, and atmosphere; and by the current use of language.

Diction is the *vocabulary,* the voice that speaks your poem. And it may range from the grandly Miltonic to the homeliness of Frostian diction—depending on whether one is writing about Olympian gods or New England farmers. Your organization of this vocabulary into phrases and lines; into stanzas, verse paragraphs, or word clusters; and, eventually, into a poem will constitute your *style.*

In the Platonic sense, *style* refers to that aptitude in creating an original verbal arrangement that precisely expresses the writer's meaning and intention—an evaluative indicator. In the Aristotelian sense, *style* is a classifying term rather than an evaluative one. We may say that a writer's style is ironic, satiric, sarcastic, Shakespearean, Latinate, or the like without passing judgment on it. It is a means of describing.

The Aristotelian concept of *style* evolves from a person's work as a whole, and this is different from the application of the term to one particular poem. For a variety of examples of individual styles of diction in the Aristotelian sense, you might compare the dictions used by Francis Thompson, Edmund Spenser, and Dylan Thomas with those of T. S. Eliot, Conrad Aiken, and William Carlos Williams.

The beginner must be more concerned with the Platonic sense of the term *style*. The other will develop of its own accord, as one continues to produce poems. Consider diction from the standpoint of whether the words are concrete or abstract, literal or figurative, common or technical, Anglo-Saxon or Latinate, formal or colloquial; and consider to what degree the words establish their denotation (a word's literal and most limited meaning) and the enhancing richness of connotation (all the associative implications and suggestions awakened by the word) in context. The nature and form you plan for your poem will also influence the diction you select. A decided difference exists between diction that is appropriate to a satirical poem and what is suitable for an elegy or ode.

In our anxiety to sound natural and unaffected in our poems (which is to be encouraged), we may overlook one of the poet's prime responsibilities—to expand the limits of contemporary language; to replenish the resource by exploring possibilities, by inventing not only original phrasing and ways of expression (when nothing extant is adequate to necessity) but words as well, new words that will help to keep the language alive and healthy. Aristotle said a writer's diction should be clear but should also raise the language above the commonplace. He felt that the writer has an obligation to introduce in diction unusual words, phrases, figures of speech, metaphors, and the like, so that the language will gain distinction. He also warned against excessive or indiscriminate reliance upon deviating from "the normal idiom"—pointing out that a diction composed entirely of such deviation would be grotesque.

In the matter of diction, there are many positions. Arguments have continued through the centuries and will, no doubt, continue. But we shall do well to heed Aristotle's point: Enough, but not too much—always the proper balance. Ornate or inflated language that may have been respectable in one age will be frowned upon in another. Inversions to suit requirements of meter or rhyme, which were acceptable once, now are out of fashion. A poet who writes today in the styles and manners of previous centuries—unless this is done deliberately for a narrative purpose—is considered guilty of *archaisms*— the use of linguistic devices from a previous time. Today's poetry mainstream expects language to be used in a natural way, stripped of decoration and without awkward syntax forced by inversions.

However much we recongize the need for naturalness, the diction of poetry will never be like that of prose. The distance between them extends or narrows in response to the requirements and attitudes toward poetry that prevail at any one time. The poet pays a debt to the language by being aware of its general state—its flexibilities as well as its rigidities— and by provoking the language now and then, perhaps nudging it in what he or she senses is the right direction. An interesting reflection: As much as we strive to avoid unnaturalness and affectation in our use of language, in the year 2580, if the works of the twentieth century are still around to be studied, our use of language *will sound* unnatural and affected. The language surviving us will continue to change and adapt, but our works, of course, will be unable to do so. It is with this parallel reality in mind that we are able to accept and appreciate the works of our predecessors.

The term *poetic diction* is used as a reference both to the vocabulary of poetry and (disparagingly) to the inflated, over-elegant, or archaic diction that is unsupported by theme or mood. Diction will be reflected in the selection and organization of words with which the poet creates the line and the poem. This diction will vary from poem to poem, based on the dictates of the work's subject, details, images, structure, and intended mood and tone. But these are internal influences, and the choice of diction will also respond to the external influences of the poem's goal: to eulogize, to mark a special occasion, to teach, to move politically, whatever. It will also be influenced by the current use of language in general. The poet's obligations are to use language in as natural a way as possible without sacrificing melody and movement and to add to the range of expression original linguistic constructions that enrich the language while projecting the poet's unique point of view. The perceptions the poet gains through experiments with language will become part of that poet's language and part of the language of the era.

While concentrating on the selection and development of a proper vocabulary diction, don't ignore the diction of the senses. The sense responses of your reader/listener will be stimulated by the qualities of your words beyond their literal meanings, by their connotations, their tonalities, their suggestiveness. Many a poem has failed because the connotations and overtones to which the poet paid little attention clashed with the intended effect. Your choice of vocabulary must demonstrate your precise meaning, must have an integrity in relation to your theme, must be consistent for the unity of the work, and must take into account all the qualities of the words in creating the right ambience for your poem.

TONE

The tone of a poem will be determined largely by the poet's relationship to the material. It is also affected by the writer's attitude toward the audience (real or imagined). The tone may be challenging, reassuring, obsequious, condescending, formal, intimate, passionate, sly, persuasive, enticing, serious, solemn, comic, ironic, sardonic, sarcastic, witty, or playful; and this will be communicated through the use of language on an inflectional level. This is not difficult when speaking to an audience or person. It is another matter to communicate it through writing. It must be achieved through the sense of context the poet establishes and through the revelation of the poet's attitude toward theme and audience. The writer sets the frame of reference. Within that frame, the writer and the audience collaborate to experience the poem.

Your ability to "convince" your audience is undermined to the degree that you exaggerate your tone. You can easily imagine the embarrassment of a poet who intended the reader to be moved to compassionate understanding if the reader burst into uncontrollable laughter. The cause may have been a poor choice of words; more likely, what escaped the poet was the tenor of the work's tone, with the result that it worked at odds with the author's purpose.

You will develop a feel for tone as you progress toward a mastery of your craft. It will seem intuitive after a while, but you should pay close attention to how you achieve it during your formative period. Not an easy term to explain, it has been variously defined as color, atmosphere, aura, spirit, impression, Gestalt-quality, shading, obliqueness, attitude, mood, and linguistic quality. Although none of these definitions is, in itself, adequate, if one were able to combine all of them into a single word, that word would be *tone*.

174   Body and Soul

Now we turn to those symptoms that prove the poem to be alive, that bring into vivid relief those pulsations and gestures, those movements and costumes, those masks that lure us into the poem's internal reality—the study of poetic devices and symbols.

7. Life Signs

The most familiar sound device in poetry is rhyme. We've already had the opportunity to observe the way rhyme works in our earlier studies of stanzas and forms. The different arrangements of matching sounds at the ends of lines made larger patterns that were not only pleasing to the ear but also helpful in revealing the forms of the poems. We called those arrangements *rhyme schemes* or *rhyme patterns*.

Rhyme can function as an elaboration of the poem's mood and tone. At its best, it contributes to and enriches the meanings of the lines; in fact, it is often the factor that is responsible for the emergence of meaning. Besides calling attention to words and syllables as musical sounds, rhymes mark the ends of rhythmic units represented by the lines. Rhymes can serve to meld the poem's lines into the pattern of the stanza or unit. Rhyme can also function as emphasis on the melodic quality of the diction of the poem. It can influence the process of intensification from stanza to stanza. And it points up the relation between the rhythmic and rhetorical quantities of the lines. Frequently, rhyme functions in several of these ways at once.

In any study of a complicated subject, a special terminology is unavoidable. The study of poetry presents additional problems because of the following: an overlapping of terms, so much disagreement on which are the correct terms, so many terms applied to more than one meaning, and other imprecisions. Let's keep in mind that terms are only devices of convenience. If you forget every term in this book but absorb all the information they represent and develop the skills to put that knowledge to use, you will write good poems, and the terms be damned. Although terms are necessary for us to discuss the ways of making, it's the actual making that is important.

In most cases, rhyme is the recurrence of duplicate or similar sounds at predictable intervals happening at the ends of lines. Such sounds may be vowels or consonants or combinations of either or both of these. The rhyming unit is our ever-important syllable. When the last syllables of a pair of lines match each other in sound, they rhyme. But there are varying criteria that determine different types of rhyming, as we shall see shortly. Before moving on to the individual types, let's recognize the fact that if a vowel sound does indeed have a melodic quality, as in a musical note's sound, then a consonant sound may be said to be percussive.

To make up for the lack of rhyming opportunities existing in English compared to other languages, poets have had to build an inventory of special rhyme types. In some forms, the rhyme requirements are met by the appearance, semblance, or *feeling* of rhyme. The repetition of end words in the sestina form, the repetition of entire lines in the villanelle or triolet or any poem that has refrain lines—such devices, although not rhymes in the strict sense, function as substitutes for rhyme because their *sound* contribution is made on the same basis as that of rhyming words. And, like rhymes, they also serve to mark the stanza, form, and rhythmic unit, as well as to help bind the stanza or poem together.

A fixed form, such as a sonnet or a Spenserian stanza, has a preestablished rhyme scheme. Departures from that are deviations, but a poet may have excellent artistic reasons for employing such deviations.

FULL RHYME

This is also called *perfect, pure, true, or complete rhyme*. It's the rhyming type with which we're most familiar in English poetry, but the origins of rhyme predate the birth of Christ by many centuries. Rhyme (along with rhythm) provided an easy way of remembering legends and prayers, especially before there was a written language.

In using full rhyme, the words you choose for your rhymes ending the lines will include final syllables that match in sound. The matching will occur from the last stressed vowels in the lines to the ends of the following consonants, if any. The stressed vowels and subsequent consonants must be identical in sound, but the consonants preceding the vowels must be different from each other. (At least one of the rhyming pair of vowels must have consonants preceding it.)

Words that are spelled differently but sound alike throughout (*son/sun*) are called *identical rhymes*. Although they're acceptable in some languages, they are considered undesirable in English poetry unless they are used to achieve some special purpose of the poet. On the other hand, words may look completely different from each other, but if they sound the same from their stressed vowels on, they form perfectly good full rhymes (*flirt/curt, pox/clocks, fate/straight, bough/prow*).

The required criteria to form full rhymes, then, are as follows: (1) The stressed vowel sounds are identical (*ow/cow*, but not *mow*); (2) the consonant sounds, if any, following the vowels are identical (*how/now/cow, catch/thatch, gruff/rough*); (3) the consonant sounds preceding the stressed vowels are not identical (*blew/blue* is not acceptable); (4) the rhyme sounds must be accented as in natural speech (*cówgirl* doesn't make a full rhyme with *whirl*); (5) you cannot make one of the rhyming sounds plural and have a full rhyme in the strict sense (*cows/now*), but it is a slight deviation and is used quite often; and (6) the stresses of the rhyme sounds must fall in parallel positions; take the lines that follow:

> It was a joyless and abandoned pláce;
> Brute anguish coiled his gut and scored his fáce.

The rhyming syllable at the end of each line is -*ace*. This is full rhyme because it meets all of our criteria: the stressed vowel in both end words (long *a*) is identical in sound and falls in the same position in each line; the consonant sounds (*ce* sounding *s*) are identical in sound, as they must be following the vowels; neither rhyming sound is a plural; and the consonant sounds before the vowels are different.

For rhyme to be truly full rhyme, the required position of the stressed syllable cannot be violated. The single-syllable word *fling* rhymes with *sing* but not with *blinking*. That's something else but not full rhyme. But rhyming *pitch* with *enrich* forms a perfectly good full rhyme because the stresses fall on the right syllables. That's what's meant by "the stresses . . . must fall in parallel positions."

MASCULINE AND FEMININE RHYMES

When the final words that form the rhyme pair are both one syllable each, the rhyme is termed *masculine*. Rhymed poetry has relied on masculine rhyme for much of its production. When the rhyming words are two or more syllables (*breaking/taking, abortion/distortion*), or when the rhyming is composed of words to make up the pair (*past her/master, to get through/forget you*), the rhyme is called *feminine*. A feminine rhyme is also called a *double rhyme* when the rhyming involves two syllables, and a *triple rhyme* when three syllables are involved in each line. Some two-syllable rhymes and many three-syllable ones often provide a humorous tone, so they must be used judiciously. As you can see from the foregoing samples, these terms apply to the rhymes from their stressed vowels on: *abortion/distortion* is a double, not a triple, rhyme; and *he chose/suppose* would be masculine, or single, because only the portions -*ortion* in the first case and -*ose* in the second form the rhymes. An example of a triple feminine rhyme would be *cluttering/buttering* where all three syllables rhyme but the first syllables have different initial consonants. Triple rhyme often must rely on the repetition of the same words in the unstressed syllables' portions, because there are so few full triple rhymes available in English; *said to me/fled to me* is an example of such a repetition. (The term *triple rhyme* is also used occasionally to designate a set of three rhyming lines, as in the rhyme royal and in the ottava rima.)

IDENTICAL RHYME

We have just seen how different words with the same sounds throughout (*main/mane*) may not be used as full rhyme. Identical rhyme also means using the same word as a rhyme two or more times, as in the limericks of Edward Lear. In general, poets avoid identical rhyme unless they can justify its use for a special purpose.

TAIL RHYME

This is also known as *tailed rhyme* or *caudate rhyme*, and is the rhyming of short lines when these are associated with longer lines in the same stanza or poem. The tail line may rhyme with another short line or with any other line in a stanzaic unit such as a couplet, triplet, sestet, and so on. It may be just a short line not rhyming with any other line—although it may rhyme with itself if it's a refrain line coming in at regular intervals—or it may be an element in the formal construction of a stanza or unit. The line *Praise him* from "Pied Beauty" by Hopkins is a tail rhyme.

BROKEN-WORD RHYME

This is generally referred to as *broken rhyme*, which is incorrect because the rhyme isn't broken at all. A word is broken in order to achieve a full rhyme, and the latter portion of the broken word is transferred to the following line's beginning:

> the mocking of the clock's face tak-
> ing my wrist's pulse, my fingers shake

LIGHT RHYME

Here the rhyme sounds exist between two lines—one of the rhyming sounds being stressed, as in normal full rhyme, and the other being the unstressed syllable of a word or element in the metrical foot. This rhyming technique was used frequently in the old ballads. Today, skilled poets use it to relieve the monotony of full rhyme when necessary.

> The preening drunk birds sing.
> Their highpitched moans
> spin in the blinking
> sunlight, bouncing off stones;
> but caught in the eye's tight ring,
> they flatten to ambushed overtones,
> return to their source: it's spring.

Whereas in full rhyme, we could not permit a pairing of words like *sing* and *blinking* for rhyme purposes, they function well as light rhyme. The other example of light rhyme is *overtones*, which rhymes with *moans* and *stones*. In the case of *blinking*, the stress comes on the first syllable, but it is the unstressed second syllable that rhymes with *sing*, *ring*, and *spring*. With *overtones*, there is a light stress on *-tones*, but it's only a secondary stress because the principal one falls on the first vowel.

RUN-OVER RHYME

Also known as *linked rhyme*, this is a device borrowed from early Welsh verse. It is formed by rhyming the final syllable in one line with the first syllable in the next line. (This introduces a new aspect to our investigation; up to now, we've been discussing what are known as *end rhymes*, those that occur at the ends of lines.) Here's an example of run-over rhyme:

> The whiskey did sustain his wit;
> bit by bit, he got funnier.

CROSSED RHYME

Also known as *interlaced rhyme*, this type of rhyme falls more or less in the middle of the lines, usually at a pause of some sort. It has the effect of breaking long lines into shorter ones, especially in couplets, where crossed rhyme makes two long lines sound like four short ones. The normal or primary rhyme scheme of the couplet is made to sound like an extended alternating one, suggestive of *abab*. Here are two samples; the crossed rhymes are italicized:

> This somber *light*, hard on the heels of day,
> Heralds the *night* and takes my joy away.
>
> Francis was a *bore*; he used to eat so fast,
> And at night he'd *snore*. I'm glad he's gone at last.

EYE RHYMES

This is a system of rhyming that satisfies the eye but not the ear. The often identical spelling of the final or rhyming syllable makes you think the words will rhyme in sound, but they are pronounced differently and are thereby unable to qualify as full rhyme. Examples are *love/prove* and *weak/break*. Eye rhymes are usually the result of obsolete or regional pronouncing styles. The words just paired *were* pronounced identically at one time. With changes in the sounding of them, they can qualify only as *near rhymes*. Eye rhymes are residue rather than invention. You can understand why such rhymes are also termed *historical rhymes*.

Historical rhymes, however, also include words that are not spelled alike but seem as though they should be pronounced alike and should therefore qualify as full rhymes. The pair *been/scene* would today be a near rhyme, because we avoid the long *e* sound in *been* so we won't sound affected, pronouncing it instead very close to *bin*. But in Spenser's time, *beene* was pronounced with the long *e*, so the pair was a legitimate full rhyme. Another near rhyme that was once a full rhyme would be *tea/away;* up to the eighteenth century, *tea* was still being voiced *tay*.

INTERNAL RHYME

Like crossed rhyme, this is a rhyme of position; it does not occur at the ends of both lines involved, but inside the lines. Occasionally, the rhyming pair will be an end word or syllable from one line, and the the second word or syllable will be inside the other line. These repeated sounds within the lines emphasize rhythmic structure, divide long lines into shorter units, and may come anywhere in the lines. Often, internal rhyme enhances the musical quality of the lines and is used purely for its tonal qualities, thereby affording increased pleasure. The following couplet provides an illustration wherein the rhymes inside the first line are feminine, and the ones in the second line are masculine.

> A *sorrow* finds this *borrowed* light,
> And *fate* will *wait* to *mate* with night.

INITIAL RHYME

Initial rhyme is also called *head rhyme* or *alliteration*. Initial or head rhyme sometimes indicates rhymes occurring at the beginnings of lines, but at other times, *initial* means the beginning consonants of words within a line—which brings it into the province of alliteration. Alliteration, in its full sense, means the repetitions of the same sounds or syllables in two or more words inside a line or group of lines. It influences the harmony and percussion of the line as well as the melody. Through the energy of similar sounds, it can add emphasis that would not be achieved in the same way by any other device. The repetition of vowel sounds may also be called alliteration, but usually only when embraced by consonants on either side. Sophisticated use of initial rhyme or alliteration can produce intricate patterns of sound that can further enhance the meaning or sense. It is possible to erect on one alliterated sound an alliterative sequence. Another skilled application is to include an alliterative pattern inside another alliterative pattern. The first of these would result in *parallel alliteration;* the second, in *crossed alliteration.*

Here is a splendid example of initial rhyme:

William Shakespeare
One Hundred and Seventh Sonnet

Not mine own fears, nor the prophetic soul
Of the wide world, dreaming on things to come,
Can yet the lease of my true love control,
Suppos'd as forfeit to a confin'd doom.
The mortal moon hath her eclipse endur'd
And the sad augurs mock their own presage;
Incertainties now crown themselves assur'd
And peace proclaims olives of endless age.
Now with the drops of this most balmy time
My love looks fresh, and Death to me subscribes,
Since, spite of him, I'll live in this poor rhyme,
While he insults o'er dull and speechless tribes:
   And thou in this shalt find thy monument,
   When tyrants' crests and tombs of brass are spent.

NEAR RHYME

This is termed variously as *apocopated, approximate, assonance, consonance, consonantal dissonance, dissonance, embryonic, half-, impure, imperfect, oblique, off, para-, par-*

tial, popular, slant, and *tangential rhyme.* Because the English language is not generous enough with rhyming words and syllables to ensure full rhymes, poets have of necessity taken advantage of poetic license and adopted near rhymes to offset the lacking resource. More than anywhere else in the terminology of prosody, near rhyme can lead to absolute confusion, as is apparent in the list at the head of this paragraph. Many terms are applied in different ways to different variations of rhyme by different prosodists and poets. Despite the spate of terms and admitting to slight differences, we can justifiably classify these types of rhymes under the general caption of *near rhyme.* We do, however, spend some extra time on some of these specific terms.

Near rhyme signifies a "rhyme substitute" for full rhyme and is distinguished by one or more variations from the criteria we considered for full rhyme earlier. The kinds of variations are largely responsible for the multiplicity of terms. Examples of near rhyme are *bite/ride* or *dated/making.* In both cases, the rhyming elements are the stressed vowels in proper position to each other, and the preceding consonants are different. So far, everything is in accord with the requirements for full rhyme. But it is in the consonants *following* the rhyming stressed vowels that the deviation occurs; they aren't identical sounds. In the second example, the final syllables are not alike in any way except that both are not stressed.

Assonance means simply that the stressed vowels in a rhyming pair of syllables agree, whereas the consonants do not, as the foregoing examples illustrate. This is also known as *vocalic assonance,* and it occurred frequently in old ballads. Hopkins and Dylan Thomas had a fondness for the technique, too; they used the device along with full rhyme, and the combination attained for them an astounding, full resonance in many of their poems.

When the consonants rather than the vowels of the stressed syllables match, this is called *consonance, consonantal rhyme, half-rhyme,* or *pararhyme.* For illustration: *boat/bait.* The consonants coincide; the vowels do not. This rhyming technique is also called *dissonance,* which is imprecise because it would depend on the types of consonants involved. It is also called *consonantal dissonance,* which is close to a contradiction in terms. And upon occasion, it's called *assonance*, which is equivalent to forcing an antonym to do the work of a synonym. This proliferation of terms demonstrates that no one has yet thought up a proper name for the technique.

 ' *Half rhyme* (or *apocopated rhyme*) describes a particular type of rhyme not restricted by the pattern of consonance. *Apocopated* literally means "cut off." One half of the rhyming pair is masculine, and the other half is feminine. The masculine portion is the short, one-syllable part of the combination, and the rhyme exists between that syllable and the stressed syllable of the feminine element. A pair such as *clip/slipping* would be described as an apocopated rhyme or a half-rhyme. Think of the technique as using double rhyme with one unrhyming syllable cut off; it doesn't matter whether this occurs in the first or second word.

Related in its effect to light rhyme is a technique called *tangential rhyme*, a glancing type of rhyming, a tentative combination of stressed and unstressed syllables—*tidal/cradle*—sometimes called *slant rhyme*.

ANALYZED RHYME

This is an intricate rhyme pattern related to near rhyme. It relies, as the term indicates, on analysis by the reader or listener. Rhymes here are apparent more readily to the eye, although the ear may detect the harmonious echo of rhyme before realizing its involved arrangements. Some of the rhyming elements are switched around so that the rhyming syllables are linked or interlocked. Demonstration will prove more useful than explanation. The rhymes function like suspensions in music, and the technique is sometimes referred to as *suspended rhyme*.

> He shyly held out a torn treasure *map*,
> shuffled his feet in the street's *dust*,
> and sighed. Weakening, I bought him a *cup*
> of soup, and said it would be his *last*.

The sequence of the rhyming vowels differs from that of their companion consonant rhymes. If we plot the rhymes of the vowels, we get *abba;* plotting the consonant rhymes gives us *abab.* The reverse of this pattern would give us the parallel rhyme schemes of—for the vowels—*abab* and—for the consonants—*abba:*

> Where is the woman who will love a man
> without money or fame or success,
> who is not a member of the upper class,
> and can only make love in his den?

Within the category of analyzed rhyme but also having some aspects of eye rhyme is *backward rhyme.* Not truly a rhyme, this involves using the same letters to end two lines, but the end words are spelled the reverse of each other. The "rhyme" is created by the use of the same letters at the ends of both lines. If you write a couplet and end your lines with words like *won/now* or *deeps/speed,* you are using backward rhyme. Less discernible at first glance than analyzed rhyme, this technique takes clever manipulation and results in an entertaining tour de force if carried through a whole poem.

METAPHOR

This device remains one of the most important and persuasive in poetry. Without stopping to reflect upon it, most of us use metaphor continually in our ordinary communication. When we say of a person: "She's a tiger!" we are employing a metaphor that enables us to convey our complex meaning in brief, visual terms. A metaphor describes—in terms of something else—some thing, person, event, or the like that would take, if described in literal terms, much more language and explanation to convey. The comprehension of the metaphor's *meaning* is based on the ability to assign the attributes of the figurative (or fictional) symbol to the intended subject. We understand, in our example, that a woman is being described in terms of a tiger, with all the connotations the term carries: she's ferocious, tenacious, predatory, fast, powerful, but also beautiful, sleek, challenging, and attractive.

So a metaphor describes indirectly. Its success depends upon tacit agreement between sayer and hearer, an agreement established on familiarity with idiom or colloquialism on the part of both, and on the sayer's assumption that the hearer is willing to comprehend a description of—in this example—a human in terms of a nonhuman. The sayer is not required to elaborate; the matter is adequately handled by the metaphor. Where an attempt at providing a literal description would have been only intellectually stimulating, the metaphor elicits from the hearer an emotional response as well; and the reward is a sharp and accurate picture of the "she."

Analytically, what do we realize about the sentence: "She's a tiger"? For one thing, it lacks logic. A human being and a jungle beast are not alike. But we are willing, for the sake of the immediacy of its meaning, to accept the metaphor and to suspend our concern with everyday logic and accept the *artistic substitution* for such logic—that is, to accept the *metaphor's logic* instead. Metaphor, in making possible the acceptance of one thing in place of another with neither resembling the other, interrupts one kind of logic to impose a logic of its own. Having achieved this much, metaphor then demands that this new logic not be disturbed.

If the poet is going to explain metaphoric attempts ("She's a tiger, beautiful and predatory"), he or she might as well just say what's meant and forget using metaphor. Poets must trust their techniques; otherwise they are not going to succeed.

Once the poet has decided to use a particular metaphor, he or she is obliged to adhere to the conventions of metaphor and must work within the perimeter of the metaphor. One cannot easily and carelessly introduce elements that would be foreign to the metaphor, even if such ideas, images, and terms are appropriate to what the metaphor represents. In other words, you cannot violate the metaphor itself. If you're giving your impression of a woman, and you choose to do it through similarities you find in her and in a tiger, you do not introduce references describing her in terms of a graceful ship: "She's a tiger when she sails into a room." The violation to the metaphor here is the fact that a tiger doesn't sail. Such an expression is called a *mixed metaphor*.

A mixed metaphor may be a curse or a blessing. At its worst (as the example above), a mixed metaphor delivers a comparison that, in one way or another, reveals itself as being so false that the two elements of the comparison cancel each other out. A bad mixed metaphor confuses rather than fuses. A line like "the seat of government has no teeth in it" is not only metaphoric nonsense but ludicrous as well; but it is only a slight exaggeration of what a mixed metaphor can sound like.

On the other hand, a mixed metaphor can attain a stimulating beauty, as in some of Hart Crane's poems (" . . . a pale balloon, . . . in shadow swims"); or an irreversible power as in *Lycidas,* where Milton describes the clergy: "Blind mouths! that scarce themselves know how to hold/a sheep-hook." At their best, mixed metaphors are termed *telescoped metaphors,* a system of metaphors in which the vehicle (the representing agent) of one metaphor is the tenor (that which is being represented) of another metaphor closely tied to it—a rather complex achievement. Telescoped metaphors flouished in metaphysical poetry.

Metaphor, then, is a device of comparison, but the comparing link is submerged. In addition to being able to see similarities between two things normally considered dissimilar, the poet must also acquire the skill to fuse two different things—one stated and the other unstated. And this must be done in such a way that the audience will accept the implied comparison without challenge, the way we're ready to accept both the "logic" and the meaning of the sentence "She's a tiger!"

The poet must also understand the differences between the two elements of the metaphor, because metaphor is also a device of contrast. In fact, metaphor is many things: in addition to similarity and contrast, metaphor may serve to express identity, tension, juxtaposition, analogy, allegory, or symbol. Metaphor makes the unknown known. The development of a body of metaphor in one's work is a step in building an individual mythology.

At the level of our "she/tiger" example, the metaphor is merely decorative, illustrative, or descriptive. We could find or choose other ways to characterize the woman. ("She's a pussycat, cow, dog, lamb.") The same is true of that other type (to return to our other example) of metaphor—"the seat of government"—which, if taken literally, is sure to provoke smirks. But in this case, the word *seat* and all it connotes (the place where government rests or is throned) comes into play and comprises the vehicle that bears the metaphor. The idea it conveys in context, in relation to *government,* is the tenor.

Some metaphors express (perhaps we should say "impress") such a complicated combination of ideas and feelings in such a subtle and exact fashion that any attempt to express that combination in any other way would ultimately be less vivid and less capable of being grasped instantly. Such a complex metaphor is known as a *structural, organic,* or *functional metaphor.*

Metaphor is also fundamentally a sign—the way a word is a sign, which makes each noun and verb a kind of metaphor for the reality, since it is language *representing* a thing or an action. This might be seen more readily if we recall the functions of pictograms, hieroglyphics, ideograms, symbols, and the like, where the attempt is to represent the thing itself visually rather than by some name for it.

In sequence, a series of metaphors may build up to a very effective encompassing metaphor. From the briefness of one word, a metaphor may eventually be enlarged into an *extended metaphor* (called also a *conceit*), a metaphor involving an entire poem wherein the shorter metaphors contribute directly to the parent metaphor.

Allegory, in which you're apt to find an elaborate vehicle representing an unstated tenor, may be classed as an extended metaphor, since it represents one thing in terms of something else. It may be the power of goodness in the form of a Samaritan (the Samaritan being the vehicle and the power of goodness the tenor). An abstract concept is represented by a concrete image. There is generally a narrative of sorts to help cloak the message, and the characters themselves—as in the Samaritan—are personifications of the abstract forces in the comparison or contrast offered. *The Divine Comedy* and *The*

Faerie Queene may be considered allegories, along with Bunyan's *Pilgrim's Progress*. Such works combine narrative with their didactic intent. Fables and myths are often allegorical in intent if not in style.

An *analogy* is a comparison based on attributes similar in two different things, thus establishing a relational kinship between the two things. In its simplest form, it is an image used to clarify a complex idea or concept. It functions on the basis of likenesses. When developed beyond immediate and brief use, it can also become an extended metaphor.

SIMILE

Where the metaphor is a relationship between an expressed vehicle and an unexpressed tenor, the *simile* is a comparison in which both elements are expressed. This is accomplished usually by using *as* or *like*, which function similarly to the equal sign between two parts of the comparison. Whereas "The Thunderbird is as fast as a Cadillac" is just a comparison, "The Thunderbird is as fast as the wind" is a simile, because the attributes of the wind are assigned to the Thunderbird.

OTHER POETIC DEVICES

A few of the devices listed next are primarily cited in criticism but are included to give the beginning poet some insight into how a poem may be received and judged.

Fallacy. There are several kinds of fallacy. *Affective* and *intentional fallacy* apply to the critical assessment of a poet's work. *Affective fallacy* is the confusion between what a poem is and what it does. The critic tends to criticize and evaluate the poem in terms of his or her individual (and often, intuitive) criteria rather than on formal standards, and the emphasis is placed on the result—the effect of the poem on the audience—instead of on the poem itself as a work of art.

Intentional fallacy is the critical judgment of a poem made by examining the poet's intention rather than what the poem is, completed and separated from its author. Critics are in disagreement on this point, some holding that poem and poet are inseparable and must be considered in tandem, whereas others claim that the poem earns a life of its own and must be judged with little or no reference to its creator. Choosing which side is a personal preference, since formidable arguments exist for both positions. (This author favors judging the poem alone.)

Communication fallacy is a misuse of medium, signifying that ideas and attitudes are being expressed in poetry that should be expressed in prose or other nonpoetic media. A propaganda poem, for instance, may arouse in the audience a strong emotional response, but usually such a response is not because of the poem but because of the current attitudes toward the theme or subject. Such a response may very well be justified on moral grounds, but too frequently, it has little to do with aesthetic experience.

Pathetic fallacy is a device many beginners seem to have difficulty with in their early poems. The device is used widely in poetry, but it can too easily turn into a snare. Pathetic fallacy is the practice of attributing human traits and feelings to natural or inanimate objects. Used skillfully, it can produce startling and profound effects, especially in surreal poetry. A justification for the use of pathetic fallacy is in the situation where the voice or narrator in the poem reaches such an intense level of emotion that reason itself is suspended. Then, indeed, stones may speak, and clouds may weep. You will find numerous examples of pathetic fallacy in the body of poetry. Homer, Dante, and Shakespeare used the device so well that no one ever questions the logic involved. Others use it to devise images of such beauty, images that are so moving that readers gladly accept the fallacy in place of more rational description. Objection to the use of pathetic fallacy arises when the result appears contrived and clumsily handled.

Today, application of the term is almost always from the standpoint of analytical description and avoids passing value judgment, since the device is apparently with us to stay. The more successful uses of pathetic fallacy take place when the fallacy is not quite so obtrusive and is less formal than in the device known as *personification*. Besides being a form of pathetic fallacy, personification also functions as a metaphor. It suggests comparison between human and nonhuman; it represents one thing in terms of another. Personification has existed as a poetic device since the art's beginnings. Simple personifications are phrases like *the sea has sung, the sun has smiled, the brook babbled;* More complex personification was an integral part of old legends and myths, where gods, heroes, and villains represented moral concepts and attitudes and the forces of nature. The talking animals in fables and children's stories and poetry are another case in point. Contemporary poets and critics regard personification, like pathetic fallacy, without judgmental bias. But when personification is used inexpertly, it results in an unconvincing—and at times silly—image or line: "A tree whose hungry mouth is prest / Against the earth's sweet flowing breast."

The *persona* of a poem is the imagined, often unidentified speaker or narrator and is not to be taken as the poet. Most of the time in "I" poems, the "I" is not the poet at all, but a persona.

In poetry, a passing reference to a person, event, or place is called an *allusion*. The poet assumes that the reader will recognize the reference because it is well known. *Literary allusion* is a reference to some character, event, place, plot, or well-known section of a longer work existing in literature or to its title or author. The value of allusion, for the poet, is that he or she can simply touch upon the reference and expect its ramifications to be recalled immediately to the reader's mind. It is an enriching device.

An *archetype* is an original or primitive form. In poetry, it suggests an ancestral quality. Archetypes may be characters, themes, or plots; and they are expressed in myths, fantasies, and dreams, as well as in poetry. Because of their representational nature, archetypes often loom a bit larger than life-size. They were described by C. G. Jung as "primordial images" formed by repeated experiences in our ancestors' lives, and we inherit them through the collective unconscious of the human race. According to Jung, archetypes evoke racial memory. In

Coleridge's "The Rime of the Ancient Mariner," the mariner is an archetype. Awakened in him is the memory of the sinfulness of man (the racial memory of man's offense against God); the mariner is, therefore, the archetype of the sinner, the individual who offends God. The journey itself is also an archetype—the spiritual journey all of us must undertake.

The device of *repetition* is basic to all the arts. A poet uses *repetends* (any repeated element in a poem may be termed a *repetend*) to provoke anticipation, to establish, familiarize, intensify, or to fulfill the demands of form. *Sequence* and *pattern* can be thought of as extensions of the device of repetition. The specific repetends in a poem are images, symbols, or motifs; words, phrases, or lines (refrains); assonance, consonance, alliteration, and rhythmic figures.

Some prosodists distinguish between *refrain* and *repetend,* reserving the former term for a line that is repeated exactly and at regular intervals, whereas the repetend permits variation and may occur wherever it suits the poem and the poet. Under this definition, a repetend lends itself to development and transference; an image or symbol early in the poem will recur later at other points in an altered or extended form or in a new context.

Incremental repetition is an intensification device that was very popular in ancient ballads. (The developed repetend already discussed may be thought of an incremental repetition.) We saw an example of incremental repetition at work in the ballad "Lord Randal" (in Chapter 4), where lines kept their key words and introduced slight variations each time to add to the suspense as the narrative was slowly revealed.

The term *transferred epithet* refers to an adjective that describes a noun to which it does not normally apply: *stony silence* is an example. The practice often results in pathetic fallacy or personification, as in *the laughing sun.*

Synaesthesia describes one sense perception in terms of another, such as attributing sound to colors, or smell to sound or to color, and so on. It need not always be primary terminology such as *blue note;* it may be *tweedy voice* or *cold tone.* Because of its implicit aspect of comparison, the device is also known as *sense analogy* or *sense transference.*

In poetic use, a *paradox* is a device of contradiction that arrives at truth. Many poets have employed paradox. In the section on sonnets, we saw how often paradox entered the form at its close or turn. This is a major device in poetry, and Shakespeare provides an excellent and easily accessible example:

Sonnet One Hundred Thirty-Eight

When my love swears that she is made of truth
I do believe her, though I know she lies,
That she might think me some untutor'd youth,
Unlearned in the world's false subtleties.
Thus vainly thinking that she thinks me young,
Although she knows my days are past the best,
Simply I credit her false-speaking tongue:
On both sides thus is simple truth suppress'd.
But wherefore says she not she is unjust?
And wherefore say not I that I am old?
O, love's best habit is in seeming trust,
And age in love loves not to have years told:
   Therefore I lie with her and she with me,
   And in our faults by lies we flatter'd be.

As you can see, paradox assumes an essential functional role; it cannot be considered merely a decorative or illustrative device when it is so finely woven into the material of the poem. Coupled with irony, paradox can achieve a tremendously expressive power.

FIGURES OF SPEECH

At one time, *figures of speech* were defined as either grammatical or rhetorical, whereas metaphor, simile, personification, and similar devices were considered *figures of thought*. Current practice has, for all intents, discarded the distinction, and all these devices are now referred to as figures of speech. These devices were originally relegated to the classification of *ornamentation* (as were most of the devices in this chapter). Since the time of Dryden and Pope, however, figures of speech have been appreciated as integral to theme and content.

In one sense, all figures of speech are types of metaphor, in that words and phrases are not only used figuratively but also express their meaning in representative terms. Figurative language is useful because it expresses a relationship between different things in terms that exceed the limits of standard constructions and literal meaning.

Using figures of speech in our daily activities is as common as breathing, and we pay little attention to the fact that we are indeed using them. When someone says "the mail poured in," we accept the statement without question. It is a figure of speech because mail does not pour; the speaker has borrowed a special verb to add color, emotion, and intensification to the expression in conveying the amount involved. The speaker could have said "Seven hundred and twenty-one pieces of mail were received," and although that would have been precise information, we would not have felt the overwhelming effect that "poured" stimulates in our mind's eye—the *image* of a *flood* of pieces of mail *inundating* desks, personnel, and everything *in its path*. In poetry, similar effects are attained through the use of figures of speech; but their use is controlled and directed by the poet, and they are newly coined to stimulate a fresh reaction in the reader.

In addition to metaphor, simile, analogy, allegory, personification, transferred epithet, paradox, and synaesthesia, here are a few additional figures with which you will come in contact in writing poetry:

Hyperbole is an exaggeration to provide intensity or force to a linguistic expression, and it occurs in ordinary language as well as poetry. Our example of the mail "pouring in" is a hyperbole.

Metonymy and *synecdoche* are forms of comparison and are directly related to metaphor and simile. *Metonymy* substitutes one thing for another, as in the sentence "The joint is jumpin'!" We know it's not the joint but the people in it who are "jumpin'." But saying "The people in the building are dancing vigorously" doesn't possess one one-hundredth the springiness, the exuberance, the musicality of "The joint is jumpin'!" because in the figurative phrase, we imagine that the building itself has been moved to join in the festivities.

The next example illustrates a complex metonymy: "Washington today announced another hike in inflation." We understand that "Washington" signifies the District of Columbia and not George or the state, and that the proper noun stands for the government, which stands for the agency responsible for the particular announcement, which stands for the specific official who released the statement to the media. (You have probably detected, also, that "hike" is a metaphor.) Yet none of us has any difficulty in understanding what is meant by the announcement. Another typical use of metonymy is to refer to a writer or artist when we mean to refer to that person's works: "I have read all of Shakespeare." You should look for examples of figures like these in everything you read for a while; that's how you will train yourself to understand and use them.

Synecdoche is a figure of speech that presents a part for the whole. It is closely allied with metaphor as well as metonymy. We're all familiar with the command: "All hands on deck!" We all understand the substitution of "hands" for "crew members." If taken literally, this figure of speech would create a gruesome image in our minds. The attempt is to emphasize the *functional* part of the whole, the hands. But in this case, the emphasis takes place at the expense of humanization.

Another extremely popular figure of speech is the *pun*—a play on words identical or similar in sound but with different meanings in their contexts. The commonest use of the pun is in the service of humor: "Men of high *rank* are a *rank* group." The pun is not limited to humor, however; it may be neutral: "My *son* is my *sun*." Or it may be serious, as when the dying Mercutio (in *Hamlet*) says, "Ask for me tomorrow and you shall find me a *grave* man." In serious use, the pun is almost always dependent on irony for its effect. As the word *grave* is used in the example, we understand its implications (its second-level meaning); the pun resides in the adjectival impossibility, which is the factor impregnating the pun with irony. If we were to use the same word in another way: "Death is a *grave* business," we would be reverting to humor again.

An *oxymoron* couples opposites to form the figure of speech and is a type of paradox: *burning ice, dead spark.* Caution must be exercised in using this figure lest you produce a "humorous grief."

When we refer to an anticipated event as if it has already happened ("Horatio, I am dead"), we're using a figure known as *prolepsis.* A prolepsis represents the use of an objective complement that anticipates the verbal outcome; the thing is presented as having taken place, but it is going to happen *as a result of action described or implied.*

Apostrophe, literally "to turn about," is in poetry a turning to and addressing an absent person or a personification of an abstraction or inanimate object. It is a digression, and often the addressee is some vague archetypal judge. By extension, it represents any similar type of break in the poem. Put simply, it's a shift in address.

Chiasmus refers to a line or passage composed of two balanced parts that demonstrate a reversal of principal elements, as in Pope's line from *Essay on Man:*

Destroying others, by himself destroyed.

A figure of speech employing one word to stand in relationship to two others while the word is syntactically related to only one of the two is called *zeugma.* In effect, the zeugma technique permits inexact syntax in order to attain an abbreviated but emotionally intensified expression. Zeugma is a form of binding; the Greek meaning of *zeugos* is "yoke." There are three main types of "yoking," which are distinguished by the position of the binding element in the sentence: (1) If the yoking word comes before the words it binds, it's called *prozeugma: "The children* hungered, and dwindled to death." (2) *Mesozeugma* signifies zeugma that occurs between the words to be bound: "The man she *worshiped,* and his wealth." (3) When the figure follows the words it binds, it's known as *hypozeugma:* "Neither land, nor sea *shall outlast time."*

The italicized words represent the zeugma agents; the binding effect itself occurs, respectively: (1) between the comma after *hungered* and the following *and,* implying the repetition of the agent; (2) with the verb *worshiped,* which is the agent and, in this case, which coincides with the point of yoking; (3) between *land* and its comma, implying the preplacement of the agent. In using this figure of speech, you must be careful not to find yourself cornered into archaic constructions. It's a delicate figure and must be treated gently.

A *rhetorical question* doesn't expect a reply but is posed to attain a stylistic effect. Its implications include that if a reply were forthcoming, it would indeed confirm the speaker's argument or point of view.

Before moving into more diffuse poetic devices, let's catch our breath and briefly summarize what we've been discussing in this section:

Figurative language is made up of figures of speech that differ from one another but have certain qualities in common. The arrangement of the words in the figures and their assimilation into the rest of the work result in constructions that deviate from standard grammatical styles of order. Figurative phrases are imaginative or fanciful expressions that add vividness, compactness, and emotional impact that would usually be lacking if literalness were strictly adhered to. The function of such figures is to point up new relationships between things and to make that kind of relationship the fulcrum on which the enhanced and multiple meaning will balance. Results are obtained through comparison, contrast, substitution, connection, or any combination of these.

The test of the technique of using figurative language is whether a figure of speech can be translated into literal terms and make strict literal sense, discounting whether the result would be emotionally pleasing or disturbing. Recall the image suggested by the command: "All hands on deck!"—it *can* be understood in strictly literal terms. Another phrase from *Julius Caesar:* "lend me your ears"; this too has an unpleasantly literal possibility. And both examples point up the fact that the literal meaning has nothing to do with *the way* the speakers intend their statements to be understood. In the first, *hands* is a substitution for crew members, and in the second, *ears* represents the abstraction attention.

Irony is a figure of speech in which the literal meaning is the opposite of the intended one. The figure often conveys an attitude of contempt, ridicule, or humor and is used in satire. Irony enables the writer to mask intended meaning behind plot or characterization portraying its opposite. The term is also applied to an outcome in opposition to what the reader was led to expect. *Verbal* (or *rhetorical*) *irony* is an expression in which the implied attitudes or assessments are opposed to those expressed literally. Your success with this figure will rely on the reader's ability to absorb the intended meaning in spite of your literal one. The briefer expressions of irony ("For Brutus is an honourable man") are easy to grasp, helped quite often by the context in which they're cast. In more developed and larger patterns, irony may be missed at first, requiring the reader's closer attention for its detection. An ironic poem is one that considers the complex incongruities of experience.

Tension can exist between several paired elements in a poem. It may develop or evolve between whole lines or sections, whole images, parts of phrases or images, internal structure and outlining form, the vehicle (concrete) meaning and the tenor (abstract) one in metaphor, or between any or all of these. A tension may also exist between the parts or a single word, phrase, or image—between its concreteness and its more diffused associative vibrations. Tone and diction can be made to produce tension. Conflict of situation or characters is one tension most readily recognized by readers. One of the best uses of tension is as an adhesive—to hold the parts of a poem together.

Imagination enables you to use all your powers to formulate in an intense fashion both what is and what is not perceived. It also directs you in the organization and unification of the details available to your memory, so that you enrich the theme you're expressing. The imagination works on at least two levels: on the more attainable level, it functions as your principal instrument of understanding; at a deeper level, it transforms those perceptions into the beginnings of a work of art. Imagination, functioning on both these levels, is responsible for true comprehension.

Fancy is a creative and unifying phenomenon of memory and association, but it doesn't provoke as deep a comprehension as does that second level of imagination. Fancy is sometimes whimsical in its selection and use of images. *Fantasy* is a bit stricter in meaning and refers to extravagant daydreaming or inventiveness. A further distinction is made for *phantasy*, which is a kind of visionary talent capable of visualizing beyond sensory perceptions.

The term *conceit* is applied to a rather fanciful and intricate (often arbitrary) system of perception leading to an elaborate, occasionally self-indulgent exploitation of private symbols and myths, as well as of one's own virtuosity. A poem or group of poems developed on such a special conceit must transcend the limitations of the figure's nature and touch upon universals to overcome the privacy of the references; otherwise, the work will not survive the author. It is difficult to separate the poems from the poet, but when the poems do transcend the limitations inherent in the conceit's technique, the results may turn out to be outstanding, even *obscuring* the poet's intent. *The Divine Comedy* was conceived and constructed on such a conceit, which Dante deliberately exploited, but that doesn't matter to us now, because the work has proved larger than its original conception.

On a narrower scale, a conceit can be a special attitude or style the poet uses for a certain subject or in poems addressed to certain persons. It may include extravagances in adoring descriptions, or it may exceed the limits of logical praise. Such poetry imposes on the reader's good-natured tolerance. If you were to write of your loved one, "Your eyes are deep pools of jade," both you and your reader/loved one would be aware that the statement is unrealistic and fanciful. It is a conceit. Petrarch's sonnets to "Laura" fall into this category; and Shakespeare pokes fun at the practice in his "Sonnet One Hundred Thirty," which begins:

> My mistress' eyes are nothing like the sun;
> Coral is far more red than her lips' red;

He himself did not hesitate to use conceits in his plays, however; *Romeo and Juliet* provides a garden of them. Conceit was a favorite device of the metaphysical poets, who regarded it as a different dimension of perception.

The *image* in poetry, one of the most important figures you will use, describes something in terms of concrete detail to form a word picture. William Carlos Williams's "red wheelbarrow" is a concrete image that translates successfully an abstract notion. On the other hand, "the short-nosed, pearl-handled revolver" is the kind of ordinary image often found in detective fiction.

Imagery is a term applied to a total family of images happening in a poem or a section of a poem. It also refers in a larger sense to the range of images favored by a poet and appearing repeatedly in his or her poems. In this latter manifestation, imagery approaches the area of symbolism.

The impressive quality of images is that they evoke mental pictures in the reader's mind: the experience is actually a visual one. This evocative system of communication remains one of the most striking and memorable systems yet devised.

Invention defines the originality with which you express yourself in form, structure, diction, the selection of images, metaphor, and other figures of speech and poetic devices. It also defines the originality of the material itself. Such invention becomes apparent through the exercise of your unique viewpoint and insight and through your individual methods of expression and use of form.

With *symbol*, we may feel that we've come full circle in this discussion on poetic devices, because in its rudimentary sense, a symbol is one thing representing something else. And a word is certainly a symbol (sign) of its meaning. Whenever we see a particular word, we associate it with the agreed-upon meaning. But symbols are radiational. They increase themselves through reappearance, communal acceptance, persistence, and metaphoric importance.

Signifying a familiar symbol, the word *cross* is different from *the Cross*. Whereas *the Cross* pertains to a narrower set of references, its evocative energy is thereby increased. Its meaning becomes more particular and lends the term more meaning (increases itself). It's a process of intensification. The capital *C* calls to mind a special set of images and associations; those recalled by the word *cross* are more general and less intense.

Traffic signals, flags, markers, logos, spires, pentagons,

crossed swords, doves—these are all symbols we understand without any problems. In art, symbols may be just as accessible to our understanding, or we may have to ferret them out of the work.

The importance of symbols in poetry, or literature in general, is that they afford the poet the opportunity to exploit their connotative or associative meanings in a wider sense for purposes of intensification, tightness, particularization, and heightening expression. Symbols serve to enrich a poem through their radiational aspects.

There may be a privacy in connection with a set of symbols appearing in a poet's work that tends to exclude the reader from the total poem or poems. In some cases, that may be necessary in order for the poet to realize personal expression in the way he or she feels it must be. The poet is likely to discover at some point in the work that he or she is developing unique points of reference. Eventually, of course, if the symbols are to attain a viable importance, they must transcend such limiting perimeters; they must, in fact, transcend the poet. The white whale in *Moby Dick* is that type of symbol.

Other symbols, such as the *cross* and *the Cross,* are considered public symbols and speak immediately and directly to the reader. In the works of skilled poets, literary symbols do move out of the private category to become integrated additions to the generally recognized symbology of literature.

Quite frequently, one of the major roles of the symbol is to signify that which cannot be defined or articulated in sufficient depth in a more direct fashion. With its multiplicity of meaning and effect, the symbol accomplishes this task for the poet artistically. When the poet has developed a system of symbology that coheres and whose individual symbols reinforce and supplement each other as well as the composite they form, that poet is on the way to establishing a personal mythology.

Now that we have traversed the way of poetic devices and figures of speech, see how many of these you can detect in the following poem by Auden. Note, too, the changes in form and tone, the absence and presence of rhyme; and speculate on why the poet handled the material differently in each section.

W. H. Auden
In Memory of W. B. Yeats
D. Jan. 1939.

I

He disappeared in the dead of winter:
The brooks were frozen, the airports almost deserted,
And snow disfigured the public statues;
The mercury sank in the mouth of the dying day.
What instruments we have agree
The day of his death was a dark cold day.

Far from his illness
The wolves ran on through the evergreen forests,
The peasant river was untempted by the fashionable quays;
By mourning tongues
The death of the poet was kept from his poems.

But for him it was his last afternoon as himself,
An afternoon of nurses and rumours;
The provinces of his body revolted,
The squares of his mind were empty,
Silence invaded the suburbs,
The current of his feeling failed; he became his admirers.

Now he is scattered among a hundred cities
And wholly given over to unfamiliar affections;
To find his happiness in another kind of wood
And be punished under a foreign code of conscience.
The words of a dead man
Are modified in the guts of the living.

But in the importance and noise of to-morrow
When the brokers are roaring like beasts on the floor of the Bourse,
And the poor have the sufferings to which they are fairly accustomed,
And each in the cell of himself is almost convinced of his freedom,
A few thousand will think of this day
As one thinks of a day when one did something slightly unusual.
What instruments we have agree
The day of his death was a dark cold day.

II

You were silly like us; your gift survived it all;
The parish of rich women, physical decay,
Yourself: mad Ireland hurt you into poetry.
Now Ireland has her madness and her weather still,
For poetry makes nothing happen: it survives
In the valley of its saying where executives
Would never want to tamper; it flows south
From ranches of isolation and the busy griefs,
Raw towns that we believe and die in; it survives,
A way of happening, a mouth.

III

Earth, receive an honoured guest:
William Yeats is laid to rest.
Let the Irish vessel lie
Emptied of its poetry.

In the nightmare of the dark
All the dogs of Europe bark,
And the living nations wait,
Each sequestered in its hate;

Intellectual disgrace
Stares from every human face,
And the seas of pity lie
Locked and frozen in each eye.

Follow, poet, follow right
To the bottom of the night,
With your unconstraining voice
Still persuade us to rejoice;

With the farming of a verse
Make a vineyard of the curse,
Sing of human unsuccess
In a rapture of distress;

In the deserts of the heart
Let the healing fountain start,

> In the prison of his days
> Teach the free man how to praise.

We understand now that the word is not simply a group of letters making a meaning. Nor is it just meaning plus associations, sound, rhythm, tone, and emotion. The word is a symbol, beyond the shape of the letters signifying the word; it is a far-reaching symbol that, to be understood, takes every faculty we possess. And multilayered symbols in combination become the lifeblood of art. Poetry is the art of the word. And even one word, in its solitude, is a poem.

There is power in the word. And nowhere is the word capable of greater power than in poetry. And this power rises out of the *everything* that is the word: the sound–the rhythm–the meaning–the echoes–the meanings of the meanings–the harmonics–the overtones—all these and more are the word; and the word is still more. The word does not rest.

Having considered the separate features of rhythms, sounds, and poetic devices, we're now ready to recognize the following:

1. The separation of different rhythms and sounds is only for purposes of study and analysis. To varying degrees and in flexing relationships, all of a language's rhythms and sounds are the foundation of the true poem.
2. Since poetry is the art of language, certain aspects may be assumed:
    a. The poems of any period not only reflect the rhythms, sounds, and usage of that period but will reflect the evolution and history of the language up to that time as well; they will, on occasion, intimate future directions for the language.
    b. The poetry of a culture influences the rhythms, sounds, devices, and figures of speech and the development and sophistication of the language of that culture.
    c. The artistic manipulation of poetic devices has or will

have results whose qualities outlast in importance the thematic matter of individual poems. The mode and method of expression are the viable final record of the language of a period. Language is its own history, as well as the recording medium for all other history—written or oral.

3. All rhythms and sounds coexist in the universe—on the verge of becoming (they are the *genes* of poems), waiting to be organized and created into composition; and

   a. Conception occurs when sufficient rhythms and sounds have gathered in proper relationship in the poet's subconscious. Inspiration (idea) comes in contact with the waiting rhythms and sounds, and the process is set in motion.

   b. A variable time follows during which the gestation of the poem-to-be takes place.

   c. The poem emerges, soft and rough shaped. It is firmed and strengthened by the poet's conscious effort.

   d. Formed and developed, the poem is released. Separating from the poet, the poem takes its place among other poems.

By having arrived at this point, you have been faithful to your commitment. You are now ready to start writing your poems.

III. Expression

8. The Consummation

No one can teach you to write poetry. You learn by writing poems. But you have now been taught effective techniques and procedures. And you have been warned about possible pitfalls. You will start with an idea, an object, an experience or memory, a witnessed event or an overheard phrase, a line you've read, or a word suddenly there in your mind.

What sort of poem will it be? Long or short? Lyric, narrative, or dramatic? Sonnet, haiku, free verse, syllabic? An experimental gamble? Sometimes the answers to these questions are not accessible at the outset. You will find yourself working with the material before recognizing what the poem's shape and style are going to be. Or you will be frustrated in your original plan for it and discover it wants to go its own way. Decisions you make when you begin are going to be altered by the subsequent development of the elements of your poem. It's best to keep yourself open, intellectually and emotionally.

The material of a poem is, as we have noted, initially raw, and we've learned that raw material is seldom poetry without the application of craft. Early attractions or shocks engendered by raw material presented as a completed poem soon fade, and one is left with fragments that might have been shaped into a poem had the poet cared or known enough concerning the art.

Your first step, then, will be to get your raw material into some temporary organization so that you can grapple with it. Occasionally, it helps to develop your idea or subject in one or two prose paragraphs from which you can begin to select and assemble, but you'll find that no two situations proceed in exactly the same manner.

Some beginners feel they'd rather just write the poem as it comes to mind, without all this preliminary organization and work. They fear that a tampering with the "inspiration" may dissipate the thrust of the material. But the poet who gains and maintains control over the material, who is familiar with the requirements and ways of the craft, will produce a greater number of valid poems than will the undisciplined or "primitive" writer.

Very well. You have recorded your thoughts and impressions concerning your subject—whether in paragraph form, as unconnected lines, phrases, or images—and you've made some marginal notes to yourself. At this point, you have some idea of how you *want* the poem to go and what its focus should be. You're making selections from your raw material and beginning to refine those selections.

This is not too early a time to start being objective and discriminating. What obviously isn't going to contribute to the poem's purpose must be discarded. It is not unusual to feel uncomfortable about doing this. One often finds oneself overly attached to an image or line, especially *la ligne donnée* ("the given line") that may have been the original inspiration. But as John Holmes said: "When the young poet recovers from blind reverence for his own words because they are his own words and therefore sacred, then he begins to grow." Take comfort in this, and don't be afraid to eliminate what you know in your heart is no longer a valid part of your poem.

You may still not be able to launch into a shaping of the form of the poem at this stage. Do not be discouraged. As you work and develop your skills, the writing will become easier to some degree. What's required from you besides true commitment are patience and persistence. You've responded to the

The Consummation

initial impulse, prompted by what seeded the poem in you. Now you may have to struggle to achieve a rough shape and a sketchy sequence of the elements that begin to make themselves recognizable as a poem, and you will have to work toward the realization of your still murky schematic.

As you write down your tentative lines, you discover more of what you're trying to express and *how* to express it. You may experience a few false starts, but if the talent for poetry is in you, soon the writing begins to flow; to your delight, development and expression evolve seemingly of their own accord. Finally, you lean back in your chair and read the poem over to yourself. It has substance. Chances are, it also has a shape that looks authentic enough. There's unity of a sort; it makes sense; it seems to move logically to its ending.

Don't relax too soon, however. What you've experienced is only the beginning of the process. There's still the matter of revision. Although it's true that now and then, a poem appears complete when it is first recorded on the page and may require no revision at all, the odds are against that happening, especially for the untrained writer. The skills required for poetry are like the skills for any other art: they must be learned and practiced. And there are other factors that will determine the degree and amount of revision a poem may need.

For instance, the less mature writer is more anxious to rush to a desk and try to write the poem from the first glimmer of an idea. This eagerness may be exactly the kind of pushing the subconscious will resist. But conscious self overrides inner reluctance, and the poem is forced into being. The writer catches an image or two, a few lines, but is frustrated by the inability to complete the poem or to make it work as it should. At this point, the poem may be given up, or language and form may be forced, which will certainly be obvious in the finished product. (That's what is meant when a poem is described as "overworked" or "strained.") Frustration is compounded if at other times poems seemed to write themselves with little effort from the author.

In the writing of poems, your most powerful genie *is* your subconscious. The times when poems seem to be born easily are probably times when an idea has taken hold of your imagination and, for some reason, you have been unable to get to your desk. Perhaps you are out shopping or fixing the stereo. The idea is there. Well, you'll get to it as soon as you can. Other circumstances intervene. Maybe by now, the poem idea has been stored so far back in your mind that you no longer think about it. Your thoughts are busy with other things.

The idea hasn't disappeared. It is in that dark room at the far end of your data warehouse. Your subconscious may have prompted it in the first place and now is busily developing it, so that you'll be more likely to read it clearly when next it surfaces. Or the idea may have come from some outside stimulus, and your subconscious is examining it with a view toward assimilating it in the store of knowledge and experience your computer brain holds in readiness for you. Without your conscious permission, associations are tested, shapes suggested, patterns developed, and emotions applied; suddenly, the embryonic idea is a full-fledged being clamoring for release. Now you find time; you set everything else aside; and at your desk, you witness the poem take form before your eager mind. So easily written, the poem appears to be truly inspired.

But you have done a great deal of the work internally. That gestation period, while you were otherwise occupied, was productive. Could we fully realize the value of allowing ideas to grow at their own pace, we would have an easier time of it. This does not imply that the subconscious part of ourselves does its task expertly every time or even that it gives us a real poem in every instance. The subconscious is servant, not master. It is the conscious mind that judges and evaluates. Without these critical applications, we will surely end up with chaotic results.

Being a careful writer, you will scrutinize everything you produce, challenge every detail—every phrase and word. Try to understand why you feel that something you've put on paper is "right," even if the reason eludes you. It may make the process a bit longer, but you will have the security of understanding specifically what it is that you are creating.

The degree of necessary revision will vary with your skill as a poet. The more experience you acquire, the more right moves you will make the first time. But there's hardly a poem that hasn't benefited (or wouldn't have) from some critical review. An imprecise word or a misplaced comma may affect the entire quality of the poem.

Being a poet means that one cares about language and finds joy in working with it. The direction of revision is always toward improvement, which is in itself sufficient justification for its pursuit. And the writer should derive as much pleasure in working and reworking of language as in expressing his or her theme effectively.

As a writing poet, therefore, your best course is to allow your subconscious enough time to do its part, then to test and challenge all aspects of the poem with your conscious mind to insure that the poem is successful. The total effect of the poem should be greater than the sum of its parts. Great care must be exercised to achieve the proper balance of all the elements. The knowledge of the craft of poetry you've been acquiring enables you to transform raw material into finished art. A poem is a live experience.

John Ciardi says: "Above all else, poetry is performance." And later, "the unparaphraseable and undiminishable life of the poem lies in the way it performs itself through the difficulties it imposes upon itself." You, as the poem's creator, give the words on paper substance, action, direction. You give them life. You invest the poem with the ability to become its own performance.

The art in poetry does not arise from putting words together to impart information and emotion; anyone can do that without writing poetry. The art evolves from the skillful arrangement of language to realize its greatest power and evocativeness, to *make* an artistic expression where before there was none (the word *poet* comes from the Greek and means "maker")—in other words, to *create* a successful illusion, an illusion that occupies space and time and has dimension. This is the skill of artists, whether they compose music, paint, or write poems. Poetry, says Susanne K. Langer, "springs from the power of language to formulate the appearance of reality, a power fundamentally different from the communicative function, however involved with it in the evolution of speech. The pure product of the formulative use of language is verbal creation, composition, art; not statement, but *poesis*."

As you go on working, you discover that quite often, revisions will be extensive—especially if you were impatient to get the poem down on paper. This means redoing . . . and redoing—as many times as necessary until you are honestly satisfied with your results. There are poets who don't believe poems are ever really finished. One changes perspective and gains new insights continually. What seems to be sufficient today may well appear less so tomorrow. Dylan Thomas's manuscripts reveal the painstaking search for exactly the right word. The wonder—and the beauty—in a true poem is the way we are impressed by the language's naturalness and the poem's spontaneity in the final version released for the public. And this is perhaps the greatest secret of real poetry. The *apparent* ease and fluidity mask the diligent application of mind and science to achieve precisely such results.

Some poems, despite revisions, will still refuse to work well. No matter. You are committed to the art; you will write others. That's why desks have waste baskets beside them. There's no shame in recognizing that you've written a bad piece and daring to throw it out. In fact, it requires a degree of courage. There are writers who've kept everything, from the very first quatrain they wrote. Having matured somewhat, they admit that much of the early stuff is worthless. But they cannot bring themselves to discard it.

You've reached the point at which you have a full-fledged first draft. If you've decided that the poem demands expression through one of the traditional fixed forms, the form is already developed for you. But you learn that casting your poem into the chosen form isn't quite as easy as pouring gelatin into a mold and letting it set. That form's conventions must be heeded, even if it's your intention to depart from some of those conventions. Of course, there must be enough discernible form elements present that the form is recognizable, however much you may experiment with it. And your experimenting with form must be justified by the demands of the text of your poem, as well as by the coherence and style of expression. If your experimental treatment of form is based on whimsy, it will prove incompatible with the sense and dynamics of the poem.

If the form involves metrics, study the metrical scheme you've chosen, and check your lines against it. Be sure the basic metrical beat is sufficiently present that it makes itself felt even when variant rhythms are employed. On the other hand, avoid the monotonous effect of total reliance on one metrical beat throughout the poem. In your study of poetry, you've observed how the masters varied metrical feet by interposing alternate feet and contrapuntal rhythms. There's nothing quite as sleep provoking as a poem cast entirely in, say, iambic pentameter. Slavishness of this sort always defeats any opportunity for rhythmic intensification, however much the sense may cry out for it.

If rhyme is an element of your poem, remember that you have a long poetic heritage with which to compete. Rhyme couplings that were fresh and interesting a century or two ago are worn and dull today. We joke about *moon/June* and *dead/head*, but the use of trite rhymes is widespread enough that editors' mail baskets are still filled with them. You must find rhymes that are alive and exciting as well as contributing to the sense's progress. As we saw earlier, English has severe limitations in rhyming compared to the Romance languages, which include thousands of words with similar endings. One way to make up for the limitation is to use the near-rhyme techniques we discussed in Chapter 7. Near rhymes often prove more intriguing than direct rhymes because of their greater subtlety. Avoid the excessive use of end rhymes that coincide with grammatical pauses. When possible, use run-on lines so that the rhymes occurring at the ends of lines have less thump, because the thoughts are carried forward to the following lines. If each and every line ends with a rhymed thump, the effect tends to be light and comical, which can be a problem if your theme happens to be a serious one.

Let us say that in the matters of rhythm and rhyme, you want enough regularity so that the poem's form, metrical scheme, and rhyme pattern are apparent to the eye and ear, but you want to include enough variety so that you don't appear sophomoric.

The tonality of your poem may be enhanced by your use of internal rhymes where this approach is appropriate. Again, be careful not to overdo this technique, especially if it also involves alliteration, lest the poem turn into a burlesque of itself. No one element of the poem shall dominate the others.

Although having decided that your poem is going to be a sonnet or a villanelle has made some portions of the task easier, you must still be sure that your work results in a logically developed poem, free of strained effort, wrenched syntax, or artificial manipulation of rhythms and rhymes. This is no simple task, but when you achieve the desired results, you will feel proud of yourself—and justifiably so.

If, on the other hand, you've decided that traditional forms would be unsuited to the expression of your theme, you will have to develop the form along with the poem. The number of options at your disposal range all the way from extensive variations on conventional forms through free verse, projective verse, concrete poetry, and on to some experimental form not yet imagined. At this stage in your development, however, you will discover quite a bit of latitude in free verse. You may be well advised to start there.

Turn your attention to the natural speech rhythms of language. The cadences will evolve from the alternation of accented and unaccented syllables that occur naturally. Your verse paragraph lengths will be determined by subject matter, dependent on sense, much in the manner of prose paragraphs. But the term *free verse* doesn't give you license to ignore the rules of composition. You must still observe the requirements of logical development and unity. Temporal dynamics are as important in free verse as in any other form. And you have the same obligations toward focus, diction, tone, rhythm, pattern, and so on. You fulfill these obligations through the wedded modulations of natural language rhythms and the sense of the words, through the pacing and sounds occurring in your lines, through the paragraphic unities leading to the final integration that defines the form. Since here you don't have measured beats and lines nor a rhyme scheme to provide formal structure, you have to rely on these different aspects to a greater degree than you would otherwise, because without form, you don't have a composition. And a poem *is* a composition.

Look closely at your poem now. If it still seems uneven, ask yourself if you have the proper arrangement. Frequently, a reordering of your verse paragraphs or a new arrangement of some of the lines will solve that problem.

One of the ways a sense of form can be achieved is through the synthesis of pattern. Pattern is an essential part of any successful composition. It may be devised in a number of ways: through the organization of the rhythmic elements the language provides and that you skillfully shape into a figure similar to a musical figure or motif; through variations of pace, rests, and timing; or through combinations of these figures and features. The figure becomes the functioning element of the pattern, to which you can introduce further variations and development so that the pattern fully deserves its functional essentiality. If the length and scope of the poem permit, you can also develop counterfigures and counterpatterns; and this will delight you, because such extensive (but discreet) manipulation, well executed, leads to very sophisticated results. And although you are using pattern in a somewhat freer style than in a form like a rondeau or a tanka, the form will be just as solid. Once again, remember that the pattern treatment must be felt without dominating the other aspects of the poem. Technique in proper balance with sense—always.

Let us turn our attention to some fundamentals that will help us to improve word choice and avoid "padding." Where diction is inappropriate to subject or mood, inflated beyond reason, archaic, or unintentionally nongrammatical, the writer will have to reconsider his or her approach and begin again. Most of the time, the problems aren't quite so severe and can be corrected with a bit of common sense. One such problem arises from too heavy a dependence on modifiers—adjectives and adverbs. Quite often, this is simply a waste of space. What easier method of filling in a missing foot or beat than by sticking in another adjective? The reason behind such subterfuge is often all too apparent. The practice is called "padding the line." And the impression it creates is that the writer hasn't thought enough, in the sense of caring as well as thinking, about the poem to work a bit harder on it. It's a lazy practice. When modifiers are overused, the writer is avoiding the need to search for the precise noun or verb that includes the modifying factor. Padding also indicates a paucity of imagination. Rather than resort to it to fill out your line's meter, consider run-on lines, or pick descriptors that add something vital to the sense without slowing down the progress of the poem.

We aren't saying that one should never use adjectives or adverbs, just that modifiers should be truly functional. How many times have you seen the phrase *the bright sun*? This tells the reader nothing beyond what can be assumed from the noun by itself. The phrase *the clouded sun*, however, does convey an unusual aspect, additional information that is crucial and unable to be anticipated. Such a modifier earns its place in the line—it is a justified descriptor. Which phrase has more emotion and life—*he ran quickly* or *he raced*? You can see that this particular adverb is unnecessary if the poet selects the correct verb.

The test of descriptors is this: Will the reader correctly assume what I am conveying without the aid of the modifier? If the answer is yes, the modifier is redundant. Another test follows: Does the descriptor show an unusual or unexpected quality or condition associated with the noun or verb being described? If the answer to this question is yes, then you are justified in giving space to the modifier. Surely you can recall many examples of redundant modifiers: *the loud crash* (have you ever heard a soft one?), *the wide ocean, a slippery eel, he floundered clumsily* (no one flounders gracefully—the sense of the modifier is inherent in the chosen verb; the writer should permit the verb to do its work), and a laughable redundancy much favored by politicians—*the future lies ahead.*

In the use of comparatives and superlatives, one's excitement may subvert common sense. Terms that do not admit the condition of degree cannot be "more" or "most" anything. Yet the phrase *most unique* is no stranger to the language. Something either is unique, or it isn't, since *unique* means "one of a kind." Nothing can be one of a kind and more or less so. Sometimes this misuse isn't quite as obvious; be careful in using comparative and superlative modifiers—be sure the words to which they are to be applied can accept them.

Always look up definitions of words you're not certain about—and occasionally check yourself on definitions you think you know. This will aid you in avoiding the misuse of several kinds of modifiers. In writing poetry, you have no alternative to the accurate use of all the words destined to find their way into your poem. Prose may escape with less scrutiny applied to it, because the reader reads with a different expectancy from when he or she reads poetry. Prose is read more quickly, primarily for information, and the reader proceeds in a discursive manner. The meaning in the sentence evolves as the mind takes in one word after another. This is true even in fine prose, though not in quite as limited a fashion. The reader does experience the multiple richness of meaning in the prose of a Kafka or Joyce, but the direction of the material is still basically linear. With poetry, one reads more slowly, more thoughtfully, and the expectancy is quite different. The words operate radiationally; the images they create are multilayered. That is why the poet must pay even more attention to connotation, suggestion, association, and innuendo as well as nuance, even the very overtones and harmonics of the words. Every word in a poem has its own rippling effect that must be taken into account when one is assessing the composition's total result. If a poem conveys only information, it has failed. It is merely prose (unimaginative prose at that!) arranged to resemble poetry.

Let's return to your poem. In this, your most recent draft, you feel sure that the focus you intend is there and have organized your material accordingly. You have given thought to the mood, tone, and diction your theme requires. You've developed a form that suits the work; the sequence is logical and well paced; intensification is present; resolution (overt or implied) occurs at the proper points. Modifiers are working for their space in the lines and are not on a "free ride"; thought pauses agree with the sense and with the structural pauses. Pattern serves your purpose effectively. Rhyme, if it is a factor, is composed of couplings that cannot be accused of being trite. Syntax and grammar have been tested. In fact, the poem looks pretty good on the page. It reads well. At last, it is finished. Not quite. The next step is to read the poem aloud. Read it aloud several times. On the page, there may seem nothing wrong with the lines, but when they are given voice, unexpected jarrings can surface. Listen carefully as you speak the poem. Do the lines, rhythms, and sounds feel right?

A good investment is an inexpensive cassette tape recorder. Record your poem-in-progress several times in succession on the tape. Pay close attention as you play it back, noting how the voiced version compares with the typed version before you. On the sheet, jot down your impressions, possible alterations, tightenings, deletions, substitutions. Then set the typed version and the machine aside for a time. Later, while you are occupied with something else, turn on the recorder again. (Your something else should be something with your hands—not trying to compose a new poem!) You want to "overhear" your poem while you're involved in that unrelated activity. You are putting some distance between you and the poem, hearing the poem without specifically listening to it. Through this technique, your critical faculties operate more freely and less defensively. This is an important phase. *The ear must be the final judge.* The "inattentive" hearing enables you to pick up, by way of a peripheral sensitivity, those almost imperceptible trip-ups or bumps in rhythms, those slightly askew sounds. You realize that some line wasn't right to begin with, now that you *hear* it. And how it should be revised becomes clear. An inappropriate image or mangled metaphor will stand out sharply. You know now that a word or phrase that seemed essential is superfluous.

You feel excitement mount. It's time to suspend your unimportant chore and get back to your cassette again. This time, listen with full attention focused on the taped poem. With the benefits of additional insights thus gained, you now know exactly how the poem must be. Startling as it may seem, it is at this stage that quite often, the poet discovers what the poem is really about. And just as often, the author is surprised to find that it's something quite different from what he or she had assumed or intended.

An additional reward of this process is the opportunity it offers poets to evaluate the way they read aloud. Mental notes on pacing, pronunciations, tone, and volume will come in handy when the poet reads that composition before an audience.

You are now ready to type your "final" version. When you've done so, check it over for the usual typographical errors. If you've used normal syntax and punctuation, check that, too. If you've omitted punctuation or used experimental syntax, make sure you don't have lines that may be misread. Many such poems include one or more dangling clauses, because the writer was concerned with the primary use of language and didn't consider potentially alternate interpretations of grammatical structure.

You've reached that stage where you feel fairly confident about your poem. Now for the acid test—bring it to a workshop. If you aren't a member of a good poetry workshop, you are denying yourself some very helpful criticism. Remember how good the poem seemed to you before you read it aloud and heard it on the cassette? And you still found things to improve. Before thinking of submitting the poem to an editor, wouldn't it be a good idea to try it out on a group of your writing peers?

Submerge your ego for a moment and choose a workshop that includes some poets who are more advanced than you are at the present time. You will reap the benefit of their experience. Make enough clear carbons or photocopies of your poem so that each member of the workshop will have one to look at. After you've read your poem aloud, give the others a chance to discuss it. Listen carefully to the responses your poem evokes, the criticism it stimulates. Take notes. When it is your turn to speak, don't be reluctant to ask questions about comments you didn't fully grasp. Later, back in your work place, look at your poem again; examine it with the workshop's comments in mind. It may be that the poem is so well made that there's little more to do. Or it may be that the discussion revealed some serious flaw that had eluded you. It needs another revision in that case. Luckily, you haven't submitted it to any magazine; there's time to correct the flaw.

It's possible the other writers in the group may have misinterpreted your poem or may, in some other way, have been remiss in their comprehension. (It does happen.) You are the one who must judge and evaluate their comments. Accept the criticisms that seem valid to you, and try to revise in that direction. The comments that seem to miss your point, to misunderstand the poem—you can forget. There may have been a comment or two that, though not directly relevant, started you thinking from a new angle, and you may revise not in accordance with such comments but because of them. It also happens that negative comments enable poets to find a defense for their work. Finding reasons for what you've done, and why you've done it, happens frequently in workshop.

In making any major changes or corrections, bear in mind that a change in one place may very well affect other places. After the obvious correction, check its impact on the logic and development with great care. You still want to end up with a cohesive composition, not a patchwork quilt. If necessary, write out the poem entirely each time you engage in a complicated revision. It's more work initially, but you are less likely to have parts of the poem not really working together.

A poem is many things at the same time: an expression of emotion, a felt experience, a performance, and a created illusion. Consider these terms: *expression, emotion, feeling, performance, illusion*—abstractions all. How does one communicate such abstractions through poetry? Concretely, of course. One picks an event, a character, a situation—to *portray* the abstract theme or subject and its subsequent development.

The poem must move the listener/reader in some way. A work of art, to complete its function, must bring about a change in the recipient. When we read *Hamlet*, listen to Beethoven's Ninth Symphony, or view Van Gogh's *Sunflowers*, we are not the same as we were before the experience. This is the function of art. After our exposure to it, we regard ourselves, our relation to humanity, the world, our universe, in a new way. If we are not the beneficiaries of some new insight, some new perspective toward or understanding of the familiar, the work may entertain us; but either we have misunderstood, or the work does not constitute a true work of art. (Even entertainment, when employed as a means and not an end, can achieve the status of art.) But these terms, too, are abstractions. These are the effects that art produces; they do not tell us how art produces them.

Poets, like everyone else, are an impatient lot. They want their works to be published, read, appreciated, understood, and applauded; and they want them to be universally applicable. It is the attempt to reach universality that leads many a novice to generalize indefensibly. Editorializing in a poem on the horrors of war is not as moving as an illustration of such horrors, as we've seen from some of the examples in this book. That's the key: *illustration*. Illustrate your thesis through a specific event, character, situation, or circumstance. Use concrete detail. The reader/listener will identify with your choices and will respond to the emotional impact of your poem if you've done your work skillfully. And the universal will evolve from the specific. If the poem fails to evoke the right response from the reader or listener, no amount of preaching, sermonizing, or editorializing is going to replace the poetry you hoped was in the composition.

You must involve the listener/reader totally, the senses and emotions as well as the intellect. After attracting his or her interest, you must hold it to the very end of your poem. This involvement on the part of your audience is of prime importance, for emotion is one of the major aspects of a poem. Emotion, not bathos. Sentiment, yes—sentimentality, no. Be as cautious in the use of sentiment as you are about the technical elements of your craft. To care about your poem, the audience must be convinced that you, too, have a commitment to that and every poem you write. Your sincerity will be sensed by a perceptive audience as a positive facet of your poem to the degree that you have exercised skill in portraying subject matter.

Feeling, by itself, does not make a poem, of course. There are any number of deeply felt writings masquerading as poems—just as there are any number of faultlessly executed "poems" that evoke little, if any, emotion. Deep feeling and dedication are not enough in themselves. Neither is skill. Both are essential. You generally come equipped with feeling and sensitivity. The skills you acquire show you how to incorporate feeling and sensitivity into your poem. And you can then write as a caring *and* knowledgeable writer. Knowledge affords you necessary control. And control introduces tension and insures the proper exploitation of conflict. It tends toward understatement (an effective tool in poetry). A controlled emotion is more powerful than one that spills itself all over the page.

Include in your poem as much as is essential to it and not a syllable more. But do not be cryptic or obscure deliberately. This approach results in an ersatz depth; it fools no one. Poetry is not a code or puzzle. Keep in mind how Kafka achieved his effects. What could be more elusive than *The Castle*? Yet you can't find a paragraph, a sentence, that isn't concrete and precise. Kafka's artistry lies in the way he created a sense of reality in his amorphous world. We never learn what the castle is, but we recognize it only too well. He touched on universals with which we all identify. The book is a novel; but it is also a poem.

In your own writing, strive to be as clear as your subject permits. But keep in mind the necessary balance. Don't overdo in either direction. The readers are participants in the experience of the poem, too—active participants. Let them do their own interpreting. Don't explain in succeeding phrases, however subtly, the images they've just read. Let the images do their work. Let the readers draw their own conclusions. Don't tie up the end of your poem too neatly for them. You have charted the direction you want interpretation to take by the manner of your portrayal, by the way you gain sympathy for one character or point of view and antipathy toward another; but the readers will feel they have truly participated. Chances are that they will remember your poem.

Sometimes facts are enough to serve your poem's theme. At other times, you will have to fictionalize to illustrate truth. The truth that applies here is the truth residing in the poem itself. Whether or not such truth coincides with factual or abstract truth is, for our present purpose, of no consequence. It's artistic integrity we're after here—the paradox of truth being revealed through illusion.

You deal in specifics and stay far from abstractions. You don't *talk* about sanity, motherhood, war, poverty. You develop poems that dramatize your position or attitude concerning any theme. You recall, invent, construct whatever is necessary to play out your condensed scene. You create the situation or event and develop it toward its climax with restraint and control. And you deal with real things—cars, rocks, chairs, pimples, bananas, roofs, refrigerators. Don't elevate your diction beyond what your subject matter will support, but don't fall short of the poem's diction demands, either. Be honest in your verbal expression. And use the simplest, the clearest, the least fancy words that will do the job. Poetry is not beautiful language but language beautifully employed.

The tension in your poem derives from the conflicts of your created situation, event, whatever device you've chosen for your vehicle; from the rhythmic syncopations you introduce; and from the compression of your textual treatment. The dynamics evolve from your progressions, pacing, pattern development, and intensification. Tone and mood come from your word meanings, style of diction, assonance, and dissonance. One mentions these things glibly, but making them function correctly takes care and sensitivity.

Remember that all these technical considerations must never intrude in the final illusion the poem creates. The structural elements in any work of art (including your poem) are like the bones in your body. They make possible the form and the variations in design. They provide essential support. But they themselves do not show. You feel their presence, their strength. You do not need to see them. You *know* they are there. So must the structure of your composition not dominate the total effect.

9. The Nurturing

Beginners frequently ask how they should schedule their work time. Since different methods suit different temperaments, there is no single answer one can give. Some writers find the discipline of a specific number of hours per day at a set time to be most productive. To others, this represents "forced labor"; they prefer to work as opportunity and mood dictate. Most successful poets depend on some compromise between these extremes.

However one schedules, a great deal of the time is spent on really working rather than sitting there daydreaming and waiting for inspiration to touch one's shoulder with its magic wand. If you're not engaged in developing a new poem, you should be busy with revisions, with preparing material for submission, with bringing your control records up to date, or with whatever else is connected with your writing efforts. The point is that you must develop the attitudes of a professional writer, that you involve yourself in activity related to writing as much as time allows. You don't want to allow yourself to become a sometimes writer, one who occasionally dashes off a poem and then ignores the whole business for months. But you will have to find your own best working routine. Quite

226

often, those more pedestrian tasks like reviewing the poems in your files will act as triggers, and you may very well find yourself sailing into a new poem as a result.

As to working environment, the place should afford privacy and quiet. A study, naturally, is the ideal solution. If that's not feasible, find a separate corner, one that you can make your own, where you won't be disturbed or disturb anyone else. If absolute privacy is impossible, learn to minimize or "tune out" distractions as much as possible.

Some poets write out one or two versions of their new poem in longhand first, postponing the use of the typewriter to when they feel they have some grasp of the potential form or direction of the new work. Others work directly at the machine. Again, this will depend on individual temperament.

As far as stimulants are concerned, there are writers who cannot function without the reinforcement of cigarettes and/or coffee. In fact, this seems to have become the characteristic stereotype in films about writers. Other drugs and liquor distort perception and disarm the critical faculty. More aesthetic stimulants vary from a cat purring in one's lap to apples gently rotting in one's desk drawer (Schiller's favorite). A good poetry workshop session sends you back to work recharged and eager, and this may be the most productive stimulant of all.

Writers dread the onset of "writer's block," a time when one finds it impossible to write anything. Your first few experiences with this phenomenon are pretty frightening. You feel as if you've written yourself out, that there's nothing left inside you to express, that the means of expression have escaped you forever. Later you learn that such dry spells come to an end, and you are able to weather them a bit better. Sometimes a block provides an unconscious rest between one stage of your writing and another, enabling you to store material for the next onrush of creativity while preparing you for the necessary gear shifting. But no matter what its unconscious legitimacy, writer's block is always frustrating. There you are, idle, when there's something you should be doing. A sense of guilt cloaks itself about you.

Revising, preparing manuscripts for submission, and the like may very well unblock the dam again, or reading other poets' works. And there are other means that can help defeat the blankness of writer's block. I have at times recommended these to various students.

1. Without any prior thought, write down the first word that comes into your mind. Then free associate, putting down words as they occur to you. After three or four minutes, consider the words you have written as a group. Examine the linkage: the words may be related in theme, tone, or through definitions. Repeat the process two or three more times. Each time, your random thinking is being influenced to some degree by your earlier attempts. If this turns out to be a technique that will work for you, you should—by the third or fourth attempt—begin to see some potential for a poem.

Take the key words in this rather elusive combination. Write a few lines suggested by each of these key words. Expand each group of lines to at least a quatrain without diluting the initial impact of each word. You may not have a poem at this point, but you will have developed a brief body of text from which a poem may be possible. The real intent is to get you writing again, even if you have to discard the first half-dozen versions of anything that results. (If this technique and those that follow appear contrived, remember that they are not designed to produce poems; their function is to simulate the production of poems in order to break through the writer's block.)

2. Leaf through the dictionary, glancing casually at the words at the top of a page here and there. If your attention is attracted—however slightly—to a particular word, stop and read the entire definition of that word. List each noun, verb, adjective, adverb, and so on, including synonyms and antonyms used in the dictionary entry. On a second sheet of paper, copy out the definition entry. Take one of the words on your list, and look that up also. From this second definition entry, add the nouns, etc., to the list on your first sheet; on the other sheet, copy out this definition entry. Repeat the process for at least another word or two on your list, each time copying out the entry involved.

Now read all the entries you've copied from the dictionary

as if they made up the unified exposition of a subject. Some poem approaches to this should occur to you at this time. Should you become intrigued by the subject matter you've developed, as sometimes happens, you may want to proceed through more words on your list with the same technique; and it may happen that a poem comes into being almost of its own accord. But just to break the block, three or four words from the list should be sufficient.

3. While you're feeling blocked, you assume it's impossible to write anything meaningful, that you probably never will again. The secret here is *not* to try to write anything meaningful but just to start writing. Don't think of poetry. Don't worry about sense, logic, or continuity. Just write—anything—whatever occurs to you, even if it seems junk or gibberish. Write; let the words flow without control or organization. If the block is too inhibiting to allow your subconscious to spew forth wantonly, invent shopping lists, menus, programs for parties, meeting agenda, anything at all. But invent. Don't copy. Don't "remember." Create even the most unlikely lists imaginable. When you begin to sense a loosening up and some coherence in your writing, abandon your "starters," and write down whatever flits through your mind. Very likely, it will be weak writing at first. No matter. Your waste basket isn't far. What you're doing is clearing away the dross to get at the molten ore.

The material now surfacing is developing a contour, is acquiring some kind of shape and cohesiveness. A logic is appearing in the sequence of the material. At last you detect the presence of patterns—rhythmic patterns, sound patterns, or sense patterns. Go on until you reach a natural stopping place. Now return to the point where the writing began truly to fit together. Concentrate on these last few pages. There's the strong possibility that you will work with the material that came to you through this maneuver. Chances are, it involves something you had mixed feelings about expressing. Seeing part of it on paper somehow lessens the reservations you felt about it, and you now dare to work on the evolving poem.

4. Pick up a favorite object, one you've never written about, and handle it. Study it; understand its form and substance, its

texture, all its features. Write down your feelings and impressions triggered by the object. To your surprise, you'll realize abruptly that you've forgotten about your writer's block.

5. Don't try to write. Refuse to write. Sit down (better yet, lie down), and let your mind wander. Meditate. Daydream. Fantasize. Let a playlet unfold in your mind. Shouldn't you be recording this experience?

Or shut your eyes and imagine pictures, colors, abstract designs, or any combination of these on the insides of your eyelids. Watch the elements form themselves, change shape, approach, and retreat. Note the weird modulations in color and tone. What do such images stir in you? Capture those feelings on paper. Is this material transformable into poetry?

6. Automatic writing is rather bizarre, but it has worked for this author, so it's included in the event that some writer needs just such a self-hypnotizing method to break out of a block. Use two simple props: a new pad of lined paper and a fresh no. 2 pencil with a point as sharp as the point of a needle. The writing hand holds the pencil and is poised over the pad. Stare at the sheet. Your other arm is down by your side. Sit in your chair without strain of any sort. Think of nothing. Become completely open and nondirectional. Your hand will start to feel a bit heavy and will come to rest on the pad. The tip of the pencil is very close to the paper without any awareness on your part as to when this sudden proximity occurred. You're not in a trance state, but it's something very like that. Do nothing. Wait. Concentrate on the tip of the pencil. It is as though the pencil is in someone else's hand. Your mind is as clear of thoughts as you can make it. The pencil's point is drawn to the top line of the sheet. Don't hurry it, and don't slow it down. Let it move of its own accord. Point and paper meet. A word forms. Force yourself to refute the word, not to become part of the process prematurely. A second word follows the first, and a third. Before the pencil has put down a dozen words, the poem is in motion.

Many students think of "assignment poems" as no more

than exercises. Even if they are only that, the discipline and insight you derive from doing them are well worth the effort. Many assignment poems by students have gone on to be published, so you may realize some fringe benefits you did not anticipate. You may also discover in yourself a heretofore unknown affinity for some particular form.

Besides providing good training, assignments open doors for many writers, introducing them to different poetry concepts and varied approaches they might otherwise not have considered.

Included are the usual traditional forms assignments, of course. Refer to the fourth chapter ("Bone and Muscle"). Write one or two poems in each of the forms described. Study the structure of these forms, and give your attention to adapting suitable ones to your themes and subject matter. The obligation to work within the prescribed limits of a fixed form forces one, as Hercule Poirot would say, "to use the little grey cells." You are encouraged to try these forms often. They are your scales and arpeggios. You are interested in developing your skills and in maintaining them in sharp working order, and that requires practice. Each progressive attempt increases your competence.

In addition to the traditional forms, the following assignments, which I have used in my own workshops, have proved to be provocative and useful as well as fun. They're listed here as a matter of interest but also as a challenge. Try them; you may enjoy the experience and learn something.

WORD ASSIGNMENTS

1. The "makeshift" poem. A nine-line poem in which each line is limited to five letters, one of which comes from the word *makeshift*. The five letters may make up one word or may be a combination of short words. Disregard normal spacing between words. The poem must make syntactical and textual sense. Here's the skeleton you will flesh:

```
M _ _ _ _ _
 _ a _ _ _ _
  _ _ k _ _ _
   _ _ _ e _ _
    _ _ _ _ s _
     _ _ _ _ h _
      _ _ i _ _
       _ f _ _ _ _
        t _ _ _ _
```

232

Working with the "Makeshift" construction and constructions similar to it will offer you opportunities for developing control over—and economy in the use of—language. Appreciate fully the space allotted, and take maximum advantage of it.

Actually, there's nothing sacred about the "starter" word *makeshift*. You might want to try the exercise using your name as the starter word, or any proper noun, some favorite word, or a brief phrase. You might also progress to the use of two or more short words producing tension in the same construction to make matters more difficult. Create your own patterns and designs. Do several of these poems. You are limited only by the limits of your own imagination and fancy. Remember, there's no law against having fun with poetry while you're developing your skills, so invent and enjoy.

Whatever the words you choose and the structures you design may be, keep in mind the basic guidelines for this assignment: normal spacing between words is not to be counted while the poem is being created, and the final result must make syntactical and textual sense. When the poem is completed, the starter word (or words) should be so well submerged inside the poem that the secret of your construction and process will not easily be revealed.

Once the poem's done, then reintroduce normal spacing between words. Here's an example by John Reed that appeared in *Pyramid* #10 (1970):

The Zamosc Rebbetzin's Birthday

My old
dance
takes
speed,
leaps
in the
faith
of the
Torah.

2. In the following nine-line poem assignment, use one of the

listed words in the order given in each line; use each of these words only once in the poem. Use any form you like, but include at least three feet or six syllables in any one line. The words: *love, recesses, bright, dark, musky, body, go, hermit, world.* (No examples will be given for this and most of the following assignments, so that your own efforts won't be influenced.)

3. Write a poem of twenty-four lines. Use no title and no true end rhymes. Either metrical measure or free verse will do. Each line must include only one of the words listed below. The chosen word may be placed anywhere in the line but can be used only once in the poem. You are at liberty to use either the noun or the verb sense of each word. The alphabetical order in which the words are listed is only for convenience. Make your own arrangement. The words: *aim, bait, balance, bear, dance, end, headline, howl, jump, light, mind, mother, move, powder, quiet, rack, service, sleep, snake, study, trip, worry, yawn, zero.*

SUBJECT ASSIGNMENTS

4. Write a poem no longer than twenty lines with an alternating stress pattern of three and five to the lines: line 1, three stresses; line 2, five stresses; line 3, three stresses; line 4, five stresses; and so on. Your subject—trying unsuccessfully to reach someone by telephone. The reason for the failure, if you decide to include it, may be expressed only through implication. The emotional reaction of the caller should be part of the poem.

5. Write an "anger" poem in two stanzas or verse paragraphs. In the first section, maintain control over the anger; in the second section, lose that control. In this assignment, do not be timid about typographic innovation if it is appropriate to your poem's development and expression.

6. Open the telephone directory at random. Without focusing on the names, poise a finger over the left column on the page. Close your eyes and touch the page. Open your eyes, and study the name just above your finger. (If by some coincidence you've picked the name of someone you know, turn to another page and go through the procedure again.) Think about the person represented by the name. Write a thirty-two-line poem fictionally developing the character suggested by the telephone-book name. Your poem should convey to the reader a sense of the character's history and lifestyle and his or her attitudes, perferences, biases, personality, and so forth.

7. Write a short poem (eight or ten lines) expressing who you are without revealing your age, sex, nationality or race, appearance, occupation, marital status, family details, or hobbies.

8. Write a poem of fourteen lines about fire. Don't use the words *fire* or *burn* or any words using those words as syllables *(burning, firemen)*. The value of subject assignments with word-use restrictions is the responsibility they place on the writer to think of imaginative word choices, the precision and accuracy of such choices, and alternate ways of illustrating what needs to be shown.

9. Review a group of your latest poems. Are there too many "I" poems? Have you concentrated almost exclusively on one particular mood? Assign yourself a series of poems of other personae in varying moods. A group of poems by any one writer should have balance and some mood relief. However fine each of the poems may be, by the bookload they will—if they are perpetually pessimistic—depress and strain the sympathy of the reader; if they are overly optimistic again and again, they will puncture the credence of the reader. Remember that reality has many faces and many moods.

10. If you notice, in reviewing your poems, that they tend to deal primarily with one specific theme or subject (nature and natural detail), write several poems that deal with other themes or subjects. (We sometimes fall into these ways without

realizing it. Looking for it awakens us to the fact.) Write poems about computers, skyscrapers, typewriters, policemen; your choices are many. Variety is as rewarding in the choice of subject matter as it is in tone and diction. Poets should not unconsciously or consciously limit their options unless they're trying to develop a particular theme through a series of poems.

VISUAL AND EXPERIMENTAL

11. Study several concrete poems until you get the feel of the genre. Then write a concrete poem, making sure that technique and visual arrangement reinforce your theme.

12. Study the requirements of projective verse. Write a poem in this style. Give thought to the energy, breathing, kinetics, and lines of force of your text. Treat the page as a musical score; your arrangement is direction for the poem's comprehension and voicing.

IDEA PROVOKERS

13. Make posters (or use large sheets of paper) on which are printed single words in large letters. Vary the size and position of the word. You can also vary ink color. Tack the posters on the walls around your work place. Study the words for several minutes; then compose poems suggested by one or more of the words. Make your own list. Here's one list I have assigned: *helmet, rope, crabgrass, beat, lace, flute, field, rabbit, six-gun, Spanish, grapefruit, spooky, nine, robot, bottles.*

14. Have a tray in the center of the table on which are a variety of small objects. Study the objects; pick them up, and feel them. Select one. Place the object on the desk or table so that you can handle it frequently during the writing of your poem. The poem should reflect your impressions about the object's substance, texture, vibrations, and so on. A variation

that's pleasant: Create a story around the object in the form of a short poem. (This assignment works very well with a workshop group, too.)

15. Using a tray similar to that for Assignment 14, improvise a poem orally into your cassette tape recorder. (This assignment also is an enjoyable challenge with a group. Here is one the author improvised. Someone in the group took the time to write it down as it was spoken.)

> *The Memory Bottle*
>
> small enough to hold in a purse or the palm of your hand
> this darkly-ancient bottle held against the light
> had I been there while it was being cased in silver
> I would have marvelled at the artisan's caprice
> to fashion so intensely a simple holder for perfume
> some after-lover would gift with passioned promises of faith
>
> you find attraction in the drop of pale blood on the cap
> and in the bottle's amber lightness a weapon
> small enough to fit as curse in the palm of a hand
> extending gracefully to drain the Italian drop of poison
> into the truthless glass behind a lover's back
> and you watch him lift the glass to his own unfutured death

16. Here's one specifically designed to be used by a group. On the table is a bowl with several small pieces of folded paper in it. Each piece of paper contains one word. Every writer in the group selects two pieces of paper without looking at the words. Once everyone has his or her words, the writers look at their words and write a poem that includes the sense of both words. How well the writers bring together two disparate ideas and form them into poems is the test of this procedure. The poets themselves may determine the words and place them in the bowl; but if someone draws any of his or her own words, they must be returned to the bowl, and the poet draws again. It's wise to include extra words in the bowl, so that choices will be more random.

238 Expression

17. Write a nonsense poem that illustrates two moods in sequence without indicating the moods involved. The moods may be associated with a place or event. Instead of words, use syllables and arbitrary combinations of letters that you feel musically express the moods you've chosen. Some letter combinations or syllables will sound harsh or discordant; others will be smooth and harmonious. Concentrate on your first mood in the first eight or nine lines; then modulate to your second mood. Be sure there's sufficient contrast between the two moods and that this contrast is an integral part of the poem. You will learn a great deal about the *sounds* of language from this experiment, and you will never be able to ignore that knowledge when you select the right words for future poems. Lewis Carroll's "Jabberwocky" demonstrates the technique.

18. This derives partly from the previous experimental assignment and is partly a subject assignment. Write a poem that will emphasize a landscape mood without using the words *sad, happy, peaceful, disturbing, shadow, dark, light,* any "color" word, or any compound word of which these words would form syllables. The poem may be in any style, form, or length.

These assignments have proven both instructive and fun. It isn't necessary to solve all of life's major problems in every poem. Relax now and then, and simply enjoy the experience of flirting with language, of teasing it into compliance. Treat language as a lover, and you will find language loving you back. Be neither a Pollyanna nor a Jeremiah. The artist is a realist who enjoys fantasy without confusing it with truth, reflecting on life as it is, as it might be, and expressing feelings about it—without sermonizing—and moving us to consider our own situations and how we may better cope with them.

In writing your poems, treat your themes and subject matter realistically and honestly. Don't strive for startling effects, but allow effectiveness to evolve as a natural consequence of your poem. Everything in a poem must belong, must spring from it at the same time as being absorbed by it.

Whatever mode of expression you decide on, make sure it

is in accord with the demands of your subject. Content needs form, and form needs content. The two are inseparable. Divided, each has little merit; together, they are powerful. All the other matters of technique we've discussed have a common goal: to insure this true marriage between content and form. The parts of a good poem are tightly spliced; you cannot pull out one strand without the whole composition coming apart.

After working so hard, why not throw caution to the winds and take some liberties with your writing? Experimentation is "new juice." It's a blood transfusion that all art needs now and then, so that it will not atrophy. Experimentation provides a body of achievement that precedes the formulation of new standards and criteria. As life around us continually undergoes change, so must poetry if it is to remain relevent. Experiment with form, with a wider variety of themes, with new terminology provided by our flourishing science and technologies, with new uses of syntax, grammar, and punctuation. The typewriter is a marvelous machine; it permits you to establish unusual margins and text spacings in a tremendously flexible way. Be daring.

Leave yourself open to new ideas. Be imaginative always. In your wildest experiments, in your playing and games, may germinate the seed of something on which you can impose control and turn into true poetry. What seems not to work can always be discarded. You may be pleasantly surprised at the results of your playing with language and form. And you'll be having a great deal of fun.

Well, you've acquired your offspring—your poems. You've nurtured them through their growing-up process, helped them through their crises of change until they're ready to stand on their own. You will still keep an eye on them as they season. Every few months, you will give them a brief review to see if everything about them is still as it should be. Now we move on to the weaning of your offspring—exposing the poems to the world of readings and publication.

10. The Weaning

Once poems are written to your satisfaction, it's necessary to think about what their fate is to be. Shall you try submitting them to magazines? Shall you, instead, just let them accumulate until you have enough for a small volume? Or shall you keep them in your files and perhaps never show them to anyone? That last proposition isn't very reasonable, but there are poets who've done exactly that. We know about more than one great poet whose work was brought to light by someone through a chance occurrence; fortunately, these great poets are now part of our poetic heritage. But suppose those particular "discoverers" hadn't happened along when they did or weren't sufficiently interested? And how many other poets are there we've never enjoyed because after they were gone, no one discovered their hidden poems? If you've had the daring to write, then have the confidence to risk exposing your work to readers. A poem, any work of art, hasn't completed its life cycle until it's found its audience.

If you are or have been a member of a writing class or workshop, chances are that you've overcome by now any reservations about having others see your work and that you will seek outlets for publication.

Reading your poems in public is a good way to start testing them. You'll have an audience reaction to guide you on their effectiveness, and you'll learn a great deal about their sonority and pacing from the actual process of reading aloud. How do you get an audience? You can participate in open readings, readings in which poets are invited to come and read some of their work. Metropolitan areas offer several opportunities for this. Check the newspapers in your area, especially the weekly "subculture" ones, for listing of poetry readings. Some listings are merely announcements that a certain poet is scheduled to read. But there are others that feature open readings, and that's where you can begin. Open readings are generally sponsored by adult education centers, the various Y's, university and college humanities or writing divisions, state poetry associations, and various private poetry groups. You will probably decide simply to observe the first time or two you drop in on one of these, but put a few poems in your pocket just in case you change your mind when you see how relaxed and easy it is.

As a rule, reading your poems in public gets less frightening each time you do it. There's nothing unique about stage fright; it's a common trauma that most performers go through. Some retain a touch of it each time they go on, but it lasts only a minute or two, so there's nothing to worry about. Usually the audience has no idea that your knees are shaking, especially if you are behind a podium. Brazen it through; once into your poems, you'll forget all about being scared. It *is* a special "high" to read before an audience, and you will probably become an addict of the practice after your "baptism of fire."

Observe the time allotted each poet in open readings. The time usually runs from five to ten minutes, depending how many poets offer to read. Don't let yourself exceed your time by more than a minute at most; better yet, stop just short of the limit. Most one-page poems take a minute or so to read, so you'll have the opportunity to show a small sample of what you can do—and to get some reading experience. Observe the rules, and you'll be remembered with favor and will very likely be invited to other readings.

Reading experience coupled with some good publication

credits (appearing in some of the better journals) may begin to earn you a following. If things work out well, you'll find you're being invited to participate in readings involving four, three, or even two poets. This means your name will be programmed for the event. Again, keep within the bounds of the time afforded you. If there are only two people reading, keep your share to no more than a half hour—twenty-five minutes is better. A program with four readers normally affords each poet fifteen minutes. When you've attained enough prominence (or notoriety), you may be asked to "solo"; the wisest decision you can make in such an event is to limit your solo reading to forty-five minutes.

Why the emphasis on time? The attention span of audiences at poetry readings seldom extends beyond an hour. The group you've been holding in the palm of your hand for three quarters of an hour will now begin to get restless; a muffled cough to the left, some shuffling of feet to the right, squirming in chairs at the rear, and near the door some people are trying to make unnoticed exits. Don't tax your audience beyond its tolerance point. And don't save your longest poem for last; at least, don't announce to a tiring audience, "My final selection is a bit long—actually it has ten sections." Be clever; leave your listeners wishing for more, and you'll see them again when you next read.

You may feel more comfortable offering some light introductory material for each poem; or you may prefer simply to read the poems, allowing sufficient time between them to let your listeners shift their emotional attention from one poem to the other. It depends on your temperament; whichever procedure feels comfortable to you is the one you should follow.

If you do decide to say a few things along with the poems, it's okay to mention how the idea came, what the circumstances were surrounding the poem, or where the poem was first published. But under no conditions should you explain the poem itself to your audience. Either you've done it in the poem or you should leave that poem out of your reading. You may decide to skip poems you've included in planning for the reading because you sense a particular type of audience, and you just know a certain poem "won't go." That's fine; you're sensing the audience and picking up guiding vibrations. You can also mention that some poem you're about to read was requested by so-and-so, if it was. Audiences seem to enjoy that personal touch.

Never apologize for a poem you are about to read or have just read. If you feel that way, you shouldn't have included it; if you've already read it, let it go, and proceed to the next. Apologies of that sort embarrass the listeners and are the stamp of the amateur; frequently, it's an attempt at mock modesty and turns into mockery of the audience. Respect your audience. They have come to listen to you. They start out rooting for you, albeit silently. When an audience turns away from a poet, it is usually the poet's fault.

Pace yourself during the reading. (Your earlier practice with the tape cassette will stand you in good stead now.) And pace yourself within the poems, too. Poetry is heavy stuff. Listeners need time to absorb, especially since they won't have printed versions to look at (and they shouldn't during a reading—the rustling of pages is distracting and a perfect mood breaker) and are trying to understand your poems by listening to you. Don't rush and don't drag beyond the sense of the words and lines. Fit the reading to the text and mood. Don't read woodenly, and don't play Barrymore. And avoid mumbling or shouting. Like it or not, when you're reading poetry to an audience, you are onstage. Every letter must be heard; the music must sing out—but all in proper balance with the sense. Remember Hamlet's advice to the players. Your audience expects the reading to be an event. Don't disappoint them.

You've decided not to let your poems gather dust in your files. How does one send to a publication? The preparation of your manuscripts is an important matter. The initial impression your poems make on editors may be the factor that encourages them to read the poems or to drop them gingerly into the "return" basket. If the sheets an editor is holding are yellow from age or gray from handling, lined with several sets of creases, have corners turned down or torn off, are splotched with corrections or—worse—rings from coffee cups, he or she won't want anything to do with them for any longer than is necessary. If writers don't have enough respect for their own work to offer it in a presentable manner, they have no right to expect an editor to show the work any respect either. Make sure your manuscript sheets are clean and neatly typed. Keep inked corrections to a minimum. Better yet, retype the poem; if it's a short one, it doesn't take long to make a fresh copy.

Roughly center each poem on its page. In the upper left corner of the page, put your name and address. If your poem exceeds a page in length, leave about an inch margin at the bottom, and continue the poem on the next page, even if it's only another two or three lines. You don't want the poems to look crowded. For all but the most traditional and old-fashioned magazines, it's perfectly acceptable to single-space your poems. For those poems that require more than one page, you need put only your last name, the title (or last word of the title if it's a long one), and the page number at the top of the second page. Then double- or triple-space down, and continue your poem. Indicate at the bottom of the previous sheet or at the top of the second one whether the page break coincides with a poem break: "no stanza break" or "stanza break." This is usually put in parentheses.

If you feel you can't live without adding footnotes to your poems, be sure you keep those to the barest minimum. They won't impress editors with your literary background; they'll only annoy them, if anything. Save that practice for the two or three times in your poetic life when they will be absolutely essential.

Proofread carefully (two or three times) before sending out your poems. And keep a true copy (carbon or photocopy) of every poem you mail. Should some question reach you from an interested editor, don't embarrass yourself by not having a copy to which to refer. Also, material does get lost. You'll feel less depressed if you've kept copies.

Okay, you've got your poems neatly typed and presentable. How many do you send? Three to five is the average; four is ideal. Poets who send only one poem at a time give the impression of being nonprofessional. However earthshaking the poem may appear to the writer, it's not true that the world has been holding its breath in anticipation. There's time to assemble two or three companion poems with your latest opus.

Besides, it's a waste of postage to send a sole effort. On the other hand, don't send your complete output; you'll scare editors right out of their seats. You want them to read what you send, not keep pushing it aside for when they're less busy. Editors are never less busy. Even eight or ten poems are too many for an initial submission. Send the others to other journals unless the market listing you've consulted indicates that a particular editor likes to look at a certain number of poems per submission. Editors' policies always override general practice.

Do you include a cover letter?—only if what you would say has significance in context. Should you have solid credits to report or your second volume has just been published—yes, editors would be interested to know that. Otherwise, your cover letter will be their first awareness of your fondness for redundancy. "Enclosed are four poems for your consideration" (many letters indeed say no more) tells editors that they aren't able to figure out why you sent them the poems, that they can't count, and that they don't know what they're supposed to do with them.

Once an editor opens the correspondence channel, that's another matter. If, instead of a standard printed rejection, you receive a note with the return of your poems saying something like: "We especially liked the Empire poem, the one with the huge gorilla and the half-naked girl, but it's too long for our magazine. Do try us again with something shorter, . . . " send that editor some more poems within a couple of weeks—you don't want to be forgotten. This time it's wise to include a note saying that you appreciate the editor's earlier interest in the poem (name it; editors tend to recall poems better than names of unknowns) and that you hope something in this new group will be better suited to the journal's needs. Don't write a long letter telling an editor all about yourself, your work, aspirations, and marital status. Editors who want more information about you will ask. All they care about at this time are your poems, and that should please you.

The worst of cover letters are those in which the poet carefully and at great length explains the poems. Don't explain. The poems should do their own work, or else they aren't any good. And avoid writing "end," "finis" or "—30—" at the end of your poems. Any editor who isn't sure when the poems end isn't going to take them anyway.

When submitting poems to a journal (without being solicited by the editor to do so), always—repeat, *always*—enclose an SASE (self-addressed stamped envelope) of the same size as the one in which you mail the poems out. If you want to prod an editor to violence, just send about twenty-five poems, flat, in a large manila envelope; and for the SASE, enclose a 3½ by 6½ inch white envelope. (It happens more often than you might think.) The editor's not going to spend time reading your poems; he or she is going to spend it vengefully folding and refolding your masterpieces into an unholy blob and stuffing them into that tiny envelope. Another cardinal sin is to send an envelope for return addressed to yourself but without postage. An editor may return your material the first time that happens, but don't count on it happening again. *Your* name will be remembered. Of course, if you don't send any SASE at all, your poems are likely to end up in the circular file. If this seems harsh treatment, think of the editors' side of it. They receive hundreds of poems every week on which they have to make some kind of decision. They're paid to be editors—not to fold, affix stamps, and the like. And there's no provision in the budget for returning manuscripts at the journal's expense.

The envelope best suited for sending out your four poems is a no. 10 white, business-size envelope. These measure about 4¼ × 9½ inches and are suitable to send to the *Atlantic* as well as the twelve-page mimeo publication of a small press. The SASE should have your name and address typed on it and *sufficient* postage pasted to it. If the magazine has to pay postage due, you're not making friends at that office. You don't need fancy paper, rag content, or anything. Plain white smooth-surfaced typing paper is fine. Editors don't like onionskin or that rough-textured stuff that strikes up a band when you handle it. Fold your little group of poems in thirds (not singly—as a group), and they'll fit nicely in the envelope. Fold the SASE in thirds also, and put that in. Ordinarily, four poems and an SASE will travel the postal system on one first-class stamp, not counting the stamp on your SASE, of course.

Whenever possible, address your poems to an editor by name. Editors' names appear in the issues of the journal you should have studied. Or they may be found along with the magazine listing in market lists.

One of the most important marketing techniques you can undertake is to study some issues of the journals in which you're interested in seeing your poems appear. This may sound so basic it shouldn't need to be said, but it's amazing how much material gets sent to markets that have absolutely no interest in or use for it. Too often, writers send off material without ever having seen an issue of the periodical and lacking any notion of what the journal's policies, audience, limits, or special emphasis might be. Don't be one of those writers; it's a waste of money, effort, and time.

Keep a record of what you send where and the date. Anything that helps you to keep track will do. Most writers prefer to create a 3- by 5-inch card file alphabetized by poem title. On each card is the title of the poem, the journal to which it was sent, the date sent, and the result of the submission: rejected, accepted, and—finally—printed. (Upon publication, enter issue number and date.) Some poets like to include the date the poem was written, details of its creation, information on readings at which it was read, and so forth. Whatever makes you happy is fine. Keep in mind that your record file is a tool to serve you. Don't become the slave of your tool. One other bit of record keeping may prove very worthwhile for you. In a small looseleaf notebook (for ease in interfiling), put the names of the periodicals, one to a page, at the tops of the pages in alphabetical order by title. Under each magazine title, list the poems sent and when they were sent. This enables you to determine at a glance whether you've sent a particular poem to that journal before, what sort of response certain poems elicited, and—from those responses and the poems marked "accepted"—the kinds of poems to which that editor is partial. Understanding an editor's preferences gives you an edge.

You've sent your first batch of poems off, and two days later you begin to watch the mailbox. A waste of time—don't be impatient. Be busy instead. Assemble other poems; send those to other magazine editors. Get your material in circulation, and keep it moving. You're going to get rejections—lots of them. Rejections will always outnumber acceptances. Don't let the return of your poems dishearten you. Keep them moving on to other editors. When material comes back, look it over, especially if some kind editor has offered a bit of free criticism. You may want to take the suggestion. Revise, if that's the case. If not, are the poems still presentable enough? Okay, send them out again. Don't let yourself be discouraged. As long as your confidence in the poems is solid, keep trying. For every good poem, there is a receptive editor. You just have to make the connection between them. And every time you do, you'll add another poem to your list of acceptances.

After you've waited two weeks, don't dash off a status query. Editors don't want to hold onto material any longer than necessary; it clutters their desks. Give them an opportunity to think about your poems. It may be a good sign if you don't hear right away; they may be considering some of your material. Or they may be holding it as "possible" to discuss at the next editorial meeting if an editorial board is involved. (Some disgruntled poets claim that a few of the national magazines have a person right in the post office to rush poems back to submitters before the things ever reach an editor's desk. That's an exaggeration, of course, but editors who know they're not going to accept certain material generally shoot it right back to the writer.)

If, however, you haven't heard a word for six weeks or so (ten to twelve weeks for little magazines), then you are entitled to submit a status query. Technically, since you did include an SASE with your submission, a postal card is enough. But if you want to ensure a quick reply, it's wiser to send a note and include another SASE. Your query should refer to the poems by title and include the date sent. Point out that an SASE was included. The tone of your query should *not* be anything like this: "Look here, jackass, you've had the damn poems for three months. How the hell long do you need to make up your mind?" Always assume the delay is not the editor's fault. You pin the blame on that great national villain, the U.S. Postal Service. Your query will state that since you've heard nothing to date, you are concerned that your poems may have been lost in the mail and never reached the editor. If, however, the delay is because the editor is still considering the material, then he or she should please take all the time necessary. But you'd appreciate a word as to the status of the poems via the SASE provided with the query. Thank editors for their courteous attention. This approach invariably gets a speedy reply.

Following these guidelines enables you to behave like a professional in a highly competitive field. The easier you make your system of working these things out, the better you'll enjoy the whole affair.

Don't send the same poems to more than one journal at the same time. Some periodicals' policies permit "multiple submissions"; but the practice does lead to complications, and editors really don't favor it. It's best to avoid doing it.

Some editors won't mind clear photocopies in place of originals, whereas others insist on originals only. You'll have to check market lists to learn which do what. When in doubt, use originals. No editor will accept carbons, which smudge badly. Not only are they difficult to read, but an editor with carbon-stained fingers isn't going to think kindly toward you.

You should always receive some form of compensation for any poems of yours that are published. It may be a few dollars, a couple of copies, a free subscription, or any combination of these. This establishes you as a professional and shows that the publisher values your work.

Of your list of magazine markets, cull out any that offer no payment at all (and that know you'll want to buy a few copies to impress your friends), those that insist you subscribe before they'll accept your material or print it, and those that ask you to help defray the expenses of publication. Their interest is in your money—not your poems. These are examples of literary rip-offs. No writer should ever have to pay for having work published in any magazine or anthology. If editors and publishers really believe your work deserves publication and accept it, they expect to stand the expense of printing it.

In compiling your list of periodicals, don't ignore the denominational magazines, periodicals with an ethnic emphasis, specialty magazines and house organs (company magazines), and newspapers that feature poetry sections.

Beware of the anthology racket and the we'll-set-your-poem-to-music scams. Here, too, you're expected to buy something or to stand the expense. They get their profit, usually for below-standard products, and you don't further your literary career in any way. Again, let your guide be: I'm not expected to pay to have my poems printed; I'm supposed to get some form of payment for allowing a publisher to print them. There are enough legitimate journal markets; you don't have to become involved with con artists.

If poets had some magic way of knowing exactly what editors are looking for, they'd score a hit every time they sent something out. Editors themselves will often tell you they're not sure, until they see it, what they do want. Just remember—one editor's trash is another editor's treasure. They're people, like the rest of us. For the poet, persistence is a virtue. But there are a few generalities that might be of benefit. We've mentioned one of the most valuable aids—reviewing issues of the journals in which you're interested. If you live near a large public library or have access to a humanities division library in a university, you can look up copies of the magazines there. Try to psyche out the editor of each magazine. Look at the contents of the issues through their eyes. Get the feel of their preferences on subject, style, experiments, themes—anything that may give you some insight into their thinking. Are the poets appearing in that journal mostly big names? Or do those names ring no bells at all? Or, best by far, is there a balance between known and unknown names? After such detailed reviewing, look over your poems again, and see if anything clicks as being of possible interest to one of those editors you want to impress.

It is said that the editor is the poet's natural enemy—that his or her sole ambition is to keep the poet's poems from cluttering up journal pages. But editors with "uncluttered" pages are not editors and are soon unemployed. They'd just love to clutter their pages with fine poems. They have to settle quite often for work they're not entirely pleased with, simply because they don't get enough top-grade poems. Editors are not the poet's enemy merely because they're such jealous guardians of journal pages. Page space, however small the publication, represents an expense—the publisher's. An editor's responsibility toward the publishers is not only to fill the space with the best poems he or she can collect but also to achieve a proper balance in the entire issue and to provide the quality material to which the readership will respond. If editors are hard to please, that's because it's their job to be hard to please. But when you do please one, you'll find that he or she will be grateful to you, and you'll have reason to be proud.

What does this benevolent ogre look for in a poem? You've sent some of your best to the editor, who likes parts of this one, and that one's good, but. . . . *You* know they're good. Why doesn't the editor say, okay, thanks—just what I'm looking for? Well, your concern—and no small one—is just with your poems; from your point of view, you feel justified in enjoying your frustration. The editor, too, is concerned with the poems, yes, but with more than that as well. The balance already mentioned, for instance, a balance that must come out of the substance of the contents as well as the quantity. Is the issue in preparation presenting a particular thematic slant? So much space has been allotted for poems—the rest for other contents. Does that mean the editor will have to leave some things out that would be included if there was room? If previous issues have concentrated on a particular current happening, is it time to shift gears—just when your fine poem on that same event hits the editorial desk? How will the poems affect the readership? Are they in conflict with the journal's policies, political viewpoints, a certain style or approach, the wishes of the periodical's advertisers?

You probably feel, at this point, a sense of outrage. We're talking about art, you say, and to hell with advertisers and politics; if something's good, it must be published. Okay, it will be—the minute your poem and the *right* editor meet. You're dealing with a real world. Don't let your feelings get so tangled that you experience more bruises than you have to. Be flexible, and ride with it; think of it from the other side—the editors'. They go out of their way to be fair, and if they can stretch a bit in the direction of a good poem, be assured they will. They'll go over your poems pretty carefully if they exhibit real talent. Do they include universal appeal and relevancy? Do they contain flaws that will jeopardize the magazine's reputation for excellence? They're well made and all that, but do they exceed those factors? Do they offer new insights, a different way of seeing and understanding? Is their expression clear and original, fresh and not imitative? Will it be of value to the journal to give these poems space? And perhaps the most important question an editor can ask: "Will I later be sorry I did not publish these poems?"

There are other things involved as well—all too human ones. The bleary brain of an editor who has just scanned four hundred poems on the visit of the Pope to America isn't going to respond alertly to your exquisite poem on the same subject. Or this person may simply hate poems about trees, or computers, or love. This particular individual may have had to miss breakfast, had a fight with his or her spouse, taken sass from the kids. And along comes your bouyant, uplifting poems. Or the editor may be in very high spirits—has just received a raise or had the last issue praised by a *New York Times* critic—and your "gloom and doom" poems land on the desk.

In dealing with an editor, you're dealing with another human being—with all the worthy strengths and debilitating weaknesses of any human being. That awareness will improve your understanding about the whole process; and the positive side of this coin is that you will realize that rejection may be due to any number of factors and is not necessarily a *critical* rejection.

Let's say you've been pretty lucky. Over a few years, you've amassed an impressive amount of respected credits. A few of your poems have found their way into legitimate anthologies. You've given frequent readings of your poems, have even been invited to travel (expenses paid, of course) outside your base of poetic operations to read to special groups. In other words, you've been building a following of admirers of your work. You think this might be a good time to issue a modest volume of your work. It's a realistic thought at this point in your career. Perhaps your writing is reaching out in new directions now; and being an orderly sort of person, you'd like the security of knowing your earlier work is neatly packaged for whatever future awaits it—a mark of respect for the work, a recognition of what it has helped you achieve.

The first step, of course, is to put together a manuscript. But even prior to that, you must ask yourself some truly hard questions. What kind of collection do I envision? Will it be thematically connected, a combination of related themes? A "straight-through," or a book divided into sections? Or will it just be a random collection of my best things? Maybe I should organize them according to the dates they were written? Or published? How long a book? How many poems make a book? And, most importantly, is there an audience for this book I envision? *Will the poems matter to that audience?* Audiences do matter; otherwise, your poems remain in suspension and do not complete their life cycles. That "good gray poet" Whitman said that great poems need great audiences. Your particular audience may be large, or it may be small; but it may not be ignored.

If you score a passing grade in the above self-testing, then you're ready to begin the actual task. Go through your poems carefully, selecting the ones you feel are your strongest—whether published in journals or not—and set them aside. As for the rest, they can go back into your files unless you have the fortitude to keep only the ones previously published for record and toss the others in the waste basket. Certainly, if they aren't good enough in your estimation to be included in your first book—before you've even considered themes, etc., and are selecting merely on the basis of individual quality—would you want their presence later, in a second book, which should be an improvement on the first? Be brave. Throw them out—unless you're sure you *will* revise them.

Now take your pile of good poems. Go through them with some rough idea of the book's silhouette; keep an eye on thematic potential, on natural groupings—anything that seems to lend a cohesive possibility. Break the big pile into smaller piles. Try organizing in smaller units, then ordering the units in different sequences. Patterns will begin to emerge soon enough if you go about the process with a degree of objectivity. The connections are there; these poems were created by one mind. They represent facets of their creator. You now have to ferret out those connections with your present goal as prime consideration. You will shuffle poems back and forth, trying to make decisions, and this is natural. Slowly the manuscript will begin to take shape and come together. Be strict with yourself. If a certain theme seems to emerge, remove the poems that do not adhere to it. These you *will* save for some future volume, because they're good; they just may not belong in this particular book. Are you noticing that the poems are dividing themselves into a number of separate sections, even though there is an overall connection? Ride with that; it will tighten the collection as well as giving your reader breathing space. But not all collections are organized in the same way. Yours may be going in a different direction. Listen to the material; find out how it's trying to direct you. You've learned that one poem is a total entity and that everything in it must contribute to the structure of that entity. In a sense, you are now dealing with a much larger "poem," and everything in the manuscript should contribute to the book's overall effect. A first book is not properly a "collected" volume. That will come later. That's why you are perhaps better off with a definite theme. You are still in the process of establishing yourself.

How many poems? Be guided by the theme or pattern of your total manuscript. Include enough to complete that—not one poem more or less. On an average, first volumes tend not to exceed fifty or so poems, but you must judge in accordance with the demands of your particular book.

When the manuscript seems to be in its proper sequence and arrangement, read the whole thing through several times. Chances are, you will still move one poem from this section to that, or switch the arrangement within a section, etc. This is still part of the process. The more critical you are in this part of the exercise, the less grief you'll have later. Just before you're ready to say "It's done!" go through the manuscript again, this time looking at each poem—as you imagine the reader will look at it—and make sure it's earning its space in furthering the effect of the book as a whole. Check for pacing, relief at appropriate stages, progression, emotion and mood intensification and easement. Check again the development of the theme if that's the basis of your organization (you can't do this too often; you must be sure), and take a good hard look at the overall form and design of the collection as it evolves during the reading.

Let the thing rest a few days; then read it through again. It's wise to do this several times over the span of a couple of weeks or so. You may decide to make some additional changes. Don't begrudge the work and time; everything you do to strengthen the collection will be, ultimately, to your benefit.

Okay, now everything seems in order. Which poems previously published will require permission to be reprinted in your book? Send out your requests for such permissions, and include an SASE with each request. And while you're waiting, start typing your manuscript.

Your title page will be your *top* page, on which you'll have your name and address and the title of the volume. Pagination starts with this page and continues uninterrupted to the end of the manuscript; don't include special page numbers for poems of more than one page. All pages are now part of this new "poem."

On the second page, type your last name, the title or the last word of the title of the collection, and "page 2"; start near the top left, and type this on one line. Farther down, type the titles of your previously published poems and the journals in which they appeared. You may want to indicate which ones you already have permission to reprint and for which ones you are awaiting permission. Don't worry about any more material that normally goes into the front area of a book. If you interest a publisher, you will be guided in that, and style varies with different publishing firms.

All the pages you're now typing will be white, 8½ × 11 inches, smooth-surfaced, regular typing paper. The upper left heading on each and every page from now on will be like page 2 but with the appropriate *consecutive* number. The third page will be your *contents* page. You may want to list only the headings describing the sections or to include the individual titles of the poems. List the contents any way you wish as long as it makes sense; but it's a good idea to omit the page numbers, since they will be different if the manuscript goes to print. The poems will be listed as they are arranged in sequence in the book, and that's a sufficient guide for the editors at this stage. If your contents page does not exceed one sheet, the page with your first poem in the collection will be 4. (Do not start paging with number 1 with the first poem, and don't indicate the earlier pages by *i, ii, iii*.)

When the manuscript is typed, proofread it carefully, especially if you've hired someone to do the typing for you. Proofread two or three times. Better yet, have your spouse or a friend proofread it also; They're not apt to anticipate the way you do and will often catch typographical errors that you might miss. Don't fasten the pages in a binder or staple them together. Leave them loose but in order. Find a suitable box—one that doesn't cramp and curl the pages but not one so big that the pages slosh around in it. The box that held the ream of paper you used is generally a fine one for the purpose, but it's usually deeper than you need. You can use the extra space for your container SASE, folded in two.

Study recent publishers' catalogs at this point. Note what the poetry picture looks like from what books have been issued, which poets, what kind of poetry. Try to pick a publisher that you think will give your material an interested look. In preparing the package for mailing, don't just address the box and stick a stamp on it. Do put your name and address as well as the title of the collection on both the cover and the bottom half of the box. A cover letter, in this case, is not only appropriate but desirable. Introduce yourself briefly (don't give your autobiography); list your writing experience and meaningful journal credits; say something (in a subtle fashion) about why you think a readership will respond to your particular group of poems and what readership you are trying to attract. If some or all of your poems deal with some current national or international situation, you might mention why you think it's worthwhile expressing some of these concerns through poetry. This will be your first contact with a book editor, so don't put that editor off with any long-winded attempt to cajole or verbally caress. Be yourself, be natural, and be brief; keep your cover letter to one page.

Take your manuscript in its box to the post office. Have the clerk weigh it, together with a mailing container large enough to hold the box. Affix the proper postage to the container you'll prepare for your SASE. Add an extra first-class stamp to pay for the editor's reply. Address the container to yourself; mark it (or have it marked by the postal clerk) in the manner you want it mailed— "First Class" or "Special Fourth Class Mail—Manuscript" (there's no stigma attached to the latter); fold the container; and place it in the box with your manuscript. Purchase from the clerk a second mailing container; place the box in it; put your return address and the address it's going to (with the editor's name, of course) on it; mark the manner of mailing on it (and also "Letter enclosed" if it's going fourth class); and have the clerk weigh the package as it now stands. You will be charged for the weight (plus the extra stamp for the letter if fourth class). You're finished for now; silently bless the thing, and leave it with the postal clerk. Again, don't be impatient, and don't sit around waiting. This may take a good deal longer than waiting to hear from a magazine. Get busy with new poems or with revising some old ones you were reluctant to throw away.

Should you have obtained the services of an agent? Would your chances have been better? Ask instead: What would I expect an agent to do with a manuscript of poems? If it's merely not to be bothered with the record keeping and the mailing chores, a clerk or secretary is what you want. With poetry manuscripts, an agent is going to encounter the same obstacles you will. The competition is tough, and the number of publishers willing to handle poetry (unless the poet is famous or notorious) keeps getting smaller. Agents depend on commissions for their livelihood. Since new poets are seldom in a position to demand an advance from a publisher, the agent's 10 or 12 percent is nothing. And the agent can't pay the rent with 10 percent of royalties realized from the sales of your first book. Unless the agent you have in mind is a relative or close friend, that individual won't be interested—and shouldn't be, logically. Agents *are* their contacts. Their value is their ability to get by obstacles, to get into editors' offices and deal with them on a first-name basis. That's a good agent, a productive one. If all one can do is mail out the material for you, you're better off doing that yourself. You can estimate an agent's worth by the degree of his or her indifference to your proposition. An agent who is eager to handle the book for you may be planning to charge you some kind of fee or is just getting started. You can sympathize with the situation all you like, but this one isn't going to do your book any good. At this stage, you are your own best agent.

If you still feel it's "classier" to have an agent, beware of the "reading fee." A real agent *expects* income from *the material he or she places.* Reading such material is part of that process. A reading fee would be a legitimate charge if you asked an agent not to try to place the material but merely to give you an opinion on its marketability. But you don't want to fall prey to those advertisements that promise that your poetry manuscript will receive all kinds of expert handling, but the agent charges an initial reading fee; and should your manuscript require editing and revision, you will be guided in that (for additional fees, of course). Such people are not agents but free-lance editors (which is a reputable profession), and they should call themselves editors without implying they have a magic entry into publishers' inner sanctums (which is what the poet secretly hopes). If a top agent does read your manuscript (usually at no charge at all) and finds it unmarketable, he or she is doing it as a favor and will recommend that you seek editorial help elsewhere. Such agents have neither the time nor the desire to assume such a role.

This brings us to the value of contacts. For placing a book of poems, one solid contact is worth six agents. The feeling that a poet should not rely on contacts, that one's masterpiece should attract and move editors and publishers on its own, is from "Unrealistic Views of Life—Course 1." Today, with the book markets for poetry diminishing, you need all the help you can get just to be read at a publishing house. And that's all you can expect (have a right to expect) as a result of using contacts. No one's going to guarantee publication. But so much material comes in to editors that there's just no way it can all be given a real study. A contact gives you an edge; it puts a little pressure on the editor when someone in the same firm or some influential person plumps your manuscript on the editor's desk and says: "What about this?" The editor will read it in order to answer that question somewhere along the way. And that's all you're asking for—a chance to be read. Don't blame the contact if it doesn't work out. What you asked has been done; the rest depends on your work. On the other hand, if it *does* work out, don't feel that your success is due to something underhanded you've done. No editor worth a paycheck is going to make himself or herself vulnerable intentionally just to do you (or your contact) a favor. You can be sure that the editor who says "yes" believes "yes." Don't be shy about approaching a possible contact who will speak on your behalf. This is the business end of poetry, and here you need guts to survive.

Major publishers are not your only option. There are alternative methods of publishing. First, there are the small presses. Some of them have shown a flair for merchandising and have been brought into "association" with larger ones. But most are still fiercely independent. There's also been aid from government funds for a few of these presses. The quality of their product runs from "inexpensive" to glossy-covered, handsomely packaged volumes. The books are mostly wrappers, library binding, or some other form of paperbound. Many well-known poets had their first book or two issued by small presses. On the other side, small presses don't have the advertising budgets, or, often, the sales abilities of the large houses. Advertising, promotion, distribution, and marketing present large problems. But if you've struck out with the major publishers, there isn't any reason you shouldn't try some of the smaller presses. What you're trying to do is get started. Always check market listings to learn all you can before sending material to any small press. Again, under no conditions should you be asked to stand the expense (unless you're employing the press as a printer rather than as a publisher) for the production of your book.

But cooperative and collaborative publishing is a legitimate way of sharing the cost of publication and of getting into print. It depends on the particular group, of course; so if this is your inclination, pick a collaborative that you feel exercises some objectivity in its publishing decisions, not one of those that—in an attempt to be "fair"—results in a "whose turn next?" operation. Publishing a person's bad poetry can in no way be considered "being fair" to that person. Financial input on your part in this kind of publishing is a legitimate expectation, and you will often be asked to give a certain amount of your time to the work of the group.

What about self-publishing? Will you be tarred with the ego brush? Isn't it the same as "vanity" publishing? No, it isn't; it's another matter altogether. Vanity or subsidy publishers promise, hint, or imply things they can't or don't (or tokenly do) deliver. The vanity publisher isn't a publisher but a printer. You pay the vanity people the cost of production of your book plus a handsome profit for themselves, and often the price is not fixed by any trade standard but by what the victim will bear. A half-dozen copies of your book may go out for review, either to very small periodicals or to places where reviewers—having seen the imprint of the "publisher"—won't touch the thing. Victims end up with several thousand copies of their book. After they've distributed fifty or so copies to family and friends, they store the rest in a closet or attic to gather dust. Any miracles that do occur from this type of publishing are rare, and they happen in spite of—rather than as a result of—this questionable type of operation.

Self-publishing is quite different. Many famous writers have started out by this route. That does not mean that everyone who self-publishes is going to crack the sound barrier. But at least you aren't being taken. You're in no way a victim of anyone's smart operation. *You are the publisher.* You're simply employing *the services* of the printer, who has no concern with the quality of your work. You've already made a decision on that, functioning as your own editor. Most metropolitan areas boast a number of reputable printers. If self-publishing is how you're going to handle your book, look at samples of the work of several printers. When you find what seems a decent-looking product at a reasonable price, you may have found the right printer. The arrangement between you two will be strictly a business one, and the printer will be guided by *your* directions on how you want the book to look.

Since your book will include a number of poems already published in various worthwhile journals, no one's going to accuse you of a vanity trip. There has been more objective evaluation in a book of this sort than of a book of poems published by a cooperative but lacking any good magazine credits.

As a publisher, you now assume the responsibilities for obtaining the copyright and for selling the book and getting it reviewed. Once your printer has printed, collated, bound, and delivered the book to you to your satisfaction, that part of the contract between you is fulfilled. The rest is up to you. You might use the same printer to make a stack of book announcements with an order blank on the bottom. You can (and should) send these flyers to libraries, bookstores and wholesalers, and to individuals you think might be interested. It doesn't hurt to put a bit of splash on the flyers, but don't overdo it. The tastefulness exhibited by your flyers will imply that of the book itself. An illustration of a reduced cover of your book is a good type of splash, plus some text (not too much) about the author and how the book may be ordered. You can contact local bookstores and ask if they'll try to sell copies for you. Most bookstores will accept such material on consignment only, which means you'll have to wait for payment until books are sold, and you'll have to accept the return (at your expense) of unsold copies. The usual discount that book dealers expect ranges from 15 or 20 percent for wholesalers to 40 percent for bookstores. Any advertising or promotion you plan will have to be paid by you, naturally. To help yourself a bit more, you might offer a bookseller an extra 10-percent discount in return for exhibiting your book in a prominent place.

In deciding what retail price to set, you'll have to take into account the cost of production (printing and related expenses) plus all your other expenses: advertising, discounts, storage, record keeping, mailings, correspondence related to sales and advertising, overhead costs attributed to the selling function, and so forth. Remember, too, that income from the book (and from journals) is reportable income and must be part of your income tax return. Be sure to take every legitimate deduction—your expenses in every stage of book production and selling. So your retail price must take into consideration all these factors. But don't make your price too high, even if it means some slight financial loss. If your paperbound volume is sitting on the store's poetry shelves next to hardbound books by other poets with twice as many pages, and if your price is double that of others, you may have a problem moving the book. And this won't make the bookseller happy, because shelf space must produce a certain amount of income for the owner. Be realistic. Notice what other books are selling for. Rather than being determined to make a slight profit, or even to make back your cost, keep your retail price within a reasonable range of similar publications, even if you have to take a loss. You do want to get the book into the hands of readers; you want them to discover your poems. That should be your first concern now—not the eighty dollars you might have made if you could have obtained your first-choice price.

Favorable reviews will help a greal deal. How do you get reviewed? For one thing, it's very good for your book if you get a plus notice in *Library Journal* and *Publisher's Weekly*, so send review copies to both these journals. Your book is almost certain to get listed; and if both or either of these publications gives it an actual review, some orders from libraries and wholesalers are bound to come in. There appears to be no problem with books for review reaching intended desks with these and other well-established journals. If you expect reviews from newspapers, you may get them, and you may not, of course; but you may not for quite a surprising reason. Mail addressed to particular departments is quite often opened by clerks in the mailroom. (This also happens in the offices of some national magazines.) Many a clever clerk has lined the shelves at home with review copies of books reaching the mailroom—and never getting to the reviewer's desk. With local papers, it might be worth hand-delivering review copies directly.

Not all reviewers are going to find your book a masterpiece. But even a lukewarm review for a first book is better than being ignored entirely. Send review copies to periodicals that specialize in reviews or that include them in a special section. And if your book *is* reviewed, appreciate the fact that the reviewer has done you a favor, selecting your book from among many eligible for review. A bit of precious space (reviewers do have limits on space) has been devoted to your book.

One excellent place to sell your book directly (no middlemen, no discounts, no hassle) is where you're giving a solo reading. People in the audience are going to be in the right mood. Some will buy the book before the reading begins, and several will buy it after you've read. Have a friend handle the selling for you; you'll have other things on your mind while preparing for the reading. Don't read the entire contents of your book, but read enough to whet your listeners' appetites. Read some new material, too. And after the reading, be approachable. Audiences like to discuss the reading and poems with the poet. But don't let one individual get you into a corner and monopolize your time. Be polite but firm. Excuse yourself, and drift toward another group. They'll welcome you and rescue you. Many who have bought your book will ask you to sign it. "Best wishes" with your signature and date is a perfectly fine inscription. You may want to include a more personal note for those people close to you. But thank them. Thank every person who praises your reading or your work. When you have been helped or encouraged, never forget to thank. Thank-you letters to editors, publishers, and reviewers are a must. And let your audiences know you appreciate their interest. Thank them for coming to listen to you. You will see them again. And again.

Some of the material in this final chapter may seem a bit harsh. It's no surprise if you say to yourself: All the way through the book, I've been encouraged to write, to express myself, to learn the craft so that I can write well. And now I'm being told not to expect immediate attention from editors, not to anticipate an eager audience for my poems. The poetry publishing picture may seem hopeless at times. It may have been more fun writing the poems than trying to sell them, but was it really any easier? You had to learn to start over again, probably discarding all you had done and cherished earlier. You had to learn parts of the craft you're not even sure you'll remember, but you tried so you could feel confident about your poetic "roots." You had to learn to be critical of your own work and to appreciate the criticism of others. You had to train yourself to revise and revise and revise. Yet if you've reached the point of being ready for publication, you've already accomplished a great deal.

If the realistic picture of the publishing status of books of poetry seems rough, it is. Consider this chapter a preparation that will minimize shattering surprises. No one ever said anything about poetry being easy—this aspect least of all. But if—battle scarred but triumphant—you've survived the earlier tasks, this too will not deter you. You are made of more ego strength than you imagine. If you *are* a poet, you cannot stop being one because of temporary setbacks. The determination to stay with it, no matter what happens, is what will make you succeed. And if you didn't possess that kind of fortitude, you would have given up long before now.

Yes, it's a harsh world. But it's the only world you've got. And if you rely on hard common sense instead of daydreaming to get your material published, you will make it. The important thing is that you have experienced a great deal of joy in writing your poems. To discover your way into the poem is the holiest adventure of all. Your journey is into your ocean-self, there to become the poem. You feel; you hear letters vibrate, taut and resilient; lines pull inward, stretch out, close to circles; circles expand, contract, come into each other; features take their own shapes, float together; rhythm and sound deliver themselves, separate and in union. Form remains fluid. Meaning bursts through your poem-skin, breaking free in moment particles of moments. And the poem, in being released, is captured forever.

Appendix i

RECOMMENDED READING LIST

Textbooks, reference books, handbooks and manuals, some anthologies and biographies. You are expected to make extensive use of your library, where you'll find volumes of poems by individual poets. Read your favorites, and extend yourself to read others, too. That's the way you'll find new favorites.

Lack of space makes the exclusion of many books unavoidable. This list does not imply that these books are superior or inferior to many that could have been listed. It's a starter list. You can add to it as your reading progresses.

Allen, Donald M., ed. *The New American Poetry* (New York: Grove, 1960).

Auden, W. H., and Norman Holmes Pearson, eds. *Poets of the English Language* (5 vols.) (New York: Viking, 1950).

Axelrod, Steven Gould. *Robert Lowell, Life and Art* (Princeton, N.J.: Princeton University Press, 1980).

Bartlett, Phyllis. *Poems in Process* (New York: Oxford, 1951).

Starkie, Enid (Charles Baudelaire). *Baudelaire* (New York: New Directions, 1958).

Beardsley, Monroe C., et al. *Theme and Form: An Introduction to Literature* (4th ed.) (Englewood Cliffs, N.J.: Prentice-Hall, Inc., 1975).

Bogan, Louise. *Selected Criticism: Poetry and Prose* (New York: Noonday Press, 1955).

Bowra, C. M. *The Creative Experiment* (New York: Grove, n.d., Evergreen E-80).

———. *Inspiration and Poetry* (London: Macmillan, 1955).

Brewer, R. F. *The Art of Versification and the Technicalities of Poetry* (Edinburgh: John Grant, 1937).

Brinnin, John Malcolm, and Bill Read, eds. *The Modern Poets: An American-British Anthology* (New York: McGraw Hill, 1963).

Brooks, Cleanth, et al. *An Approach to Literature* (5th ed.) (Englewood Cliffs, N.J.: Prentice-Hall, Inc., 1967, 1975).

Burden, Jean. *Journey Toward Poetry* (New York: October House, 1966, 1969).

Ciardi, John. *Dialogue with an Audience* (Philadelphia: Lippincott, 1963).

———. *How Does a Poem Mean?* (Boston: Houghton Mifflin, 1959).

Cooke, M., ed. *Modern Black Poets: A Collection of Critical Essays* (Englewood Cliffs, N.J.: Prentice-Hall, Inc., 1971).

Deutsch, Babette. *Poetry Handbook* (3rd ed.) (New York: Funk & Wagnalls, 1969).

Dickey, James. *Babel to Byzantium: Poets and Poetry Now* (New York: Farrar, Straus & Giroux, 1968).

Drew, Elizabeth, and George Connor. *Discovering Modern Poetry* (New York: Holt, Rinehart & Winston, 1961).

Eliot, T. S. *On Poetry and Poets* (New York: Farrar, Straus & Giroux, 1957).

———. *The Three Voices of Poetry* (New York: Cambridge University Press, 1954).

Matthiessen, F. O. (T. S. Eliot). *The Achievement of T. S. Eliot: An Essay on the Nature of Poetry* (3rd ed.) (New York: Oxford, 1959, 1960).

Tate, Allen (T. S. Eliot). *T. S. Eliot: The Man and His Work: A Critical Evaluation by Twenty-Six Distinguished Writers* (New York, Delacorte, 1966).

Ellmann, Richard, and Charles Feidelson, Jr., eds. *The Modern Tradition: Backgrounds of Modern Literature* (New York: Oxford, 1965).

Empson, William. *Seven Types of Ambiguity* (3rd ed.) (New York: New Directions, 1953).

Golino, Carlo L., ed. *Contemporary Italian Poetry: An Anthology* (Berkeley & Los Angeles: University of California Press, 1962).

Graves, Robert. *The White Goddess: A Historical Grammar of Poetic Myth* (London: Faber & Faber, 1948).

Hardison, O., Jr., and J. Mills, eds. *The Forms of Imagination: An Anthology of Poetry, Fiction, and Drama* (Englewood Cliffs, N.J.: Prentice-Hall, Inc., 1972).

Heidegger, M. *Poetry, Language, Thought* (New York: Harper & Row, 1976).

Hollander, John. *Vision and Resonance: Two Senses of Poetic Form* (New York: Oxford, 1975).

Holmes, John. *Writing Poetry* (Boston: The Writer, 1960).

Honig, Edwin. *Dark Conceit: The Making of Allegory* (Evanston, Ill.: Northwestern University Press, 1959).

Hyman, Stanley Edgar. *Poetry and Criticism: Four Revolutions in Literary Taste* (New York: Atheneum, 1961).

Jarrell, Randall. *Poetry and the Age* (New York: Vintage Books, 1955).

Kennedy, X. J. *An Introduction to Poetry* (4th ed.) (Boston: Little, Brown, 1978).

Langer, Susanne K. *Problems of Art* (New York: Scribner's, 1957).

Gregory, Horace (D. H. Lawrence). *Pilgrim of the Apocalypse* (New York: Grove, 1957).

Lewis, D. B. Wyndam, and Charles Lee. *The Stuffed Owl: An Anthology of Bad Verse* (New York: Capricorn, 1962).

Lucas, F. L. *The Criticism of Poetry* (Folcroft, Pa.: Folcroft Library Editions, 1976).

Maritain, Jacques. *Art and Scholasticism and the Frontiers of Poetry* (tr. Joseph W. Evans, two vols. in one) (Notre Dame, Ind: Notre Dame University Press, 1974, reprint of 1962 edition by Scribner's).

———. *Creative Intuition in Art and Poetry* (New York: World, 1953, 1961).

Maritain, Jacques, and Raissa Maritain. *The Situation of Poetry: Four Essays on the Relations between Poetry, Mysticism, Magic, and Knowledge* (New York: Philosophical Library, 1955).

Minot, Stephen. *Three Genres: the Writing of Poetry, Fiction, and Drama* (2nd ed.) (Englewood Cliffs, N.J.: Prentice-Hall, Inc., 1971).

Murray, Gilbert. *The Classical Tradition in Poetry* (New York: Vintage Books, 1957).

Nabokov, Vladimir. *Pale Fire* (New York: Putnam's, 1962).

Nemerov, Howard. *Reflexions on Poetry and Poetics* (New Brunswick, N.J.: Rutgers University Press, 1972).

———, ed. *Poets on Poetry* (New York: Basic Books, 1966).

Nims, John Frederick. *Western Wind: An Introduction to Poetry* (New York: Random House, 1974).

Packard, William. *The Craft of Poetry* (New York: Anchor/Doubleday, 1978).

Perrine, Laurence. *Sound and Sense: An Introduction to Poetry* (New York: Harcourt Brace Jovanovich, 1956).

Pinsky, Robert. *The Situation of Poetry: Contemporary Poetry and Its Traditions* (Princeton, N.J.: Princeton University Press, 1977).

Poulin, A., Jr., ed. *Contemporary American Poetry* (Boston: Houghton Mifflin, 1971).

Pound, Ezra. *A. B. C. of Reading* (New York: New Directions, 1951).

Preminger, Alex, ed. *Princeton Encyclopedia of Poetry and Poetics* (Princeton, N.J.: Princeton University Press, 1974).

Ransom, John Crowe. *New Criticism* (New York: New Directions, 1941).

Raymond, Marcel. *From Baudelaire to Surrealism* (London: Peter Owen, 1961).

Rexroth, Kenneth. *One Hundred Poems from the Chinese* (New York: New Directions, 1959).

Richards, I. A. *Practical Criticism* (New York: Harcourt Brace Jovanovich, 1939).

Starkie, Enid (Arthur Rimbaud). *Arthur Rimbaud* (New York: New Directions, 1961).

Rosenthal, M. L. *The Modern Poets: A Critical Introduction* (New York: Oxford, 1960).

———. *The New Poets: American and British Poetry Since World War II* (New York: Oxford, 1967).

Sanders, Gerald DeWitt, et al. *Chief Modern Poets of Britain and America* (5th ed.) (New York: Macmillan, 1970).

Atlas, James (Delmore Schwartz). *Delmore Schwartz: The Life of An American Poet* (New York: Farrar, Straus & Giroux, 1977) (Avon, 1977).

Scott, W. S. *Skills of the Poet* (New York: Harper & Row, 1977).

Shapiro, Karl. *English Prosody and Modern Poetry* (Baltimore: Johns Hopkins University Press, 1947).

———. *Essay on Rime* (New York: Reynal & Hitchcock, 1945).

———. *The Poetry Wreck: Selected Essays, 1950–1970* (New York: Random House, 1975).

Shumaker, W., ed. *An Approach to Poetry* (Englewood Cliffs, N.J.: Prentice-Hall, Inc., 1964).

Solt, Mary Ellen, ed. *Concrete Poetry* (Bloomington, Ind.: Indiana University Press, 1969, © 1968).

Spender, Stephen. *The Still Centre* (London: Faber & Faber, 1939).

Stevens, Wallace. *The Necessary Angel: Essays on Reality and the Imagination* (New York: Vintage Books, 1951).

Strachan, W. J. *Apollinaire to Aragon: Thirty Modern French Poets* (London: Methuen, 1948).

Untermeyer, Louis. *Lives of the Poets: The Story of One Thousand Years of English and American Poetry* (New York: Simon & Schuster, 1959).

———. *The Pursuit of Poetry* (New York: Simon & Schuster, 1969).

Van Doren, Mark, ed. *An Anthology of World Poetry* (rev. ed.) (New York: Reynal & Hitchcock, 1936).

Waggoner, Hyatt H. *American Poets, from the Puritans to the Present* (Boston: Houghton Mifflin, 1968).

Waley, Arthur. *Chinese Poems* (London: George Allen & Unwin, 1946, 1948).

Walsh, Chad. *Doors Into Poetry* (2nd ed.) (Englewood Cliffs, N.J.: Prentice-Hall, Inc., 1970).

Wheelwright, Philip, Cleanth Brooks, I. A. Richards, and Wallace Stevens. *The Language of Poetry* (ed., Allen Tate) (New York: Russell & Russell, 1960).

Williams, Oscar, ed. *Master Poems of the English Language* (New York: Trident, 1966).

Wilson, Edmund. *Axel's Castle* (New York: Scribner's, 1931).

Ellmann, Richard (William Butler Yeats). *The Identity of Yeats* (New York: Macmillan, 1954).

RECOMMENDED LISTENING LIST

This list consists of poetry on records and cassette tapes. Many large libraries now have poetry on records and tapes in separate listening areas. Their holdings are usually listed in a card catalog near the audio equipment. You can find your favorites there and enjoy hearing the poems, often read by the poets themselves. There is no greater pleasure. You can find out what is available commercially by sending for catalogues issued by companies that record poetry. Here are two major companies: Caedmon, 1995 Broadway, New York City 10023; and Spoken Arts, 310 North Avenue, New Rochelle, New York 10801.

There are also several series of records issued by Laboratory P of the U.S. Library of Congress. Poets read their own works. Contents and poets vary. Your library's catalog will list individual recordings. In addition, here are some of this author's favorite recorded readings.

Conrad Aiken reading his own poetry (Caedmon TC1039/ CMS Records CMS677).

W. H. Auden reading his own poetry (Caedmon TC1019).

———, *Selected poems* (Spoken Arts SA999-HS).

E. E. Cummings reading his own poetry (Caedmon TC1017).

T. S. Eliot reading his own poetry (Caedmon TC1045).

Robert Frost reading his own poetry (Caedmon TC1060).

Marianne Moore reading her own poetry (Caedmon TC1025/ CMS Records CMS678).

Sonnets of William Shakespeare read by John Gielgud (Shakespeare Recording Society: Caedmon SRS-M241, 2 LPs).

Edith Sitwell reading her own poetry (Caedmon TC1016).

Dylan Thomas reading his own poetry (Vols I-IV, Caedmon TC1002, TC1018, TC1043, TC2005; Vol IV on 2 LPs).

Poems of William Butler Yeats (Spoken Arts SA753).

Special recordings and collections:

Baxter, Frank C. *The Nature of Poetry* (Spoken Arts SA703).

Great Poems of the English Language read by David Allen (CMS Records CMS544, CMS545, CMS546).

Schreiber, Morris. *Understanding and Appreciating Poetry* (Folkways FL9120).

The Spoken Arts Treasury of 100 Modern American Poets (Vols I–XVIII; 18 LPs).

The World's Great Poets (Vols I–VII, various poets/various nationalities; CMS Records).

Yale Series of Recorded Poets (contemporary poets reading from their own works; CMS Records/Carillon Records, 202 Davenport Avenue, New Haven, Connecticut).

PERIODICALS

Following is a small list of worthwhile journals. Again, this is just a list to start you off. Sources offering comprehensive listings will be found under the market listing section (Appendix ii). You are all aware of *New Yorker, Harper's, Atlantic, Mademoiselle*, etc., so we won't list those.

Arizona Quarterly, University of Arizona, Tucson, Arizona 85721.

Beloit Poetry Journal, P.O. Box 2, Beloit, Wisconsin 53511.

Carolina Quarterly, Box 1117, Chapel Hill, North Carolina 27514.

Chelsea, Box 5880, Grand Central Station, New York, New York 10017.

Chicago Review, University of Chicago, Faculty Exchange, Chicago, Illinois 60637.

Field, Rice Hall, Oberlin College, Oberlin, Ohio 44074.

Hudson Review, 65 East 55th St., New York, New York 10022.

Invisible City, 6 San Gabriel Dr., Fairfax, California 94930.

Iowa Review, EPB 321, University of Iowa, Iowa City, Iowa 52240.

Kayak, 325 Ocean View, Santa Cruz, California 95062.

Massachusetts Review, Memorial Hall, University of Massachusetts, Amherst, Massachusetts 01002.

New, The Crossing Press, Trumansburg, New York 14886.

New Orleans Review, Loyola University, New Orleans, Louisiana 70118.

New Renaissance, 9 Heath Rd., Arlington, Massachusetts 02174.

Northwest Reveiew, 369 P.L.C., University of Oregon, Eugene, Oregon 97405.

Paris Review, 541 East 72nd St., New York, New York 10021.

Ploughshares, Box 529, Cambridge, Massachusetts 02139.

Poetry, 1228 N. Dearborn Pkwy, Chicago, Illinois 60610.

Poetry Northwest, Parrington Hall, University of Washington, Seattle, Washington 98195.

Prairie Schooner, Andrews Hall 201, University of Nebraska, Lincoln, Nebraska 68588.

Pyramid, 39 Eliot St., Jamaica Plain, Massachusetts 02130.

Quartet, 1119 Neal Picket Dr., College Station, Texas 77840.

Sewanee Review, Sewanee, Tennessee 37375.

Southern Humanities Review, 9090 Haley Center, Auburn University, Auburn, Alabama 36830.

Southern Review, Drawer D, University Station, Baton Rouge, Louisiana 70893.

Sou'wester, Dept. of English, Southern Illinois University, Edwardsville, Illinois 62026.

Virginia Quarterly Review, One West Range, Charlottesville, Virginia 22903.

Wormwood Review, P.O. Box 8840, Stockton, California 95204.

Yale Review, 1902A Yale Station, New Haven, Connecticut 06520.

Yankee Magazine, Dublin, New Hampshire 03444.

Appendix ii

MARKET LISTS

Since prices of reference items listed are subject to change, it's suggested that you query publishers about the costs of those publications in which you may be interested.

1. *International Directory of Little Magazines and Small Presses.* Annual. From Dustbooks, P.O. Box 1056, Paradise, California 95969. Len Fulton, Editor/Publisher. Over 3000 entries, including many foreign publications. The most comprehensive list available.

Other Dustbooks publications: *Directory of Small Magazine/Press Editors & Publishers* (Annual); *Small Press Record of Books* (Annual); *Small Press Review* (a monthly magazine listing new magazines, new presses, address changes, reviews of small press books & little magazines, & news from the small press world.

2. *Writer's Market.* Annual. From Writer's Digest, 9933 Alliance Road, Cincinnati, Ohio 45242 or from your local library or bookstores. Check under headings *General Interest Publi-*

cations & Women's Magazines for national publications like *Atlantic, Harper's, New Yorker* & *Mademoiselle; Poetry* for the bulk of magazines looking for poetry; *Literary & Little Magazines* for periodicals that devote a number of pages to poetry. For specialized poetry and verse, check trade journals, house organs, newspapers, and denominational magazines under their respective headings. For those of you preparing book-length poetry manuscripts, check under *Book Publishers.* Another heading to consider for specialized verse: *Greeting Card Markets.*

3. *The Writer.* (March issue, each year) The Writer, Inc., 8 Arlington Street, Boston, Massachusetts 02116 or your local library or newspaper/magazine vendor. This magazine lists a different market list each month, and the March issue is the poetry markets list. Much more condensed than either 1 or 2 above, it includes *General Magazines, College, Literary and Poetry Magazines, Greeting Card Markets,* and *Prize Offers, Market News,* and *Fellowships and Grants.* (These last three categories appear in other issues during the year as well as in the March issue.) The periodical also includes "The Poet's Workshop" by Florence Trefethen, a discussion of poems submitted by readers.

4. *Literary Market Place.* From R. R. Bowker, 1180 Avenue of the Americas, New York, New York 10036 or your local library. (Somewhat similar to *Writer's Market.*)

5. *Writer's Digest.* From Writer's Digest, Inc., 9933 Alliance Road, Cincinnati, Ohio 45242. The poetry listings in this monthly aren't very helpful, but Judson Jerome's poetry column is usually worth reading.

6. Many individual journals offer brief reviews or mentions of new magazines as well as items of interest to poets.

INFORMATION SOURCES

1. Poets and Writers, Inc., 201 West 54th Street, New York, New York 10019. *Coda: Poets and Writers Newsletter; Dispatch: Poets and Writers Bulletin; Poets and Writers Infor-*

mation Center. (For general information about the literary world, call 212-757-1766.)

2. *Newsart, The New York Smith.* The Smith, 5 Beekman Street, New York, New York 10038. National news, reviews, columns about the literary scene.

3. *Beyond Baroque.* Beyond Baroque Foundation, 1639 W. Washington Blvd, P.O. Box 806, Venice, Calif. 90291. West Coast news items, readings, workshops of interest to poets.

4. The Poetry Society of America, 15 Gramercy Park, New York, New York 10003.

5. The Academy of American Poets, 1078 Madison Avenue, New York, New York 10028.

6. National Endowments for the Arts, Washington D.C.

7. Your own state Council for the Arts.

8. Your local library.

CONFERENCES, RETREATS, SEMINARS

1. The MacDowell Colony, Peterborough, New Hampshire 03458.

2. Bread Loaf Writer's Conference, Box 500, Middlebury College, Middlebury, Vermont 05753.

3. Several other conferences, seminars, retreats, etc. Check, with *Coda: Poets and Writers Information Center;* check the advertisements in various issues of *The Writer*, your own state Council for the Arts, state Poetry Society, colleges and universities, local libraries, bookstores, Y's, and poetry clubs.

4. Poetry workshops and courses. Check with your local adult education center, with the continuing education divisions of nearby colleges and universities, and investigate creative writ-

ing courses offered by many undergraduate departments. (For a complete list of university level courses or courses leading to a degree, write to Kathy Walton, Executive Secretary, Associated Writing Programs, c/o English Department, Old Dominion University, Norfolk, Virginia 23508, or phone 804-489-6705.)

Appendix iii:
The Workshop Connection

I do think, as I look back, that there was no writer of any consequence in history who was not at some time a member of a group.... And it occurs to me, therefore, that after that the man might leave and go live on a mountain, but he needed some period of social cross-fertilization, you know, because the arts are socially transmitted.

JOHN CIARDI

He [the apprentice-poet] will never know what he himself *can write* until he has a general sense of what *needs to be written*. And this is the one thing his elders cannot teach him, just because they are his elders; he can only learn it from his fellow apprentices with whom he shares one thing in common, they are his contemporaries.... The apprentices do each other a further mutual service which no older and sounder critic could do. They read each other's manuscripts. At this age a fellow apprentice has two great virtues as a critic. When he reads your poem, he may grossly overestimate it, but if he does, he really believes what he is saying; he never flatters or praises merely to encourage. Secondly, he reads your poem with the passionate attention which grown-up critics only give to masterpieces and grown-up poets only to themselves. When he finds fault, his criticisms are intended to help you to improve.

W. H. AUDEN

...poetry not being a self-expression alone but a celebration of life itself....

DYLAN THOMAS

Some poets shy away from poetry workshops. One of the reasons most often given is that creative writing is a solitary endeavor, and distractions are inimical to composition. Of course, fine writing is accomplished in solitude. One's study, however, must not be permitted to become the fatal ivory tower. Any poet who avoids interacting with life will have difficulty in making the work relevant, and his or her poems will reflect such a lack all too readily. Once a poem is written, or even just a fairly good draft of it, a poetry workshop provides a bridge between the private act of writing and the time when the finished piece finds its page in a journal or is read before an audience.

Poetry workshops provide an effective milieu in which poets with honest talent can further their art. Poets participating in such workshops are able to gauge the response to their efforts, to learn how much of what was intended to be expressed is actually conveyed by their poems, to rethink certain parts of their poems that may need to be pruned or strengthened. They have the benefit of an attentive group truly interested in seeing their poems succeed.

If the group has been meeting over a period of time, it will furnish the poet with a balance of individual critical strengths. Members exercise unique points of view in their criticism. One will test the logic of the piece; another will seek out visual images and specific details; a third will challenge overreliance on poetic devices; a fourth will look for mythic overtones; another will comment on metrical rhythms, natural rhythms, and sounds, analyzing speech cadences and questioning line breaks; still another will consider stanzaic order and sequence of pattern. If you are lucky enough to be in a workshop like this, you will do well to take into account these various observations by your fellow members when, in the privacy of your study, you set about the final revision of your poem. You may take one, two, or none of the suggestions offered—such decisions are between the poet and the poem—but your point of view will have been broadened from your having looked through the eyes of others. And your future poems will also benefit from what you learn at each meeting.

Most workshop members admit that assignments (they are not usually obligatory) provide stimuli to their writing. Assignments are a challenge; they provoke the poet-members into new fields and modes of expression. The introduction of improvisation is a new feature in some workshops. In earlier times, poets were expected to improvise on the spot, to win some fair lady's love, to celebrate some king's conquests, to mark some special occasion. Can one forget Cyrano's composing a ballade as he duels? From antiquity, poets as bards and prophets were expected not only to repeat the legends of their cultures—embellishing them with cumulative personal touches—but also to compose orally ballads and epics to fit almost any occasion. The improvisational aspect of poetry must not be allowed to disappear.

The members of your workshop may sit in a circle on the floor and take turns improvising poems aloud on people or objects in the room. Or a tray with a variety of small objects can be placed before them, and each member selects one of the items for consideration. Some poets will concentrate on their selections without actually touching them. Others will pick up the objects of their choice and fondle them. After an allowable interval for silent contemplation, time is called, and the poets are asked to improvise on the items they've considered. After each improvisation, there is a brief critique by the group. Not only does this technique afford opportunity to flex one's poetry muscles; it also turns out to be fun.

There are different kinds of workshops. Each serves a

purpose, even if they are little more than gatherings of poets who want simply to listen to each other read. For your purposes, look for one with a more clinical and objective style, one where real criticism is offered, where even syntax and punctuation are discussed, where the emphasis is on the "work" half of "workshop."

It is not an easy matter to be on the receiving end of criticism. In a productive workshop, the poet generally gets more criticism than he or she bargains for. Though constructive criticism is still painful at times, there's no doubt as to its benefits. A good group gets into the very bones and muscles of a poem. But every effort is made (it is a dictum in well-run workshops) to keep comments directed toward the poem itself. Never should the discussion focus on the writer; it is the poem that is under scrutiny. That's one of the redeeming features of accepting criticism in such an environment—personal beliefs and themes never come under attack. What matters is how well the poets express what they have to say. And each member gets the opportunity to critique the work of the other members in the group.

As to whether a poetry workshop is worthwhile only for beginners—some advanced poets continue to meet regularly because they enjoy the high-powered discussions that arise as well as each other's company. Workshops are not for everyone. For some, they are a helpful interim until the writers feel more confidence in themselves. Others say that having meetings to look forward to prevents them from putting off writing, so it helps their productivity. And there are those poets for whom the getting together, the give-and-take that ensues, is all an exciting part of the process. Fortunately, we live in a world in which differing temperaments can coexist.

One of the best services a workshop offers poets is to lure them into a more objective stance toward their own work. They are often too close to their material to see faults that too frequently find their way into poems. Yet identical faults in the work of others will be obvious to them. When poets learn to regard their poems the way the others regard them, they are on their way to attaining objective distance and a clearer perspective toward their own writing.

Having copies before you as you criticize a poem is an important feature of the workshop technique. It is too difficult to try to retain the entire poem in one's mind as the discussion progresses. It is also important to consider how the poem is presented on the page. Members should bring enough carbons or photocopies to go around.

After a poet has read a poem aloud, he or she maintains a difficult silence while the group studies the poem and furnishes comments. The temptation to plunge into the discussion and show the group how it's misinterpreting the poem or it is too dense to see the writer's intent is very strong. But if that temptation is not resisted, the writer limits drastically what he or she may be able to learn about the poem. If the poem, in its present state, isn't clear to a group of peers, it may very well be as unclear to other poetry readers. If the piece is published, the author will not be at each reader's elbow, explaining exactly what was meant by this image or that phrase. (The poem *must* eventually stand apart from the poet.)

After the group's discussion, which may run from five to twenty-five minutes in most cases, the poet is offered the opportunity to reply, to voice rebuttal or disagreement with what has been said. He or she may admit the validity of some of the remarks. The workshop's treatment of a poem may at times present the author with a new approach to the subject, and a final version of the poem may very well result in something quite different from the earlier effort.

Some thought should be given to the makeup of the membership in a workshop. A better group results if it is made up of writers who are not too far apart in their stages of development.

Transmission of an emotion, an idea, or an experience into poetry requires a knowledge of the poet's craft. This book has attempted an exposition of that craft, with special emphasis on lines, phrases, words, syllables, and even the letters themselves and how they function in poetry. After all the other definitions are stripped away, one discovers that poetry really is a love affair with language.

Index

Ab Intra, 23
Abstract concept, 189
Abstractions, 96, 197, 222
 in figurative language, 198; in writing poems, 224
Abstract sense (*see* Meaning)
Abstract truth, 224
Accent(s), 94–95, 136, 138 (*see also* Beat in poetry; Foot in poetry; Rhythm, accent in; Stress[es])
 in free verse, 116–17, 119
 as rhythmic beats, 119
Acceptance:
 of logic, of artistic substitution, in metaphor, 187; of physical universe, 96; reader's, 8–9; of symbols, communal, 201
Action, 64, 166, 169
 in prolepsis, 197
Adjectival impossibility in pun, 196
Adjectives, 96, 217–18, 219
Adverbs, 96, 217–18, 219
Affective fallacy, 190
After a Game of Squash (Samuel L. Albert), 119–20
After-song, 82
Agent, 257–58 (*see also* Contacts)
 reading fee, 258
Aiken, Conrad, 68–69, 170
 (poem), 68
Aiming (Richard Gillman), 153
Albert, Samuel L. (poem), 119–20
Alcestis (Euripides), lines, 48–50
Alexandrine, 74, 145
Alighieri, Dante (*see* Dante Alighieri)
Allegory, 188

Alliteration, 182–83, 193, 216
 in free verse, 118; in Welsh poetry, 100
Allusion, 192
Alphabet, 160–61, 165
Alternative methods of publishing, 259–62
Ambience, 166, 173
American Indians—songs, 78
Amoretti—Sonnet LXXV (Edmund Spenser), 88
Amphibrach, 142, 144
Amphimacer, 142, 144
Analogy, 188, 193
Analysis, 7–8, 136, 138, 205
Anapest, 139, 142, 144, 148, 149
Anapestic meter, 139, 140–41
Anapestic rhythm, 102
Anapestic tetrameter, 102
Anthology(ies):
 legitimate, 252; racket, 250
Antistrophe, 82
Apocopated rhyme (*see* Rhyme, near)
Apollinaire, Guillaume, 58, 63
Apostrophe, 197
Appearance(s) of poetry, 27, 29, 61
Approximate rhyme (*see* Rhyme, near)
Aragon, Louis, 58
Archaic construction, 198
Archaic diction, 172, 217
Archaisms, 171
Archetype, 192–93
Ariosto, 33
Aristotle, 171
Arnold, Matthew, 118
Artaud, Antonin, 58
Artistic integrity, 224
Assignments, 230–38

Association(s), 205, 219
  fancy a phenomenon of, 199; free, 228; of symbols, 201; in writing poems, 228
Assonance, 184, 185, 193, 225
  in Welsh poetry, 100
Atmosphere, 22, 25, 64, 166, 170
Attitude(s), 26, 166, 169, 191
  toward audience, 173
    when reading aloud, 243
  conceit as a special, 200; of professional, 226; in sonnet, 86; in verbal (rhetorical) irony, 199
Auden, W. H., 41, 86, 94, 101, 202, 278–79
  (poems), 114–15, 203–05
Audience, 9, 18, 22, 173, 190
  importance of, 253; involvement of, 223; relationship between poetry and, 5, 8–9; sincerity sensed by perceptive, 223; tolerance of, at readings, 242–43
Autobiography in poetry, 4
Automatic writing, 230

Backward rhyme, 185–86
Balance, 53, 78, 167, 171
  to achieve, 213; in chiasmus, 197; in free verse, 217; in writing poems, 224
Ballad, 79–81, 180, 184, 193
  folk, 33, 79; literary, 33
Ballade, 101, 102–03, 105
  double, 102
Ballad measure, 80–81
Ballad of Dreamland (Algernon Charles Swinburne), 102–03
A Ballad of François Villon (Algernon Charles Swinburne,) envoi, 72
Ballad rhyme, 79
Ballad stanza, 66, 80–81
Barker, George (poem), 92–93
Bashō (haiku), 99
Bathos, 223
Baudelaire, Charles, 58
Beat in poetry, 41, 77, 116–17, 136, 137, 145
  in duple rhythm, 144; in free verse, 119, 216; measured, 216; metrical, 138, 215; natural, 138; stressed, 145, 168; in triple rhythm, 144
Beat poets, 18
Beauty (Sappho), 34
"Because I could not stop for Death" (#712) (Emily Dickinson), 81
The Beginning of the End: 2 (Gerard Manley Hopkins), 91–92
Beloit Poetry Journal, 124
Biblical poetry:
  free verse in, 117–18; in Old Testament, Songs, 36
Bishop, Elizabeth, 101
Blake, William, 73, 78, 118
  (poems), 37, 73, 141
Blank verse, 76–77, 146
Bolton, Stanwood K. (poem), 152
Boncho (haiku), 99
Book manuscript, 252–56, 257, 259–62
Book of Songs (Chinese poetry), 97
Braga, Edgard, 123
Breath intervals in projective verse, 128
Bremer, Claus, 123

Breton, André, 58, 78
Brewer, R. F., 131
The Bridge of Sighs (Thomas Hood) first 3 stanzas, 141–42
Bridges, Robert (poem), 105
Broken rhyme (*see* Rhyme, broken-word)
Browning, Elizabeth Barrett, 69, 86
  (poem), 91
Browning, Robert, 47, 55, 69, 74
  (poems), 47–48, 69
Bunyan, John, 190
Burns, Robert, 31, 33, 74
Buson (haiku), 99
Butler, Samuel, 31
Byron, George Gordon Lord, 33, 54, 73, 74
  (poem), 73

Cadence:
  in free verse, 119, 151–52; of natural speech, 116, 138–39, 216
Cadenced verse, 119
Calligramme, 63, 123
Campos, Augusto de, 123
Campos, Haraldo de, 123
Canto, 66, 77
Carew, Thomas (poem), 71
Carroll, Lewis, 238
Casey, Michael, 47
Cassette tape recorder, use in poetry, 220
Caudate rhyme, 179
Censor, personal, 20, 131
Chant royal, 101
Character(s):
  in allegory, 189; as archetype, 192; delineation of, 41, 64, 224
    in irony, 199; tension in, 199
  humor as revealer of, 55; pastoral, 109; revelation of, 47
Characteristics of poetry, 34, 43, 56
Characterization (*see* Character[s], delineation of)
Chaucer, Geoffrey, 33, 72, 101
Chiasmus, 197
Chinese poetry, 96–97
Choriamb, 142–43
Ciardi, John, 213
Cinquain, 94–95
Classical meter, 137, 139
Classical poetry, 32–33, 53–54, 136, 145
Classical poets, 54
Classical verse (*see* Classical poetry)
Classicism, 56
Climax, 64, 168
  in writing poems, 224
Closet drama, 33, 52 (*see also* Dramatic poetry; Verse drama)
Clothes Do But Cheat and Cozen Us (Robert Herrick), 55
Coleridge, Samuel Taylor, 18–20, 54, 148, 193
  (poem), 18–20
Collaborative publishing, 259–60
Collage poetry, 124–28, 131
Collective unconscious, 192
Collins, William, 75, 82
Colloquialism, 161
  in metaphor, 187

Colloquial words, 170
Color, 64
  in figures of speech, 195
Commitment, 3, 4, 11, 26, 132, 206, 210
Communication:
  in concrete poetry, 124; imagery as evocative system of, 201
Communication fallacy, 191
Comparatives, 218
Comparison:
  in allegory, 189; in analogy, 190; in figurative language, 198; in metaphor, 188; metonymy as, 195–96; in personification, 192; in simile, 190; in synaesthesia, 193; synecdoche as, 195, 196
Compensation, 145
Complete rhyme (see Rhyme, full)
Composite sonnet, 93
Composition:
  criticism on, effects of, 222; pattern in, 217; poem as a, 28, 216; rules of, 216; structure of, 225; total result of, 219
Composition by field (see Projective verse)
Comprehension, 199–200
Compression, 28, 225
Conceit, 189, 200
Conception, 8, 200, 206
Conclusion, 26, 224
  in projective verse, 131
Concrete image, 98, 189, 201
Concreteness, 96, 199
Concrete poetry, 122–25, 131
Concrete words, 170
Concretists, 123
Condition of degree, 218
Conflict, 164, 169, 199, 223, 225
Congreve, William (poem), 56
Connotation, 170, 172, 219 (see also Meaning)
Conscious effect, 206
Conscious level, 15–16, 57, 136, 212
Conscious permission, 212
Conscious self, 211
Consonance, 184, 193 (see also Rhyme, near)
  in free verse, 118; in Welsh poetry, 100
Consonantal dissonance (see Rhyme, near)
Consonantal rhyme (see Rhyme, near)
Consonants (see Letters; Sound[s], consonant; Syllable[s], sounds)
Contacts, 258–59 (see also Agent)
Contemporary poetry, 146
Contempt, in irony, 199
Content, 3, 4, 21, 63, 75, 76, 239 (see also Subject matter; Theme)
  emotional, 36, 156; in figures of speech, 195; in free verse, 119
Context, 169, 193
  irony in, 199; metaphor, 189
Contrapuntal rhythm, 215
Contrast:
  in allegory, 189; in figurative language, 198; in metaphor, 188
Control, 210, 223, 224–25, 239
Control records, 226 (see also Record keeping)
Conventions of poetry, 29, 82, 101
Cooperative publishing, 259
Copyright, 261

Coronach, from *The Lady of the Lake* (Sir Walter Scott), 42
Correspondence with editors, 245
Cosmopolis, 63
Counterfigures, rhythmic, 217
Counterpatterns, 217
Counterpoint, 95, 139
Counterrhythms, 135
Counter-turn, 82
Couplet, 61, 64–66
  in sonnet, 85, 88–89; in villanelle, 106
Cover letter, 245–46, 256
Cowley, Abraham, 84
Cowleyan mode, odes in the, 84
Cowper, William, 30
Crane, Hart, 188
  (poem), 42–43
Crapsey, Adelaide, 95
  (poem), 95
Created illusion, 213, 222, 225
Creation:
  act of, 8; artistic, 16; of situation or event, 224–25
Creative intellect, 16
Creative process, 15, 63
Cretic, 142
Criteria, new, 239
Critical faculty disarmed by stimulants, 227
Critical judgment, 7, 212
Critical process, 16 (see also Critical judgment; Skill[s], critical)
Critical review, 213
Criticism:
  poetic devices cited in, 190–202; workshop, 221–22
Crossed alliteration, 183
Crossed rhyme, 100, 181
Cross-rhyme, 100
Crown of sonnets, 93
Cummings, E. E., 63
Curtal sonnet, 93
Cynghanedd, 100

Dactyl, 139, 142, 144, 148, 149
Dactylic meter, 139, 141–42
Dance, 132
Dance measure, 41
Dance movement, 82
Dante Alighieri, 31, 33, 66, 77, 86, 114, 191, 200
  (poems), 66, 111–12
Daydreaming, 226, 230
  in fancy, 200
Definition of poetry, 27–28
Degree, condition of, 218
Denotation, 170 (see also Meaning)
Denouement, 64
Density, 28, 94
Dependence on modifiers, 217
Description, in conceit, 200
Descriptive poetry, 29, 32
  in free verse, 118
Descriptors (see Modifiers)
Detail(s), 153, 167, 172
  concrete, 201; in haiku, 98; imagination in organization and unification of, 199; interpretation of, 64; in projective verse,

Detail(s) (cont.)
128; selection and arrangement of, 26; in writing poems, 212
Development:
of diction of the senses, 172; of poetry, 28, 29, 64, 90; of projective verse, 131; of villanelle, 107; of vocabulary diction, 172; in writing poems, 209, 211, 216, 224
Diagram, 64
sestina, 110–11
Dialogue:
ballad, 79; in free verse, 118
Dibrach, 143
Dickinson, Emily (poem), 81
Diction, 64, 96, 170–73, 175, 216 (see also Language; Style; Words)
archaic, 172, 217; in free verse, 118, 217; inappropriate, 217; inflated, 217; invention in, 201; nongrammatical, 217; in projective verse, 129; tension in, 199; in writing poems, 219, 225
Didactic intent, 190
Didactic poetry, 29–31, 78
Digression, apostrophe, 197
Direct address, 42
Discipline, self, 226
Discordants (Conrad Aiken), stanza, 68
Discursive reading, 219
Dissonance, 156, 164, 184, 225 (see also Rhyme, near)
The Divine Comedy (Dante Alighieri), tercets, 66
Dobson, Austin, 103
Don Juan (George Gordon, Lord Byron), excerpt, 73
Donne, John, 93
(poems), 74–75, 90–91
Do not go gently into that good night (Dylan Thomas), 106–07
Double ballade, 102
Double refrain, 102
Double rhyme (see Rhyme, feminine)
Doubt:
beneficial, 4; of relationship between poetry and audience, 5
Draft, 214, 219 (see also Poem, versions; Revision; Writing poems)
Drama, 29, 56, 168
in free verse, 118
Dramatic effect, 72, 147
Dramatic meaning, 147
Dramatic monologue, 47
Dramatic poetry, 29, 32, 33, 47–53, 77 (see also Closet drama; Verse drama)
in ballad, 79
Drayton, Michael, 32
Dream, 18–21
archetype in, 192; world, in surrealism, 56
Dryden, John, 31, 68, 75, 84, 118, 195
Dry spells (see Writer's block)
Dynamics, 138, 215, 225
in concrete poetry, 124; in projective verse, 128, 131; temporal, 216

Editorial comments in poem, 26
Editorializing, 223
Editors, 243–52, 258–59

Ego, 21, 26, 221, 264
Elegy, 41–43
Eliot, T. S., 33, 55, 78
Éluard, Paul, 58
Embryonic rhyme (see Rhyme, near)
Emotion, 4, 21, 22, 54, 64, 108, 167, 168, 169, 205, 223
in concrete poetry, 124; controlled, 224; expression of, 222; in figures of speech, 195; in free verse, 118; in haiku, 98; in projective verse, 129; in rhythm, 134–35
Emotional impact, 223
in concrete poetry, 124; in figurative phrases, 198
Emotional involvement, 101, 160, 223
Empson, William, 101
End rhyme, 68, 177, 181, 186, 215
End words in sestina, 110–11
Energy:
evocative, of symbol, 201; in projective verse, 129; of similar sounds, 183
Englyn, 100
Englyns, from *The White Goddess* (Robert Graves), 100
Enjambment, 64, 76, 147
in couplet, 64–65; in free verse, 218; in villanelle, 108; in writing poems, 215
Envelope stanza, 67
Envoi, 71, 102
Epic, 32–33, 62
Epigram, 65
Epitaph, 65
Epitaph (J. M. Synge), 140
Epithet, transferred, 193
Epode, 82
Essay on Criticism (Alexander Pope), lines, 30–31
Euripides, lines from *Alcestis,* 48–50
Evaluation, 190, 212
objective, in self-publishing, 261; in surrealist poetry, 57
Exaggeration (see Hyperbole)
Exclusive poetry, 17–18
Expectancy in reading, 219
Experience, 26, 108, 192, 209, 212, 222
aesthetic, 192; incongruities of, in ironic poem, 199; parallel, 4; personal, 17, 21, 22; poem as a live, 213; reader's participation in poem's, 224; truth of, 24; in writing poems, 211
Experiment(s), 29, 128, 131–32, 239 (see also Poetry, experimental)
with form, 214
Experimental assignments, 236, 238
Explanation, 224
of poems, in cover letters, 245
Exposition, 64
Expression, 8, 16, 21, 26, 108, 132, 171, 172, 195, 213, 222, 252
in figurative language, 198; in free verse, 118; integration of, 64; limited, 160; logic of, 7; in metaphor, 188; methods of, 205
individual, 201
misuse of medium of, 191; mode of, 205
verbal, honesty in, 225
personal, 202; in sonnet, 86; style of, 170;

symbols in, 202; totality of, 64; tradition of poetic, 132; verbal arrangement in, 170; in writing poems, 238–39; in zeugma, 197
Extravagances, 200
Extended metaphor, 189, 190
Eye rhyme, 181—82

Fables, 190, 192
The Faerie Queene (Edmund Spenser), stanza, 74
Failed poem, 219, 223
Fallacy:
  affective, 190; communication, 191; intentional, 190–91; pathetic, 191–92, 193; personification, 192, 193
Fancy, 199–200
Fantasizing, 230
Fantasy(ies), 192, 200, 238
Feeling, 22, 26, 82, 108, 134, 168, 222, 223
  in Oriental poetry, 96; of rhythm, 176; in sonnet, 86
Feminine rhyme, 178–79, 182, 185
Fictionalizing in poetry, 4, 21
  to illustrate truth, 224
Figurative language, 195, 198
Figurative phrases, 196, 198
Figurative words, 170
Figures of speech, 171, 194–98, 205
  invention in, 201
Figures of thought, 194
Final pauses, 147
Finlay, Ian, 123
Finnish poetry, 78
"*First/immacu-/late pearl-*" (Valerie Jayne), spiral poem, 125
The Fish (Marianne Moore), 150–51
Fixed form, 62, 63, 104, 108, 176, 214
Floyd, Bryan Alec, 47
  (poem), 45–47
Focus in writing poems, 210, 216
Foot in poetry, 65–69, 72, 137, 139–40, 142, 143–45 (*see also* Accent[s]; Beat in poetry; Measure; Meter; Rhythm; Scansion; Stress[es])
  amphibrach, 142; amphimacer, 142; anapestic, 139, 140–41; choriamb, 142–43; cretic, 142; dactylic, 139, 141–42; dibrach, 143; iambic, 68, 139, 140, 146, 167; Ionic, 143; paeon, 143, 149; pyrrhic, 143; spondaic, 140, 142; in sprung rhythm, 148–49; substitution, 144–45, 146; tribach, 143; trochaic, 139, 141, 145
Footnotes, 244
Forcing the poem, 211
Foreign-language forms, 96–116
Foreshadowing, 168
Form, 28–29, 41, 62–64, 75, 108, 170 (*see also* Poem's shape)
  character of, 101; classical, 53; consciously shaped, 16; conventions of, 62, 98; emergent, 117; fixed, 62, 104, 108, 176, 214
  nonmetric, 63
  invention in, 201; mastery of, 105; metrical, 118, 215; organic, 27, 62, 63, 117, 118, 129;

outlining, 199; projective verse, 128–31; sense of, 217; stanza, 75, 176; story in verse, 43; strict, 102; in surrealist poetry, 57; syllabic, 27; tension in, 199; traditional, 27, 28–29, 62, 64, 76, 118, 142, 214
  evolution of, 63; stylized, 105
  visual, 63 (*see also* Concrete poetry; Visual poetry); in writing poems, 219, 225, 239
Forms:
  ballad, 78–81; ballade, 102; blank verse, 76–77; Chinese, 96–97; cinquain, 94–95; collage, 124–28, 131; concrete poetry, 122–25, 131; foreign-language, 96–116; found poetry, 124–28, 131; free verse, 116–22, 216; French, 101–16, 131; haiku, 98–99; Japanese, 96–99; ode, 82–84; Oriental, 94, 96–99; pantoum, 101; projective verse, 128–31; rondeau, 103; rondeau redoublé, 104; rondelet, 104; roundel, 101, 104; roundelay, 104; sestina, 110–16, 131; sonnet, 85–93; syllabic, 94–100; tanka, 97; triolet, 104–05; villanelle, 105–10, 131; Welsh, 94, 100
Found poetry, 124–28, 131
Fox, Siv Cedering (poem), 147
Free association, 228
Free verse, 27, 64, 76, 116–22, 151–52
  writing, 216–21
French forms, 101–06
French poetry, 94
Frost, Robert, 55, 77, 139
Full rhyme, 40, 177–82, 184
Fun:
  of poetry, 101; in writing poems, 238, 239
Functional essentiality, 217
Functional metaphor, 189
Functional modifiers, 218

Garnier, Pierre, 123
Gascoyne, David, 58
Generalizations, 223 (*see also* Abstractions)
Ghosts (Anne Sexton), 121
Gillman, Richard (poem), 153
"*Go and catch a falling star*"—song (John Donne), 74–75
Goldsmith, Oliver, 32
Gomringer, Eugen, 123
Gosse, Sir Edmund, 103
Grammar, 169, 219
Grammatical styles of order, 198
Graves, Robert, 77
  (poems), 38, 100; translator (Welsh poetry), 100
Gray, Thomas, 75
Greek choric songs, 82
Greenberg, Barbara L., 109
  (poem), 109–10

Haiku, 94, 97–99, 123
Half-rhyme (*see* Rhyme, near)
Half-stanza, 102
Hamlet (William Shakespeare)
  death scene, lines, 167–69; *speech to the players*, 29–30
Hands (Siv Cedering Fox), lines, 147
Hardy, Thomas (poem), 67

Harmonics of words, 205, 219
Harmony, 164, 166–67
  imitative, 166–69; in rhyme, 183; in Welsh poetry, 100
Hearing Margaret, Aged Four (John Holmes), 120–21
Heart's Needle (W. D. Snodgrass), stanzas, 76
Hebrew poetry, 78, 94
Heine, Heinrich, 118
Henley, William Ernest, 103
  (poem), 103–04
Herbert, George, 63
Heroic couplet, 65
Heroic poetry, 32
Herrick, Robert, 39, 55, 65
  (poems), 34, 55
Historical rhymes (see Eye rhyme)
Hokku, 98
Holmes, John, 210
  (poem), 120–21
Holy Sonnets—X (John Donne), 90–91
Homer, 32, 191
Hood, Thomas (poem), 141–42
Hopkins, Gerard Manley, 93, 117, 143, 148–50, 179, 184
  (poems), 91–92, 93–94, 149–50
Horace, 82, 84, 137
  (poem), 84–85
Houèdard, Dom Sylvester, 123
Howes, Barbara, 101
Humor, 55–56
  in irony, 199; in pun, 196
Hymnal stanza, 66–67
Hyperbole, 195

Iamb, 139, 142, 143, 144, 146, 148, 149
Iambic meter, 68, 139, 140, 146, 167
Iambic pentameter, 68–69, 73, 74, 76, 144, 215
  in sonnet, 85
Iambic rhythm, 102, 144
Iambic tetrameter, 102
Idea(s), 8, 9, 33, 57, 64, 78, 190, 191 (see also Inspiration)
  in Oriental poetry, 96; in sonnet, 85–86; in triolet, 104–05; in writing poems, 239
Idea provokers, 236–38
Identical rhyme, 177, 179
Identification with poem's elements, 223
Identity in metaphor, 188
Idiom in metaphor, 187
Illusion, created, 213, 222, 225
Illustration, 223
  fictionalizing for, of truth, 224
Image(s), 21, 76, 78, 128, 153, 172, 201, 224
  in analogy, 190; concrete, 98, 189, 201; in fancy, use of, 200; in figures of speech, 195, 196, 198; in free verse, 118, 119; in haiku, 98–99; multilayered, 219; in pathetic fallacy, 191; primordial, 192; as repetend, 193; tension between, 199
Imagery, 64, 201
  in haiku, 98; and symbolism, 201
Imagination, 4, 21, 24, 94, 199
  paucity of, 218; writer's block, to defeat, 230; in writing poems, 212
Imagists, 99
Imitation, 9, 53

Imitative harmony, 166–69
Impact:
  emotional, 223
    in concrete poetry, 124; in figurative phrases, 198
  visual:
    in concrete poetry, 124; in projective verse, 128–29
Implication (see also Meaning)
  associative, 170; in rhetorical question, 198; second level, in pun, 196
Impure rhyme (see Rhyme, near)
Incantation (rune), 77
Incantatory effect, 78
Incremental repetition, 193
Indentation in free verse, 118
In Honour of St. Alphonsus Rodriguez, Laybrother of the Society of Jesus (Gerard Manley Hopkins), 149–50
In Memoriam (Alfred Lord Tennyson), stanza, 67
In Memory of W. B. Yeats (W. H. Auden), 203–05
Insight, 98, 214, 222, 252
  in found poetry, 126, 128; invention in, 201
Insight line, 98
Inspiration, 206 (see also Idea[s])
  tampering with, 210; in writing poems, 210, 227
Instinct, 17
Integration in free verse, 216
Integrity:
  artistic, 224; in the poem, 4, 138
Intellect, 21, 22, 223
Intensification, 64, 78, 107, 136, 175
  emotional, 41, 42, 134–35; in figures of speech, 195; by incremental repetition, 193; rhythmic, 215; symbol as process of, 201, 202; in writing poems, 219, 225; in zeugma, 197
Intensity (see Intensification)
Intention, 191, 200
Intentional fallacy, 190–91
Interlaced rhyme, 181
Internal rhyme, 68, 182
  in writing poems, 215
Interpretation, 22, 64, 221, 224
Interpretive phrases, 26
Intuition, 6–7, 17
  in free verse, 118; in projective verse, 129; in surrealism, 57, 58
Intuitive level, 136
Innuendo, 219
Invention, 201, 224
The Invention of Comics (LeRoi Jones), 121–22
Inventiveness, 4, 21, 171, 200
Inventive writing, uncontrolled, 229
Inversions, 169, 171
Invocation to Misery (Percy Bysshe Shelley), stanza, 70
Ionic foot, 143
Irony, 198–99
  paradox, coupled with, 194; in pun, 196
Irregular stanza, 75
Isolation, 10

Jandl, Ernst, 123
Japanese forms, 94, 97–99

Japanese poetry, 96-99
Jayne, Valerie (poem), 125
Jazz Fantasia (Carl Sandburg), 154
Jazz rhythm, 153
Jones, LeRoi (poem), 121-22
Journals (*see* Magazines)
Joyce, James, 27, 60, 219
Julia (Robert Herrick), 34
Jung, C. G., 192
Justified modifiers, 218
Juxtaposition(s), 26, 56, 166
  in collage poetry, 126; in concrete poetry, 124; in found poetry, 128; in metaphor, 188; of Oriental characters, 96; in surrealism, 57-58

Kafka, Franz, 27, 60, 219, 224
Keats, John, 33, 54, 74, 76, 89
  (poem), 89
Kennedy, Terry, 116
Kinetics in projective verse, 129
Kubla Khan (Samuel Taylor Coleridge), 18-20

The Lake Isle of Innisfree (William Butler Yeats), 37-38
Lament for Banba (Egan O'Rahilly), stanza, 140-41
Lament in Spring (John Logan), 35
Langer, Susanne K., 213-14
Language(s), 3, 6, 21, 116-17, 138, 146, 153, 160-61, 169, 205-06
  accented, 94; accents, 94-95, 116-17, 119;
  alternation:
    of accented syllables in, 119; of beats in, 116
  arrangement of, 213; ballad, 79; cadence in, 119; colloquial, 161; constructions in, 172, 195, 198
  archaic, 198
  contemporary, expanding, 171; current use of, 170, 172; of dialogue, 79, 118; diction in, 64, 96
  regional, 118
  directional and nondirectional, 28; dynamics of, in projective verse, 128; experiments in, 172; figurative, 195; in free verse, 116-17, 119, 216; French, 94-95, 116; future directions of, 205; hieroglyphics as, 124, 189; history of, 205, 206; inflated, 171; Japanese, 94-95; jargon, 18, 169; in living action, 28; a living entity, 161; modulation of natural rhythms, 216; naturalness of, 171, 172, 214; natural rhythm of, 119; of natural speech, 116; nondirectional, 28; Oriental, 96-97
    ideograms, 96, 124, 189; pictograms, 96, 189; script characters, 96, 124; vocabularies, 96
  ornate, 171; particular and universal, 28; phrasing, 171; playing with, and form, 239; poetry as the art of, 205; in projective verse, dynamics of, 128; regional, 161; rhythmic elements of, 217; rhythm of, 135; Romance, 215; sophistication of, 205; spoken, 161; terminology, new, 239; translation of, 96-97, 100; treatment of, 238; universal, 28; variations in, 161; working with, 213
Lattimore, Richmond, translator (Euripides), 48-50

Lax, Robert, 123
Lear, Edward, 179
Let Me Enjoy (Thomas Hardy), 67
Letters:
  in alphabet, 160-61, 165; consonants, 161-64, 167, 168, 184, 186
  in full rhyme, 177-78; percussive, 176
  creating syllables and words, 160-64;
  diphthongs, 161, 163; pronunciation of, 165; redundancies in, 160; sounds of, 160-66; vowels, 161, 162-63, 164-66, 167, 184, 186
    in full rhyme, 177-78; melodic quality of, 176; pronunciation of, 161, 162-63; tonal quality of, 165; versatility of, 161
Lewis, C. Day, 148
Library Journal, 262
Light rhyme, 100, 180
Light verse, 101
Limericks, 179
Line, 63, 145-48, 166, 167-69, 172, 220
  acatalectic, 145; Alexandrine, 74, 145; arrangement of, 41
  in Chinese poetry, 97; in free verse, 117, 118, 217; in haiku, 98-99; in tail rhyme, 179; in tanka, 97-98
  catalectic, 145; construction of, 166; decasyllabic, 145; dimeter, 145; end-stopped, 64; fourteener, 145; in free verse, 216; half-, 93, 103, 104; headless, 145, 146, 168; hendecasyllabic, 145; heptameter, 145; hexameter, 145, 146; insight, 98; metrical, 144-45; monometer, 145; octameter, 145; padding the, 217; pentameter, 64, 68-69, 73, 74, 76, 85, 101, 144, 145, 146; refrain, 102; repeated, 105-10; as repetend, 193; run-on (*see* Enjambment); staccato effect in, 145-46; tail, 103; tetrameter, 65, 67, 101, 102, 145, 146; trimeter, 145, 146; truncated, 145
Line endings, 147-48
Line lengths, 153
Linear direction, 219
Lines:
  intricate pattern of, 75; as rhythmic units, 175; tension between, 199; in writing poems, 211
Linked effect (*see* Linking effect)
Linked rhyme, 180-81
Linking effect, 65, 76, 85, 88
  in crown of sonnets, 93; in villanelle, 106
Li Po, 97
Listener's involvement, 223
Literalness (*see* Meaning, literal)
Literary allusion, 192
Literary journals (*see* Magazines)
Logan, John, 40, 41
  (poem), 35
Logic, 7, 9, 21, 211, 219
  in conceit, 200; discursive, 28; in metaphor, 187, 188; in pathetic fallacy, 191; suspension of, 187
Longfellow, Henry Wadsworth, 69
Long measure, 67
Lorca, Federico García, 33
Lord Randal (Anonymous), 79
Love (Ottone M. Riccio), concrete poem, 125
Love Poem (John Frederick Nims), 35-36
Love's Inconsistency (Francesco Petrarca), 87

Lowell, Amy, 99, 119
Lowell, Robert, 33
Lowenfels, Walter, 126
Lyricism, 29, 56
  in free verse, 118, 119
Lyric poetry, 29, 32, 34-43, 53, 62, 78
  ballad, 79; ode, 82; roundelay, 104; sonnet, 86

Magazines, 241, 247, 249, 252
Magic in poetry, 9, 21, 28, 58, 160, 169
  formula (rune), 77; in Welsh poetry, 100
Mailing requirements for manuscripts:
  to book publishers, 257; to magazine editors, 246-47
Mallarmé, Stéphane, 63
Mangan, James Clarence, translator (O'Rahilly), 140-41
Manuscript:
  book (*see* Book manuscript); preparation of, 243-46, 252-56
Marketing techniques, 247
Market lists, 249
Marlin, Laura (poem), 23-24
Marlowe, Christopher, 156
  (poem), 155-56
Masculine rhyme, 178, 182, 185
Masefield, John, 72
Masks of poetry, 132
Masters, Edgar Lee, 41
Meaning, 22, 23, 64, 138, 154, 156, 160, 166, 168, 169, 175, 205, 215
  in allegory, 189; associative, 202; changing during poem's development, 220; in concrete poetry, 124; connotative, 170, 172, 202; denotative, 170; descriptive, 166; in haiku, 98; in irony, 199; literal, 170, 172, 195, 198; in metaphor, 186-87, 188; multiple, 198; mystical (rune), 77; in projective verse, 131; in prose, 219; in pun, 196; second level, 196; symbol of, 201; word, 225; in writing poems, 211
Measure (*see also* Beat in poetry; Foot in poetry; Meter; Rhythm)
  ballad, 80-81; dance, 41; metric (*see* Metric measure); pentameter, 168; syllabic, 95, 150-51; in time, 136
Medieval tales and romances, 62
Meditation, 230
Melody in poetry, 34, 132, 156, 172, 175, 183
Memory, 17-18, 21, 199, 209 (*see also* Racial memory)
The Memory Bottle (Ottone M. Riccio), 237
Merwin, W. S. 77-78
Metaphor, 27, 28, 64, 171, 186-90, 194, 195, 196 (*see also* Simile)
  in concrete poetry, 124; extended, 189, 190; in free verse, 118; invention in, 201; mixed, 188; organic, 189; in Oriental poetry, 96; personification as, 192; in sestina, 114; symbol in, 186, 188; telescoped, 188; tenor of, 188, 189, 199; vehicle of, 188, 189, 199; violation of, 187-88
Meter, 27, 77, 138, 145, 168, 171 (*see also* Beat in poetry; Foot in poetry; Metric measure; Rhythm)
  anapestic (*see* Anapestic meter); classical, 137, 139; in couplet, 64; dactylic (*see* Dactylic meter); in free verse, 116-17; in French forms, 101; iambic (*see* Iambic meter; Iambic pentameter); mixed, 148; monotony of, 144, 148; in odes, 75; Sapphic, 137-38; in sonnet, 85; and speech rhythm, 148; spondaic (*see* Spondaic meter); as structural element, 63; strict, 116, 144; trochaic (*see* Trochaic meter); variety in, 140, 142; in *vers libre*, relaxation of, 116
Metonymy, 195-96
Metrical beat, 138, 215
Metrical design, 136, 138, 145, 215
Metrical pattern, 84, 118, 139, 147
Metrical poetry, 139
Metrical pulse, 117
Metrical relief, 67, 144
Metrical rhythm, 102, 136
Metrical stress, 136
Metric measure, 82, 136, 137
Metric value of pause, 147
Midnight Mass for the Dying Year (Henry Wadsworth Longfellow), stanzas, 70-71
Milton, John, 31, 32, 33, 52, 75, 76-77, 89-90, 93, 94, 118, 146-47, 188
  (poems), 50-52, 76-77, 89-90; translator (Horace), 84-85
Miles, Josephine, 25
  (poem), 25
Miltonic sonnet, 85, 89, 93
Mist (Henry David Thoreau), 142
Misuse of modifiers, 218-19
Mixed metaphor, 188
Mock epic, 33
Modified sonnet, 53, 86, 93
Modifiers, 217-18, 219
Momentum, 153
Monotony, 146, 215
  of full rhyme, 180; of meter, 144, 148; rhythmic, 135
Mood, 28, 40, 41, 64, 168, 169, 172, 175
  diction, 170, 172
  inappropriate to, 217
  in writing poems, 219, 225
Moore, Marianne, 94
  (poem), 150-51
Morgan, Edwin, 123
Morning and Evening Song (Dolores Stewart), 38-39
Motif:
  repetend as, 193; rhythmic, 217
Motives, 5-6
Movement, 132, 172
  dance, 82
Multiple submissions, 249
Music of poetry, 28, 39-41, 43, 77, 105, 145, 148, 153-54, 160, 166
  in free verse, 118; jazz rhythm, 153; in metonymy, 196; in rhymes, 175, 182, 185
Music terminology in poetry, 137
Mystery, 7-9
  of result, 8
Mystique, 9
Myth, 9, 28, 190, 192
  as archetype, 192; personal (*see* Mythology, personal); private (*see* Mythology, private)

Mythology:
personal, 8, 202; private, 200

Nabokov, Vladimir (poem), 65
Narration, 29, 56, 171
Narrative poetry, 29, 32, 43-47, 53
in allegory, 189-90; in ballad, 79, 193; in free verse, 118; in sestina, 114; in sonnet, 86
Nash, Ogden, 55
Naturalness in language, 171, 172, 214
Natures of poetry, 27, 29, 32, 56, 61, 79, 170
dramatic, 29, 32-34, 47-53, 77, 79, 86; lyric, 29, 32-42, 78, 79, 82, 86; narrative, 29, 32-34, 42-47, 79, 86
Near rhyme, 40, 183-85
Newspaper poetry sections, 249
Night (William Blake), stanza, 73
Niikuni, Seiichi, 123
Nims, John Frederick, 40
(poem), 35
Nine-line stanza, 74-75
Ninety-Eighth Sonnet (William Shakespeare), 88-89
Nisetich, Frank J., translator (Pindar), 83-84
Notation in concrete poetry, 124
Nuance, 219
Number of poems:
for book manuscript, 254; per submission to magazine editors, 244-45
Nurse's Song (William Blake), 37

Oates, Joyce Carol (poem), 22-23
Objective complement (prolepsis), 197
Objective evaluation in self-publishing, 261
Objective poetry, 25, 54
Objectivity, 6-7, 24-26, 54
in writing poems, 210
Oblique rhyme (*see* Rhyme, near)
Obscurity, 200, 224
Observer, invisible, 25
Octave, 73
in sonnet, 85-87
Ode, 62, 70, 74, 82-85
irregular, 75, 82, 84
Off rhyme (*see* Rhyme, near)
Olson, Charles, 129
On a Mourner (Alfred Lord Tennyson), stanzas, 69-70
One Hundred and Seventh Sonnet (William Shakespeare), 183
One Hundred Thirty-Eighth Sonnet (William Shakespeare), 194
On First Looking into Chapman's Homer (John Keats), 89
On His Blindness (John Milton), 89-90
Onomatopoeia, 166, 167, 169
Open verse (*see* Projective verse)
O'Rahilly, Egan (poem), 140-41
Orchestration, 156
Organic form, 27, 62, 63, 117, 118, 129
in projective verse, 129
Organic metaphor, 189
Organization:
analysis of, 64; of elements, 57; in free verse, 118, 217; in projective verse, 128-29; of rhythmic elements, 217; of sounds and rhythms, 62; in surrealism, 57; temporary, 210; for visual impact, 128-29; of word clusters, 129
Oriental forms, 96-99
Oriental poetry, 78, 96-99
Ornamentation, 195
Ottava rima, 73, 179
Overtones:
in concrete poetry, 124; of words, 172, 205, 219
Overuse of modifiers, 217-18
Overworked poem, 211
Oxymoron, 197

Pacing, 168
in free verse, 152, 216, 217; in projective verse, 129; at readings, 243; in writing poems, 219, 225
Padding, 217
Paeon, 143, 149
Pale Fire (Vladimir Nabokov), couplets, 65
Pantoum, 101
Paradise Lost (John Milton), lines, 76-77
Paradox, 193-94
in oxymoron, 197; in sonnet, 85-92, 194 (*see also* Turn)
Parallel alliteration, 183
Parallelism, 78, 147, 153
Pararhyme (*see* Rhyme, near)
Parker, Dorothy (poem), 56
Partial rhyme (*see* Rhyme, near)
Parting at Dawn (John Crowe Ransom), 92
The Passionate Shepherd to His Love (Christopher Marlowe), 155-56
Pastoral poems, 32, 105, 106, 109
Pathetic fallacy, 191-92, 193
Pattern, 28, 41, 62, 76, 78, 146, 175 (*see also* Rhyme scheme)
alliterative, 183; counter-, 217; development of, 217, 225; in free verse, 118-19, 151-53 rhythmic, 119, 138
intricate, 74; in irony, 199; metrical, 84, 118, 139, 147; repetition as, 193; rhythmic, 119, 133, 134, 135
figure as element of, 217
in sestina, 110, 111; in sonnet, 85-89, 93; sound, 63, 101, 156; syllabic, 94; in syllabic verse, 150; synthesis of, 217; variation in, 217; in Welsh poetry, 100; in writing poems, 212, 219
Pause(s), 40, 138, 140, 145-48
as compensation, 145, 146, 168, 169; grammatical, 215, 219; in Welsh poetry, 100
Payment for publication, 249
Paysage Moralise (W. H. Auden), 114-15
Penance (Laura Marlin), 23-24
Pentameter (*see* Iambic pentameter: Line, pentameter)
Perception, 5, 172
conceit as system of, 200; distorted by stimulants, 227; imagination transforms, into work of art, 199; in projective verse, 129; sensory, visualizing beyond, 200; truth of, 24
Percussion in rhyme, 183
Periodicals (*see* Magazines)
Permissions to reprint, 255
Persona, 192

Personal poetry, 54
Personals (Dolores Stewart), 126-27
Personification, 189, 192, 193, 194, 197
Perspective, 6-7, 214, 222
Petrarch (Francesco Petrarca), 86-88, 200
    (poem), 87
Petrarchan sonnet, 85-88, 89
Phantasy, 200
Photocopies and carbons for submissions, 249
Phrases, word, 153, 170
Phrasing, 171
"Picture" poems, 63
Pied Beauty (Gerard Manley Hopkins), 93-94
Pignatari, Decio, 123
Pindar, 62, 82-83
    (poem), 83-84
Pindar's Victory Songs (Pythian 2—first triad), 83-84
Pious Celinda (William Congreve), 56
The Piper (William Blake), stanzas, 141
Pitch, 136, 138
The Place of the Carp (Stanwood K. Bolton), 152
Plato (on rhythm), 134
Players (Josephine Miles), 25
Playing with language and form, 239
Poem:
    captured, 264; evolution of, 8; as performance, 213; seasoning the, 239; version of, 221, 227
Poem on His Birthday (Dylan Thomas), 156-59
Poems-set-to-music scams, 250
Poem's shape, 16, 27, 28, 43, 62-63, 209, 210, 211, 212 (*see also* Form)
    in concrete poetry, 123-24; external, 64; "picture" poems, 63; in surrealism, 57
Poet:
    attitudes of the, 223; being a, 213, 264; career of, 250, 252; professional, 249
Poetic beat (*see* Beat in poetry)
Poetic devices, 28, 118-19, 174-202, 194, 198, 205
    in Auden, 202
Poetic diction, 171, 172
    archaic, 172, 217
Poetic foot (*see* Foot in poetry)
"Poetic Trifles," 131-32
Poetry:
    appearances of, 27, 29, 61; characteristics of, 34, 43, 56; classical, 32-33, 53-54, 136, 145; contemporary, 146; conventions of, 29, 82, 101; definition of, 27-28; denouement in, 64; development of, 28, 29, 64, 90; dramatic (*see* Dramatic monologue; Dramatic poetry); experimental, 10 (*see also* Experiments) variations in, 63
    by field (*see* Projective verse); fun of, 101; lyric (*see* Lyric poetry); narrative (*see* Narrative poetry); natures of (*see* Natures of poetry); personal, 54; process in (*see* Process, in poetry); resources of, 169; romantic, 33, 53-54; sounds of (*see* Sound[s]); statement in, 85; surrealist, 56-60, 124; symbols, the importance of, in, 202; traditions of, 28, 29, 105, 117; universal, 54 (*see also* Universality); virtuosity in, 101, 200; visual aspects of, 27, 28, 43, 61-64, 122-31

Poetry community, 10 (*see also* Readings; Workshops)
Poetry style (*see* Style)
Poetry traits (*see* Poetry, characteristics of)
Point of view, 21, 26, 172
    invention in unique, 201; in rhetorical question, 198; in sestina, 113; sympathy toward, 224
Pope, Alexander, 31, 32, 33, 75, 78, 94, 195, 197
    (poem) 30-31
Popular rhyme (*see* Rhyme, near)
Pound, Ezra, 77, 78, 99, 101, 113-14, 118
    (poems), 78, 113-14
Praise for an Urn (Hart Crane), 42-43
Presentation of poetry, 61
Primordial images, 192
Privacy, 4, 10
    of symbols, 202; of working environment, 227
Process:
    in poetry, 64, 128, 206; in projective verse, 129; in sestina, 110; in surrealist poetry, 57-58
Productivity, 226
Progression, 108, 138, 225
    discursive, 28; in projective verse, 131; in sestina, 111; in villanelle, 107
Projective verse, 128-31
Prolepsis, 197
Proofreading, 244
    book manuscript, 256
Propaganda in poetry, 47, 191
Proportion, 53 (*see also* Balance)
Prose:
    arranged to resemble poetry, 219; of poetic quality, 27-28, 60
Prose paragraph, 75, 117, 216
Prose poem, 29
Protagonist, 54
Publication:
    payment for, 249; techniques to achieve, 243-49 (*see also* Submissions)
Publication credits, 241-42, 245, 252
Publication markets, 249
Publishers:
    book, 258-60; magazine, 250, 251
Publisher's Weekly, 262
Publishing options, book manuscripts, 259-62
Publishing picture for poetry, 263-64
Pun:
    as figure of speech, 196; in rondeau, 103
Pyramid, 124-25, 126, 128, 233
Pyrrhic, 143
Pythian 2 (*Pindar's Victory Songs*) first triad, 83-84

Quantity (*see* Rhythm, quantity)
Quartet in One Movement (Ottone M. Riccio), 58-60
Quatrain, 66-69, 76
    in free verse, 119; in rondeau redoublé, 104; in sonnet, 85-86; in villanelle, 105
Query letter, status, 248-49
Query (Joyce Carol Oates), 22-23
Quintain, 69-71

Racial memory, 17, 192-93 (*see also* Memory)
Radiational direction, 219

Index 293

Radiational effect, 96 (*see also* Rippling effect of words)
 in projective verse, 131; of symbols, 201, 202
Radiational level, 28
Raleigh, Sir Walter, 156
Ransom, John Crowe (poem), 92
The Rape of Lucrece (William Shakespeare), stanza, 72-73
Reading aloud, 39, 219-20 (*see also* Readings)
 before an audience, 220-21, 241-43
Reading alternatives in projective verse, 131
Reading in discursive manner, 219
Reading other poets, 9-10
Readings, 241-43, 252 (*see also* Reading aloud)
Realism, 56-58
Reality, 9, 224
 in surrealism, 56
Recollection, 224 (*see also* Memory)
Recording poem-in-process, 220-21
Record keeping, 247 (*see also* Control records)
Redundancy of modifiers, 218
Reed, John (poem), 233
References:
 privacy of, 200; private, 18; symbols as, 201; unique points of, 202
Refrain, 102, 104, 105, 118, 176, 179, 193
Rejections, 248, 252
Relevancy, 251
Renga, 97
Repetend, 193
Repetition, 78, 105-16, 193
 of detail, 41; in free verse, 119; as rhyme substitute, 176; of sounds, 183; in Welsh poetry, 100; of words, 39
 in rhyming, 78-79
Resolution, 219
Resolution and Independence (William Wordsworth), 72
Resources of poetry, 169
Response, 147
 emotional, 53, 191
 to metaphor, 187
 failure to evoke, 223; sense, 172
Restraint, 53, 224
Reversal of elements (chiasmus), 197
Review-copies (book) distribution:
 by self-publisher, 262-63; by vanity publishers, 260
Revision, 4-5, 136, 211, 212-14, 220-22, 226, 253
 to defeat writer's block, 227-28
Rexroth, Kenneth, 97
Rhetorical irony, 199
Rhetorical quantities of lines, 175
Rhetorical question, 198
Rhetorical unit, 76
Rhyme, 27, 40, 63, 138, 171, 175-86
 alliteration, 182-83; analyzed, 185-86; appearance of, 176; in Auden, 202; ballad, 79; broken-word, 179-80; in couplets, 64; criteria for, 64; cross-, 100; crossed, 100, 181; deviation in, 176, 177, 184; as elaboration, 175; end, 68, 177, 181, 186, 215; eye, 181-82; feeling of, 176; feminine, 178-79, 182, 185; in French forms, 101; full, 40, 177-82, 184, 215; functions of, 175; identical, 177, 179;
 initial, 182-83; interlaced, 181; internal, 68, 168, 182, 215; license in, 184; light, 100, 180; limitations in, 215; linked, 180-81; masculine, 178, 182, 185; near, 40, 181, 183-85, 215; in nine-line stanza, 74-75; in octave, 73; origins of, 177; patterned, 118; patterns of, 68-69, 100, 103-06, 175; in quatrains, 66-68, 76; in quintains, 69; random, 118, 151; in rondeau, 103-04
 redoublé, 104
 run-over, 180-81; in sestet, 71-72; in septet, 72; in sonnet, 85-91, 93, 176; stresses in, 177-79, 180, 184; substitute, 184; tail, 179; in tercet and terza rima, 66; terminology of, 176, 184-85; in triolet, 105, 176; in villanelle, 105-06, 109, 176; in Welsh poetry, 100; in writing poems, 215, 219
Rhyme royal, 72, 179
Rhyme scheme, 66, 85, 93, 102, 106, 175, 176, 181, 216
 deviations in, 176
Rhyme sound(s), 101, 102, 103, 109, 176
Rhythm, 28, 39, 40, 62, 63, 132, 133-54, 168, 205, 206, 220 (*see also* Beat in poetry; Foot in poetry; Meter; Scansion)
 accent in, 136; anapestic, 102; contrapuntal, 215; as dance measure, 41, 82; duple, 144; falling, 139; in free verse, 119, 216; iambic, 102, 144; metrical, 102, 136; modulation of natural language, 216; natural, 119, 138, 139; of natural speech, 136, 144, 148, 152, 153, 216; of prose, 135; quantity in, 136, 137-38, 139; rising, 139, 145; rocking, 142; running, 148; sprung, 117, 143, 148-50; stress in (*see* Stress[es]); syncopated, 135, 225; triple, 144; variations in, 134-35, 147, 215; wave-sense in, 134, 135; in writing poems, 216
Rhythmic action, 135
Rhythmic counterfigures, 217
Rhythmic elements in free verse, 217
Rhythmic figures, 144, 193, 217
Rhythmic quantities of lines, 175
Riccio, Ottone M.:
 (poems), 58-60, 125, 129-31, 237; translator (Dante Alighieri), 111-12
Richards, I. A., 148
Ridicule, in irony, 199
Rilke, Rainer Maria, 41
Rimbaud, Arthur, 58
Rip-offs, literary, 249, 250, 258, 260
Rippling effect of words, 219 (*see also* Radiational effects)
Robinson, Edwin Arlington, 76
Roethke, Theodore, 101
Romantic epic, 33
Romanticism, 53, 56
Romantic poetry, 33, 53-54
Romeo and Juliet (William Shakespeare), excerpt, 52-53
Rondeau, 101, 103-04, 105, 128
 redoublé, 104
Rondeau (William Ernest Henley), 103-04
Rondel, 103
Rossetti, D. G., 86
 translator (Sappho), 34, 39

294 Index

Roundel, 101, 104
Roundelay, 104
Rühm, Gerhard, 123
Rune, 77
Rune (Robert Graves), 77
Running rhythm, 148
Run-on lines (*see* Enjambment)

Salutation (Ezra Pound), 78
Samson Agonistes (John Milton), lines, 50–52
Sandburg, Carl (poem), 153–54
Sapphics, 77, 137
Sapphics (Algernon Charles Swinburne) stanza, 137
Sappho, 39, 137
  (poem), 34
Saroyan, Aram, 123
Satire, 31, 199
Sayers, Dorothy, translator (Dante Alighieri), 66
Scansion, 136–37, 139, 143, 146–47, 148, 168
  rove-over (in sprung rhythm), 149
Scheduling work time, 226
Scott, Sir Walter, 54
  (poem), 42
The Secular Masque (John Dryden), lines, 68
Selection of materials:
  in surrealist poetry, 57; in writing poems, 210
Self-discipline, work time, 226
Self-publishing, 260–62
  reviews, 262–63
Selling your book, 261–63
Sense analogy, 193
Senses:
  diction of, 172; involvement of, 223
Sense transference, 193
Sensitivity, 28, 58, 223
Sentiment, 85–87, 223
Sentimentality, 223
Septet, 72–73
Sestet, 71–72
  in sonnet, 85–86, 87–88, 93
Sestina, 27, 62, 71, 85, 101, 105, 110–16, 131
  repetition of end words, 110–16, 176
Sestina (Dante Alighieri), 111–12
Sestina: Altaforte (Ezra Pound), 113–14
Sexton, Anne (poem), 121
Shakespeare, William, 32, 55, 56, 72, 76, 86, 146, 168–69, 200
  Hamlet:
    death scene, lines, 167–69; *speech to the players*, 29–30
  The Rape of Lucrece, stanza, 72–73; *Romeo and Juliet*, excerpt, 52–53; sonnets, 88–89, 183, 194; *Twelfth Night*, songs from, 37
Shakespearean sonnet, 85, 88–89, 93
Shelley, Percy Bysshe, 54, 66, 69, 74, 75
  (poem), 70
Shift in address (apostrophe), 197
Sibilance, 164, 168
Sidney, Sir Philip, 86
Sign(s):
  concrete poetry as art of, 124; metaphor as, 189; word as, 189
Simile, 190, 194, 195 (*see also* Metaphor)
Skill(s), 16, 21, 22, 211, 223 (*see also* Critical judgment)
  critical, 10 (*see also* Critical process)

Slant rhyme (*see* Rhyme, near)
A Slumber Did My Spirit Seal (William Wordsworth), 34–35
Small-press publishing, 259
Snodgrass, W. D., 76
  (poem), 76
Soliloquy of the Spanish Cloister (Robert Browning), stanzas, 47–48
Song (John Donne), 74–75
Songs, 36–41, 131, 134
  American Indian, 78
  Greek choric, 82
Sonnet, 62, 71, 72, 85–94, 128, 176
  modified, 53, 86, 93
Sonnet of Fishes (George Barker), 92–93
Sonnet One Hundred and Seven (William Shakespeare), 183
Sonnet One Hundred Thirty-Eight (William Shakespeare), 194
Sonnets, crown of, 93
Sonnet sequence, 86, 93
Sonnets from the Portuguese—XXVI (Elizabeth Barrett Browning), 91
Sound(s), 153–54, 168, 169, 205, 206, 220
  conflict of, 164; consonant, 183; dissonant, 164; in free verse, 118, 136, 138, 165, 152, 216; harmony in, 164; harshness of, 164; letters, produced by, 160–64; patterns of, 63, 101, 156; of poetry, 61, 62, 132, 160; quality of, 164–66; repetition of, 183; sibilant, 164; smoothness of, 164; vowel, 183; of words, 26, 40, 41, 101, 136, 168, 175
Space, white, in projective verse, 128, 129
Spacing, typewriter as aid in, 239
Specifics, in writing poems, 224–25
Spenser, Edmund, 33, 72, 74, 170
  (poems), 74, 88
Spenserian sonnet, 85, 88
Spenserian stanza, 74, 176
Spondaic meter, 140, 142
Spondee, 139–40, 142, 143, 144, 147, 148–49
Spontaneity, 6–7, 214
Sprung rhythm, 117, 143, 148–50
Stand (in ode), 82
Standards, new, 239
Stanza(s), 63, 65, 66, 75, 77, 137, 170, 175, 176, 179
  ballad, 66; in ballade, 102; couplet, 64–65, 66, 75; envelope, 67; envoi, 71, 102; half-, 102; hymnal, 66–67; length of, 75; nine-line, 74–75; octave, 73, 85–87; in ode, 82
  irregular, 75, 82, 84
  ottava rima, 73; quatrain, 66–69, 75; quintain, 69–71; rhyme royal, 72; septet, 72–73; sestet, 71–72, 85–86, 87–88, 93; Spenserian, 74; tercet, 65–66, 75, 85, 105–06, 110–11, 112–14; terza rima, 65–66; in Welsh poetry, 100
Statement in poetry, 85
Stewart, Dolores, 41, 116, 128
  (poems), 38–39, 126–27
Stimulants, 227
Stimuli, 4, 134–35, 212
Stress(es), 68, 95, 136, 137, 138, 139, 143, 146 (*see also* Accent(s); Beat in poetry; Foot in poetry; Meter; Rhythm)
  metrical, 136; in rhyme, 177–79, 180, 184; in

sprung rhythm, 148–49; in substitution, 144; variable, 143
Strope:
 in free verse, 117; in ode, 82
Structural elements, 62–64, 77, 225
Structural metaphor (see Metaphor, organic)
Structural pauses, in writing poems, 219
Structure, 22, 28, 61, 101, 105, 172 (see also Form; Structural elements)
 erectile, 64; formal, 216; of haiku, 99; internal, tension in, 199; invention in, 201; rhythmic, 135; of sestina, 110; tension in, 199; of villanelle, 107
Style, 170, 211
 Aristotelian sense, 170; conceit as, 200; Platonic sense, 170; in sonnet, 90
Subconscious, 15–16, 17, 60, 206
 in automatic writing, 229; in surrealism, 57–58; in writing poems, 211, 212, 213
Subject (see Subject matter)
Subject assignments, 234–36, 238
Subjective poetry, 25, 54
Subjectivity, 24–26, 54
 in reading, 33
Subject matter, 4, 28, 78, 86, 108, 138, 153, 169, 172, 210, 225 (see also Content; Theme)
 characteristics of, 170; classical, 54; diction inappropriate to, 217; and form, 108, 109; in French forms, 105, 107; nature as, 170; in sestina, 114; skill in portraying, 223; sonnet, 90; technology as, 109; and verse paragraph length, 216; in writing poems, 238–39
Submissions, 226, 243–59
Subsidy publishing, 260
Substitution, 144–45, 146
 artistic (of logic in metaphor), 187; in figurative language, 198; in synecdoche, 196
Suggestiveness of words, 170, 172, 219
Superlatives, 218
Surrealism, 56–60, 124, 131
 pathetic fallacy in, 191
Surrealist poetry, 56–60, 124
Suspended rhyme (see Rhyme, analyzed)
Suspense, 193
Suspension, 168
 in projective verse, 129, 131; in rhyme, 185
Swift, Jonathan, 31
Swinburne, Algernon Charles, 71–72, 77, 104, 110, 137–38
 (poems), 71, 102–03, 137
Syllabics (see Syllabic verse)
Syllabic verse, 27, 94–100, 150–51
Syllable(s), 68–69, 137, 138, 144, 145, 160, 164–65
 accented, 117, 119, 165, 216; in Chinese poetry, 97; compensating, 145; in free verse, 119; in full rhyme, 177; in haiku, 98–99; hangers (in sprung rhythm), 149; long, 136; mono-, 149; outrides (in sprung rhythm), 149; pronunciation of, 165; rhyming, 101, 177, 178; short, 136; sounds of, 136, 161, 166, 175, 184; in sprung rhythm, 149; stressed and unstressed, 68–69, 139–40, 146, 177–78, 180, 184, 185; in syllabic verse, 94–100, 150–51; in

tanka, 97; in translation, 97; unaccented, 117, 119, 165, 216; uncounted (in sprung rhythm), 149; in Welsh poetry, 100
Symbol(s), 7, 8, 119, 174, 186, 189, 193, 200–02
Synaesthesia, 193
Syncopation, 135, 225
Synge, J. M. (poem), 140
Synonyms as end words in sestina, 116
Syntax, 64, 138, 169, 171
 in concrete poetry, 96; in haiku, 99; in Oriental poetry, 96; in writing poems, 216, 219; in zeugma, 197

Taigi (haiku), 99
Tailed sonnet, 93–94
Tail rhyme, 179
Tangential rhyme (see Rhyme, near)
Tanka, 94, 97–98
Tape-recording poem-in-progress, 220–21
Taste, personal and popular, 9–10
Tate, Allen, 84
Technical devices, 118
Technical elements, 223
Technical features, 22, 138
Technical words (see Vocabularies; Words, technical)
Technique(s), 3, 4, 76, 101, 105, 169, 209, 239
 collage, 126; figurative language, of using, 198; open, 27; projective verse, 129, 131; sonnet, variations of, 90; syllabic verse, 94; zeugma, 197
Teika, Fujiwara (tanka), 98
Telescoped metaphors, 188
Tempo, 168
Tennyson, Alfred Lord, 33, 74, 76, 167
 (poems), 67, 69
Tenor (see Metaphor, tenor of)
Tension, 41, 108, 167, 168, 169, 199, 223, 225
 in metaphor, 188
Tercet, 65–66
 in sestina, 110–11, 112–14; in sonnet, 85; in villanelle, 105–06
Terminology:
 new, provided by science and technology, 239; of rhyme, 176, 184–85
Terrell, Mary (poem), 95
Terzain, 65
Terza rima, 65–66
Tetrameter (see Line, tetrameter)
Texture, 164
Thematic sources, 24–26
Theme, 8, 26, 28, 41, 55, 63, 105, 166, 169, 199, 215, 219, 224, 238, 239 (see also Content; Subject matter)
 archetype as, 192; in classical poetry, 53, 54; diction of, 172; elevated, 32; and figures of speech, 195; in free verse, 118; movement of, in villanelle, 107; in sestina, 114; in sonnet, 85, 86
Thin Ice (Ottone M. Riccio), 129–31
Thomas, Dylan, 40, 63, 101, 106–08, 144, 156, 170, 184, 214, 279
 (poems), 106–07, 156–59
Thompson, Francis, 170
Thomson, James, 74, 76
Thoreau, Henry David (poem), 142
To a Skylark (Percy Bysshe Shelley), stanza, 70

A Toast (Anonymous), 55
To My Inconstant Mistress (Thomas Carew), 71
Tonality, 43, 64, 216
  melodic, 34; of words, 172
Tone, 33, 39, 69, 105, 168, 170, 172, 173, 175, 205, 216, 219, 225
  in Auden, 202; exaggeration in, 173; in French forms, 101, 105; humorous, 178; in sonnet, 90; tension in, 199
To Pyrrha (Horace), 84-85
Traditional form (*see* Form, traditional)
Traditions of poetry, 28, 29, 105, 117
Transferred epithet, 193
Translation, problems in, 96-97, 100
Triad, 82-84
Triad (Adelaide Crapsey), 95
Tribach, 143
Triggers, 227
  in surrealist poetry, 58
Triolet, 101, 104-05
  refrain lines in, 176
Triolet (Robert Bridges), 105
Triple rhyme (*see* Rhyme, feminine)
Triplet, 65
Trochaic meter, 139, 141, 145
Trochee, 139, 142, 144, 146, 148, 149
Troubadours, 101
Truth:
  abstract and factual, 224; paradox to express, 224; in writing poems, 224, 238
Turn:
  in ode, 82; in sonnet, 85-92, 194 (*see also* Paradox)
The Twa Corbies (Anonymous), 44
Twelfth Night (William Shakespeare), songs from, 37
Twinned Heart (Robert Graves), 38
Two in the Campagna (Robert Browning), stanzas, 69
227-2272 (Barbara L. Greenberg), 109-10
Typographic arrangements (*see* Concrete poetry; Form, visual; Visual poetry)

Understanding, 222, 252
  imagination as instrument of, 199
Understatement, 223-24
Unfortunate Coincidence (Dorothy Parker), 56
Uniqueness, 5, 8, 9, 21, 172
  misuse with condition of degree, 218
Unity, 53, 172
  in form (syllabics), 94; in free verse, 119; paragraphic, in free verse, 216; in projective verse, 131; of sense and sound, 138
  in projective verse, 129
  structural, 41; tonal, 167; in writing poems, 211, 216
Universality, 108, 251
  attempt to reach, 223; in conceit, 200; in Kafka's writing, 224; from the specific, 223
Universal poetry, 54

Vanity publishing, 260
Variable stress, 143
Variations, experimental, 63
Vehicle (*see* Metaphor, vehicle of)

Verbal irony, 199
Verse drama, 33, 47, 53, 62 (*see also* Closet drama; Dramatic poetry)
Verse paragraph(s), 63, 76, 77, 118-19, 147, 152, 170, 216, 217
Verse plays (*see* Closet drama; Dramatic poetry; Verse drama)
Vers libre (*see* Free verse)
Vibrations, associative, 199
Villanelle, 62, 101, 105-10, 131, 176
Villon, François, 101
Virelay, 101
Virgil, 32
Virgule(s), 137, 138, 139
Virtuosity in poetry, 101, 200
Vision, 4, 5, 9, 20-21
Visual arrangements, in projective verse, 129
Visual aspects of poetry, 27, 28, 43, 61-64, 122-31
Visual assignments, 236
Visual impact:
  of concrete poetry, 124; of projective verse, 128-29
Visualizing in phantasy, 200
Visual poetry, 63 (*see also* Collage poetry; Concrete poetry; Form, visual)
Vocabulary(ies), 169, 170
  of Oriental languages, 96
Vocalic assonance (*see* Assonance)
Voicing the line, 166
Voicing of multisyllabic words, 165
Voltaire, 103
Volume (sound), 136, 138, 165
Vowels (*see* Letters, vowels; Rhythm, quantity; Sound(s), vowel; Syllable[s], sounds of)

Waley, Arthur, 97
White, E. B., 160
White space in projective verse, 128, 129
Whitman, Walt, 41, 78, 117, 153, 253
Wilde, Oscar, 33
Williams, William Carlos, 170, 201
Word association, 219
Word clusters, 170
  in projective verse, 129, 131
Words, 39, 40, 95, 139, 160, 166, 170, 172, 198, 205, 219, 225
  abstract, 170; Anglo-Saxon, 170; assignments on, 231-34; choice of, 217; colloquial, 170; connotations of, 170, 172, 219; end, in sestina, 110-11, 113, 116; in free verse, 216; harmonics of, 205, 219; inventing new, 171; juxtaposition of, 26, 139; overtones of, 172, 205, 219; picture, 201; polysyllabic, 136; power of, 205; as repetends, 193; rippling effect of, 219; sense of, 216; sounds of, 26, 40, 41, 101, 136, 169, 175; suggestiveness of, 170, 172, 219; as symbols, 201; technical, 170; tension in, 199; in Welsh poetry, 100
Wordsworth, William, 30, 39-40, 54, 72, 76, 84, 93
  (poems), 34-35, 72
Working environment, 227
Workshops, 221-22, 240
  bringing poem to, 221-22; as stimulant, 227

Work-time scheduling, 226
Wormwood Review, 124
"*Wrinkles/gray hair, dry bones*" (Mary Terrell), cinquain, 95
Writer's block, 227, 228–30
Writing:
  automatic, 230; inventive, uncontrolled, 229
Writing poems, 209–25, 238–39
  assignments for, 231–38
Wyatt, Sir Thomas, 87–88
  translator (Petrarch), 87

Xisto, Pedro, 123

Yankee, 116
Yeats, William Butler, 33, 40
  (poem), 37–38

The Zamosc Rebbetzin's Birthday (John Reed), 233
Zeugma, 197–98